PAUL TINGAY

TRAVELLER'S GUIDE TO ZIMBABWE

STRUIK

Struik Publishers (Pty) Ltd
(a member of The Struik Publishing Group (Pty) Ltd)
80 McKenzie Street
Cape Town 8001

First published in 1996

Reg. No.: 54/00965/07

ISBN 1-86825-833-5

Managing editor: Annlerie van Rooyen
Editor: Glynne Williamson
Design and DTP: Peter Bosman
Cover design: Peter Bosman
Assistant designers: Chris Abrahams and Lellyn Creamer
DTP assistant: Deirdré Geldenhuys
DTP maps: Renée Barnes
Picture research: Arlene de Muijnk

Reproduction by cmyk prepress
Printed and bound in Singapore by Tien Wah Press (Pte.) Ltd, Singapore

Every effort has been made to ensure factual accuracy in this book. However, with the rapid changes that are taking place in Zimbabwe, it is inevitable that information in this book will become outdated. The author and publishers invites any comments or suggestions for future updates. Please write to: The Editor, Traveller's Guide to Zimbabwe, Struik Publishers (Pty) Ltd, P O Box 1144, Cape Town 8000.

ACKNOWLEDGEMENTS

The author and publishers would like to thank the following persons for their invaluable assistance:

Jeremy Brooke of Shearwater
Lance Reynolds of Europcar
Ann Smythe of Zimbabwe Sun Hotels
Sarah-Jayne Lightfoot

Paul Tingay has written several novels, films and travel books, including *Wildest Africa, Globetrotter Travel Guide Seychelles* and *Handy Guide Victoria Falls*. He enjoys nothing more than being in the wild with camera, notebook and binoculars. He and his wife, Ann, a teacher, have been married for 30 years. They have a son and three daughters.

PHOTOGRAPHIC CREDITS

Copyright for the photographs rests with the photographers and/or their agents as listed below.

ABPL = Anthony Bannister Photo Library
PA = Photo Access SIL = Struik Image Library

Daryl Balfour 14 bottom; 56 top right; 61 bottom; 80 top; 90; 101; 106 top; 155; 176 **Batoka Air** page 38 **Keith Begg** spine; 12; 15; 20; 23 bottom; 25 top right; 27; 36; 37; 87; 89 top; 132; 135; 136; 137 top right and bottom; 140; 141; 142 top and centre; 146; 149; 151 bottom; 152; 153 bottom; 154; 165 top; 166 top left (all SIL) **David Bristow** 34 (PA) **Gerald Cubitt** 8; 16; 17; 18 bottom; 19; 22; 39; 52; 56 top left; 60; 62; 63; 64 right; 71 top; 72 top right and bottom; 74; 75 bottom; 79; 80 bottom; 84; 91; 100; 104 top; 105 top left; 113 top; 114 bottom; 120 bottom; 123; 126 bottom left; 137 top left; 139; 142 bottom; 150; 153 top; 164; 165 bottom; 168; 169 bottom; 170 bottom **Roger de la Harpe** front and back cover (all SIL); 6 (SIL); 7 (SIL); 13 top (SIL) and bottom; 14 top (SIL); 18 top (SIL); 23 top (SIL); 29 (SIL); 30 (SIL); 33 (SIL); 35 (SIL); 43 bottom (SIL); 44 (SIL); 45 top left (SIL); 46 (SIL); 47 bottom (SIL); 48 (SIL); 49 (SIL); 57 (SIL); 58 (SIL); 59 (SIL); 61 top; 64 left (SIL); 68 (SIL); 72 top left (SIL); 73 (SIL); 75 top and centre (SIL); 76 (SIL); 77 (SIL); 81 (SIL); 89 bottom (SIL); 92 (SIL); 105 bottom; 110 (SIL); 115 top (SIL); 116 (SIL); 117 (SIL); 120 top and centre (SIL); 121 (SIL); 125 (SIL); 126 top and bottom right (SIL); 129 (SIL); 133 (SIL); 158 (SIL); 159 (SIL); 161 left (SIL); 163 (SIL); 166 top right and bottom (SIL); 169 top (SIL); 170 top (SIL); 171;
Nigel Dennis 3; 47 top left; 61 centre; 65 (SIL); 104 bottom; 151 centre; 167 top **Peter Lawson** 119 (SIL); **Colin Paterson-Jones** 25 top left; 43 top; 71 bottom **Peter Pickford** 55; 115 bottom; 118; 162 (all SIL) **Mark Skinner** 177 **Lorna Stanton** 96; 103; 106 bottom; 107 **David Steele** 47 top right (PA)
Paul Tingay 32; 41; 56 bottom; 99; 105 top right; 113 bottom; 114 top; 161 right; 167 bottom **Lanz von Hörsten** title page; 88; 138 **Patrick Wagner** (both PA) 42; 45 top right **B & L Worsley** 151 top (PA).

Front cover: Top left: Great Zimbabwe Ruins; Top right: Victoria Falls; Middle left: Tea pickers in the Honde Valley; Middle right: Elephant at Matusadona National Park; Bottom left: White-water rafting on the Zambezi River; Bottom right: Makishi dancers, Victoria Falls Hotel; Spine: Sculpture at the Chapungu Kraal and Sculpture Park, Harare; Back cover: Nyamandhlovu game-viewing platform, Hwange National Park; Half-title page: Impala drinking at water hole; Title page: Drowned forest, Lake Kariba.

CONTENTS

PART ONE

An Introduction to Zimbabwe

Zimbabwe, named after the largest ancient man-made structure south of the pyramids, Great Zimbabwe, is synonymous with the Victoria Falls and the inland sea of Lake Kariba, the mighty Zambezi River, the vast tracts of game-rich wilderness and the great granite boulders of the Matobo Hills. Set on a high plateau 500km (311 miles) inland from the Indian Ocean, Zimbabwe is a woodland of tiny-leafed msasa trees, of tumbled rock formations, tobacco farms, gold mines and misty mountains. It averages eight hours of sun daily, but winter nights can be freezing. Its population of some 13 million is mainly Shona-speaking but most, due to 19th-century British colonization and massive expenditure on schooling since independence, are fluent English-speakers. Good air, rail and road routes link its game reserves and towns.

LEFT: *The magnificent Main Falls and a traditional Makishi dancer (above) capture the vibrant spirit and splendour of the Victoria Falls.*

THE LAND

Zimbabwe lies firmly between the Limpopo and Zambezi rivers in southern central Africa. Nearly as big as California and about three times the size of England, much of Zimbabwe lies 600m (1 968ft) above sea level, while its central Highveld crescent, where the main towns, heavy engineering industries and commercial farms are sited, lies at 1 500m (4 921ft). This plateau, with its rich central ridge, or Great Dyke, of minerals, consists of a belt of woodland interspersed with maize, tobacco and cattle farms running southwest to northeast for 650km (404 miles).

It is bordered by country that is not quite as high, descending through hot, baobab-covered Lowveld with its sugar plantations and game reserves, to the great river valleys that frame the country. Massive granite outcrops that look as if giants have been piling boulder on precarious boulder dot the landscape. About 30 000 of these house San (Bushman) paintings dating back to the time of Jesus Christ. In the west, the country beyond Bulawayo is an ancient granite wilderness, Kipling's 'great spaces washed by the sun'. This is the Matobo National Park, burial place of British imperialist and diamond magnate Cecil John Rhodes, who for a 100 years gave his name to the country. Nearby are the *zimbabwes* of Kame and Naletale, stone ruins in the tradition of Great Zimbabwe of which there are nearly 150 in the country. The west is also the site of the country's finest game reserve, Hwange, where generators pump water for the world's largest concentration of elephant.

The Zambezi forms the country's northern border and gives it its most renowned attraction, the World Heritage Site of Victoria Falls, where explorer David Livingstone's bronze statue gazes stoically over the turbulent Devil's Cataract and a mile-wide splendour of water, spray and thunder. One of Africa's largest lakes, 282km-long (175 miles) Kariba, is also on the Zambezi. The flooding of the Zambezi Valley 35 years ago encouraged the

World's View, Nyanga National Park, overlooking Nyanga communal lands and Ziwa Ruins.

growth of wide shores of torpedo grass and attracted great quantities of game, while its drowned forests and *kapenta* sardines ensured an explosion of the tigerfish population. Downstream from Kariba is the Zambezi's second World Heritage Site, the wild and remote Mana Pools National Park, a riverine forest of mountains, huge trees, hippo, more than 400 bird species, and nearly the entire range of Africa's wild animals.

The Eastern Highlands, bordering Mozambique and covering the Nyanga, Bvumba and Chimanimani national parks, seem more like Scotland than Africa. Rolling moorland covered with ferns, forests, coffee farms and trout lakes stretch for 300km (190 miles) and rise as high as 2 593m (8 508ft) at wind-buffeted Inyangani, the country's highest massif.

WHAT TO EXPECT

Although Zimbabwe can still be terribly British with Barclays Bank, Parliament, polite policemen and business suits, it is also vibrant Africa where women dress colourfully, the music pulsates and the climate is near perfect. Every modern convenience is available, from wide-body jets, metal roads and automated cash dispensers, to British Sunday papers, American popcorn and elegant shopping malls. The cost of living for visitors, based on favourable exchange rates, is bargain basement and you will seldom meet the rapacity of countries gutted by tourism.

Zimbabwe can trace its trading, city-building and cultural history back 1 000 years. It has a record of nearly two decades of nation-building and with the exception of a short conflict in Matabeleland 10 years ago, has had continuous peace after the long struggle for self-determination. Culturally, it is largely homogenous and renowned for its unusually confident and welcoming population. Few visitors fail to comment on the friendly reception, be it in a clothes boutique, roadside stall, country hotel or city banking hall.

The climate is equable by day, hot but not humid, and cool at night. The health facilities, which include medical air rescue, are excellent, food inexpensive, shopping easy, and its wide open, sunny spaces and relaxed atmosphere are unusually free from crime and the excesses of urban life.

THE LIE OF THE LAND

Zimbabwe can be divided into six main areas: the Victoria Falls; Hwange National Park in the northwest; the northern boundary consisting of Lake Kariba and the Zambezi River; the Eastern Highlands bordering on Mozambique; the central plateau, the country's granary; and finally, the Great Zimbabwe Ruins and the Lowveld game reserve of Gonarezhou.

THE VICTORIA FALLS

The Victoria Falls is where the Zambezi River, 1 000km (621 miles) from its source, opens out into an extravaganza of roaring, spray-tumbled water, *Mosi-oa-Tunya*, 'smoke that thunders'. Standing before the brooding statue of David Livingstone, who in 1855 named the Falls after his Queen, part of the raging river is compressed into a massive surge of green-white water known as the Devil's Cataract. It lies between the bank on which visitors stand (with only a woven boma of thorn scrub to protect you from the edge) and Cataract Island. Few sights are as awe-inspiring, even frightening, as the ground shakes and rumbles with the force of the water. In November, 20 000m^3 (706 292ft^3) per minute hurtles over the brink but this can increase 25 times in flood seasons.

The walk through the rain forest, a tangle of lianas, fig trees and riverine jungle perched on the lip of the chasm, is a fairytale experience as the paved path winds in and out to a dozen viewpoints, and the billowing upsurge of the spray causes rainbows to compete with the butterflies and dappled shafts of sunlight in the jungle. 'Views so lovely must have been gazed upon by angels in their flight', Livingstone wrote as he was poled down the Zambezi in a dugout canoe, thence to creep to the chasm's edge and lying full length, peer into the awesome, thundering abyss. A

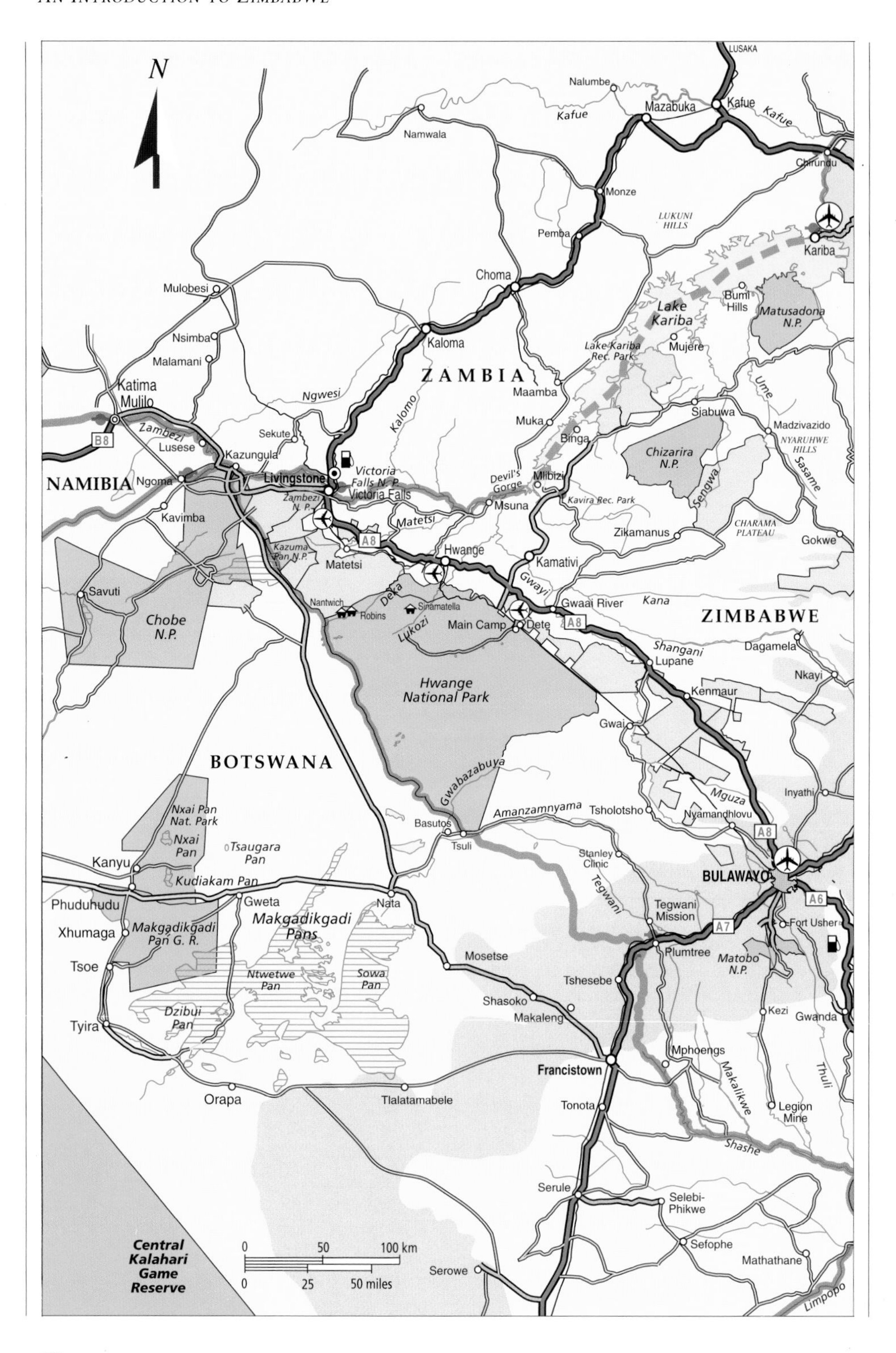
N
ZAMBIA
ZIMBABWE
NAMIBIA
BOTSWANA
Lusaka
Nalumbe
Mazabuka
Kafue
Namwala
Chirundu
Monze
Lukuni Hills
Pemba
Kariba
Choma
Mulobesi
Lake Kariba
Bumi Hills
Matusadona N.P.
Nsimba
Kaloma
Mujere
Malamani
Lake Kariba Rec. Park
Katima Mulilo
Maamba
Ngwesi
Kalomo
Ume
Sjabuwa
Muka
Madzivazido
Nyaruhwe Hills
B8
Zambezi
Sekute
Binga
Lusese
Kazungula
Chizarira N.P.
Sasame
Victoria Falls N.P.
Livingstone
Devil's Gorge
Mlibizi
Ngoma
Victoria Falls
Sengwa
Zambezi N.P.
Kavira Rec. Park
Msuna
Kavimba
Matetsi
Zikamanus
Charama Plateau
Gokwe
A8
Kazuma Pan N.P.
Hwange
Kamativi
Matetsi
Savuti
Gwayi
Nantwich
Deka
Sinamatella
Gwaai River
Kana
Robins
Main Camp
Dete
Chobe N.P.
Lukozi
Shangani
Dagamela
Lupane
Hwange National Park
Nkayi
Kenmaur
Gwai
Gwabazabuya
Inyathi
Mguza
Amanzamnyama
Tsholotsho
Nxai Pan Nat. Park
Nyamandhlovu
Basutos
Nxai Pan
Tsuli
Tsaugara Pan
Stanley Clinic
Kanyu
Bulawayo
Kudiakam Pan
Tegwani
Phuduhudu
Gweta
Nata
A6
Makgadikgadi Pans
Tegwani Mission
Xhumaga
Makgadikgadi Pan G. R.
A7
Fort Usher
Plumtree
Tsoe
Mosetse
Matobo N.P.
Ntwetwe Pan
Sowa Pan
Tshesebe
Shasoko
Kezi
Gwanda
Dzibui Pan
Tyira
Makaleng
Mphoengs
Makalikwe
Francistown
Thuli
Orapa
Tlalatamabele
Tonota
Legion Mine
Shashe
Serule
Selebi-Phikwe
Central Kalahari Game Reserve
0
50
100 km
Sefophe
Mathathane
0
25
50 miles
Serowe
Limpopo

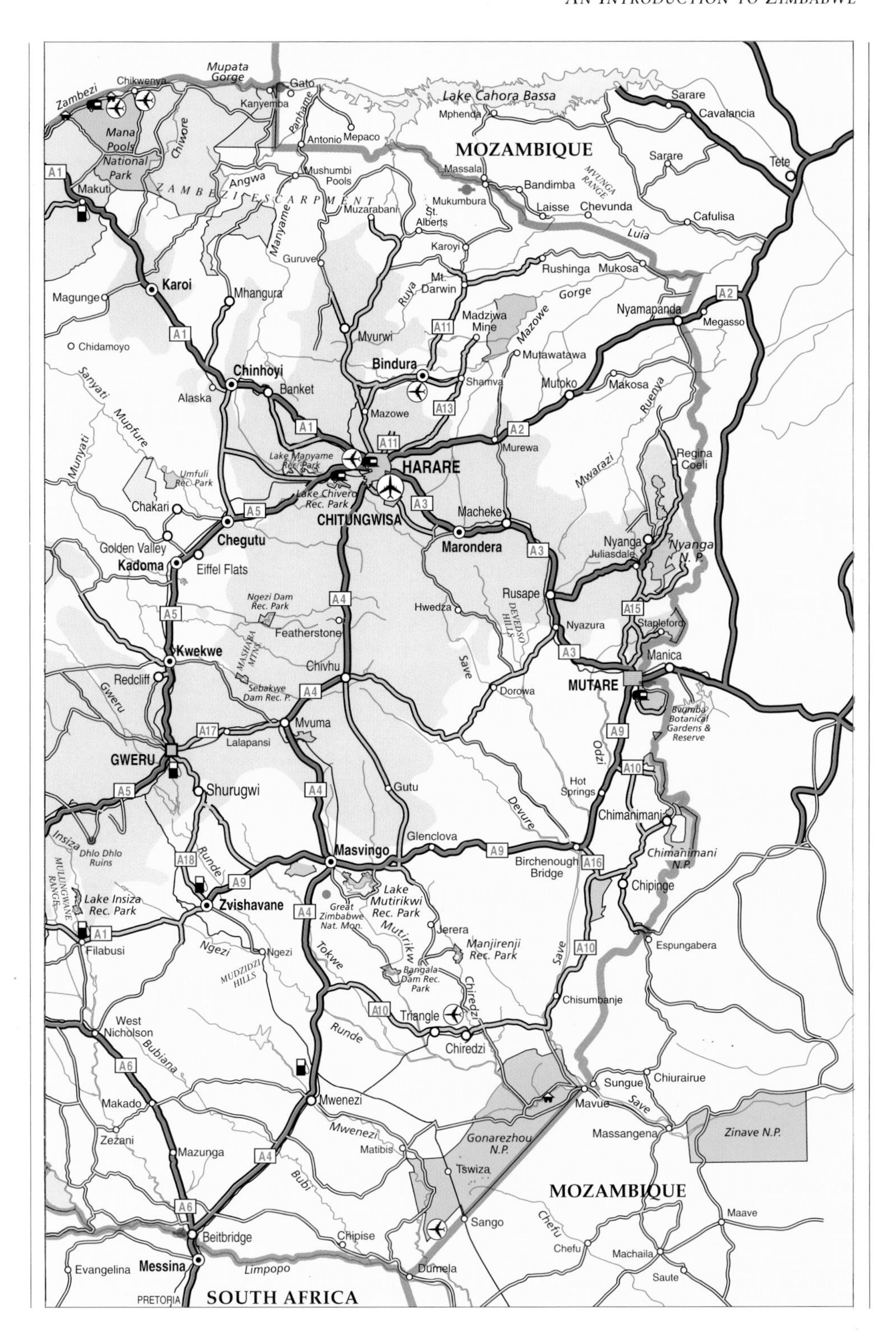
Mupata Gorge
Zambezi
Chikwenya
Gato
Kanyemba
Mana Pools National Park
Chiwore
Panhame
Antonio
Mepaco
Lake Cahora Bassa
Mphenda
Sarare
Cavalancia
MOZAMBIQUE
Tete
Massala
Bandimba
MVUNGA RANGE
Mushumbi Pools
Angwa
ZAMBEZI ESCARPMENT
Makuti
Mukumbura
Muzarabani
St. Alberts
Laisse
Chevunda
Cafulisa
Luia
Manyame
Karoyi
Guruve
Rushinga
Mukosa
Mt. Darwin
Gorge
Karoi
Magunge
Mhangura
Ruya
Nyamapanda
Megasso
Madziwa Mine
Mazowe
Chidamoyo
Mvurwi
Mutawatawa
Bindura
Chinhoyi
Banket
Alaska
Shamva
Mutoko
Makosa
Sanyati
Mupfure
Mazowe
Ruenya
Munyati
Lake Manyame Rec. Park
Murewa
HARARE
Regina Coeli
Umfuli Rec. Park
Mwarazi
Lake Chivero Rec. Park
Chakari
CHITUNGWISA
Macheke
Chegutu
Marondera
Nyanga
Juliasdale
Nyanga N. P.
Golden Valley
Kadoma
Eiffel Flats
Rusape
Ngezi Dam Rec. Park
Hwedza
DEVEDSO HILLS
Featherstone
Nyazura
Stapleford
Kwekwe
MASHABA MTNS
Save
Manica
Chivhu
MUTARE
Redcliff
Sebakwe Dam Rec. P.
Dorowa
Gweru
Mvuma
Bvumba Botanical Gardens & Reserve
Lalapansi
Odzi
GWERU
Shurugwi
Gutu
Hot Springs
Devure
Chimanimani
Chimanimani N.P.
Insiza
Dhlo Dhlo Ruins
Glenclova
Masvingo
Birchenough Bridge
Runde
MULUNGWANE RANGE
Lake Insiza Rec. Park
Zvishavane
Lake Mutirikwi Rec. Park
Great Zimbabwe Nat. Mon.
Chipinge
Mutirikwi
Jerera
Espungabera
Filabusi
Ngezi
Tokwe
Manjirenji Rec. Park
MUDZIDZI HILLS
Bangala Dam Rec. Park
Chiredzi
Chisumbanje
West Nicholson
Triangle
Runde
Chiredzi
Bubiana
Sungue
Chiurairue
Mwenezi
Mavue
Save
Makado
Massangena
Zinave N.P.
Zezani
Mwenezi
Gonarezhou N.P.
Matibis
Mazunga
Tswiza
Bubi
MOZAMBIQUE
Sango
Chefu
Maave
Beitbridge
Chipise
Chefu
Machaila
Evangelina
Messina
Limpopo
Dumela
Saute
PRETORIA
SOUTH AFRICA
A1
A2
A3
A4
A5
A6
A9
A10
A11
A13
A15
A16
A17
A18

Bull elephant taking a bath, Mana Pools.

national park now surrounds and protects the Falls and no buildings are allowed anywhere near it. The only evidence of man's presence is the narrow paved walkway and the great span of the bridge across the gorge, starting point of white-water rafting runs.

The Victoria Falls cannot claim to be the world's highest, widest or largest waterfall, but with a natural amphitheatre in the form of the rain forest from which to witness its grandeur, it is probably the world's most visible spectacle, a thunderous, endless turmoil of water and spray, beautiful to behold.

HWANGE NATIONAL PARK

The Zambezi is a sinuous wilderness of game parks and safari areas. Its natural partner is the Hwange wildlife area which, for the migratory animals, stretches from the river through the Zambezi National Park, Kazuma Pan, two indigenous forests and Matetsi hunting concessions for a distance of 280km (124 miles). Hwange, pronounced Hwang-geh and formerly Wankie, means peace in the Nambya dialect of the area. The park alone covers an area of over 14 620km^2 (5 645 miles^2) and takes a day to negotiate. Everything about Hwange is on a giant scale. It contains at least 17 000 elephant during drought years, 15 000 buffalo, 5 000 kudu, 3 000 zebra, lion, leopard, giraffe and hundreds of bird species. Divided into three areas or camps – Main, Sinamatella and Robins-Nantwich – it has 480km (298 miles) of roads linking the pans, forests, plains and *vleis* (marshy ground), such as Dete in the south where many luxury safari lodges are sited.

The railway line from Bulawayo cuts through Hwange's eastern flank to the Victoria Falls and you can travel by old-fashioned steam train to view the game. National Parks lodges and restaurants are available at each of the camps. The park sits on a deep strata of coal and, during the time of Mzilikazi, warrior-king of the Matabele who considered the area to be his private hunting preserve, it was known as the area of burning rocks. Hwange's small town, the centre of the area's coal mining industry, lies 50km (31 miles) outside the park. With good air and road connections, Hwange, Lake Kariba and Victoria Falls form an ideal touring combination.

LAKE KARIBA AND THE ZAMBEZI

Cahora Bassa in Mozambique and Kariba in Zimbabwe are the two great lakes on the Zambezi River. Kariba Dam was constructed between 1955 and 1959 to provide hydro-electric power for Zimbabwe and her neighbour, Zambia. More than a million cubic metres (35.3 million ft^3) of concrete were needed to construct the massive arch which curves 579m (1 900ft) along its crest and stands 128m (420ft) high. It has a capacity of 180 600 million m^3 (180 billion ft^3).

The wall holds back the Zambezi at a narrow, 100m-wide (330ft) precipitous neck which was first explored 300 years ago by Portuguese discoverer Manuel Baretto, while Livingstone and his brother shot the rapids here in 1860. Kariba's gorge, 620km (385 miles) downstream of Victoria Falls, is only 366m (1 200ft) above sea level and the temperature in summer can reach up to 57 °C (135 °F). The Zambezi continues to run beneath Lake Kariba. Its wide shores of green *Panicum repens* grass are grazed by elephant and buffalo, while fish eagles build their big fussy nests in the steel-hard skeletons of drowned trees that stick out the water along the shoreline of the Matusadona mountains. Kariba is the inland water playground of Zimbabwe and South Africa. A host of safari lodges have been built on Kariba's shores and islands where the game-viewing is excellent and the tigerfishing the best in the world.

Kariba is also renowned for its houseboats, ranging from small, double-deck boxes powered by the family outboard, to multi-deck, multi-cabin Missisippi-style paddle boats. Yachts, windsurfers, hobiecats, catamarans and every shape of power cruiser grace the waters of Kariba. The Kariba car ferry, the *Sealion*, plies the length of the lake, a 22-hour journey and the ideal way of getting from Harare to Hwange and the Victoria Falls.

Kariba town, with its bowling club on the Heights, Italian-built cofferdam church and tiny cluster of shops, is scattered over a series of hills above the lake and Andora fishing harbour. A string of holiday hotels overlook the waters where as evening falls, the lights of *kapenta* rigs twinkle like fireflies.

The Zambezi, having provided the watery palm-fringed wonderland above the Victoria Falls, followed by Lake Kariba's endless pastel vistas, continues from below the dam wall through the Kariba and Mupata gorges. Here, canoeists make their way downriver to Chirundu Bridge and beyond to Mana Pools National Park, the ideal way of seeing the Zambezi. The great river, 5km (3 miles) wide in parts, absorbs a host of other rivers including the Kafue and Luangwa from Zambia, the Chobe in Botswana, the Shire from Malawi and from Zimbabwe, the gold rich Mazowe and Angwa rivers. The Manyame, which provides Harare with its recreational lake and water supply, also flows into the Zambezi.

The Zambezi is deep only in the gorges below the Falls where it can reach depths of 50m (165ft). It is usually a lazy, shallow river interspersed with sand banks and islands where hippo and crocodiles bask in the sun. It is often lined with giant acacia, mahogany and sausage trees, the latter danced around by local women, hoping that their bosoms will emulate the luxuriant fruit. Mana Pools National Park, Zimbabwe's most untouched preserve, occupies 50km (30 miles) of the Zambezi's most beautiful and pristine frontage. Here there are only a few camping sites, two luxury safari lodges, and access only permitted to a strictly limited number of people and cars. A World Heritage Site, Mana Pools' Garden of Eden fragility is periodically threatened by oil, coal, power and uranium projects, elephant over-grazing and rhino poaching, but to date Mana has miraculously survived the depredations of man.

TOP: *Marina and pleasure craft at Lake Kariba.*
ABOVE: *Pausing on the Zambezi, Mana Pools.*

THE EASTERN HIGHLANDS

Lovely mountain ranges and passes stretch along the 500km (300 mile) length of the northern Zambezi escarpment, the roof of Zimbabwe. They include the Mavuradonha above Cahora Bassa Lake, the Matusadona mountains at Lake Kariba, the Chizarira barrier further west and the great gorges along the Zambezi itself. Equally splendid are the jumbled hills of the Matobos near Bulawayo. Beautiful ranges in the mineral-rich Great Dyke run from north of Harare through the Ngezi and Sebakwe lakes to Matabeleland. None, however, really match the unique chain of high, misty mountains and open highlands of the east that stretch 300km (190 miles) from little visited Nyanga North to Chirinda Forest in the far south.

The range includes Mount Inyangani, at 2 593m (8 508ft) the country's highest mountain. It is situated in the Nyanga National Park, its grassy, rolling hills similar to those in Scotland but on a larger canvas.

Also in the east is the lush coffee, fruit and protea-growing Bvumba (with a silent B), the deserted Himalaya, Hot Springs near the pretty town of Mutare and finally the jagged range of mountains known as the Chimanimani, haunt of lovely trout pools, mysterious caves and challenging cliff-edge climbs bordering on Mozambique.

The Eastern Highlands have always been the holiday retreat for city dwellers and farmers. This is horse-riding and trout-fishing country, with a wide choice of hotels and resorts, including one of the country's most scenic golf clubs at the Bvumba's Leopard Rock. All of them are accessed by good metal roads from Harare, Masvingo and Beitbridge.

RIGHT: *Bunga Forest in the Bvumba forms a cathedral canopy across the road.*
BELOW: *The Chilojo Cliffs stand sentinel in Gonarezhou National Park.*

GREAT ZIMBABWE, GONAREZHOU AND THE LOWVELD

The Lowveld, south of the Great Zimbabwe Ruins, stretches as far as Gonarezhou National Park in the east, and the game and cattle ranches to the Limpopo River in the southwest. It is hot mopane country, rich in game and thin in population, and leads down to Zimbabwe's lowest point, the confluence of the Save and Runde rivers where at 200m (660ft), it is a hop to the Indian Ocean.

Halfway between Harare and Beitbridge border post is Masvingo, formerly Fort Victoria. It sits on the edge of the high plateau and is ideal for cattle ranching. It was, in fact, cattle wealth that enabled the ancestors of today's Shona people to build, 700 years ago, the stone walls and 18 000 strong town of Great Zimbabwe, 'houses of stone'. This magnificent monument, after which the country is named, lies very near Lake Mutirikwi with its game park and popular bass fishing. The Great Enclosure, Valley and Hill complexes of Great Zimbabwe are spread over 720ha (1 779 acres). An estimated million granite slabs were used to build the 11m (36ft) high walls of the Great Enclosure.

A variety of dams, Manyuchi, Bangala and Manjirenji – not easily accessed but each unique and in lovely settings – lead through Zimbabwe's cattle ranching Lowveld to the sugar cane-growing areas of Chiredzi and Triangle. Many ranches have now amalgamated into huge game conservancies where the viewing is often better than at Gonarezhou National Park, the 150km-long (95 miles) 'place of elephant' facing the Mozambique plains. Save Conservancy is also a huge citrus plantation. Gonarezhou has always been a hideout for gun-runners, ivory and slave traders and game poachers, going back to the days hundreds of years ago when, local legend would have us believe, Arab dhows sailed up the Save River from the Indian Ocean.

Although Gonarezhou game is depleted, it is still a refreshing and deserted wilderness, its often sandy riverbeds rich in bird life, lush marshy pans and riverine forest. Diamonds are now being found in the Lowveld, as well as many a dinasour bone, a new bridge is open at Beitbridge and the weekly train to Johannesburg cuts through its stark baobab and mopane plains.

Harare's historical Africa Unity Square.

A CRESCENT OF TOWNS

Harare, the nation's capital, is really two towns: the sleek, metropolitan area with its futuristic pods of angled blue glass buildings shaped like pyramids, rockets, hexagons, and, the tallest, the Reserve Bank, a giant tennis racquet handle. Beyond Harare's industrial area is the second city, the huge dormitory town of Chitungwisa on the southern fringe. The combined population is about 2.5 million people. Apart from Harare, there are a dozen other towns on the crescent-shaped Highveld plateau. Some 30% of Zimbabwe's population is urban; 60 000 rural migrants arrive in Harare annually and the city's water and housing reserves are feeling the strain.

Bulawayo, the railway city, is the second largest town. To Westerners, its gracious streets, wide enough to turn a span of oxen, retain a lot of its turn-of-the-century past: Bulawayo Club, railway station, High Court and City Hall are all gems. The town's elderly cars, preserved by the dry air of the Highveld, and its unhurried ambience gives it a special cachet much loved by movie-makers and visitors. The Matobo National Park, burial ground of Cecil John Rhodes and Mzilikazi, founder of the Matabele nation, lies to the south of the city, a smouldering lunarscape of hills, lakes and rugged wilderness.

Kame Ruins, centre of the Torwa culture and Zimbabwe's other man-made World Heritage Site, lies just west of the city on the Kame River. Bulawayo's Natural History Museum has the largest collection, 75 000 animals, in the southern hemisphere, while the open-air Railway Museum includes among its nine vintage locomotives, one Jack Tar dating back to 1896.

Between Bulawayo and Harare lies a line of rail settlements born from a hundred years of mining and farming. Gweru is the largest with a population of 350 000. It forms the main railway link to South Africa, and is rich in minerals, including iron ore, chromite, asbestos, quartz and nickel, while shoe manufacturing, clothing, glass and engineering are some of its products. Gweru is the centre of the country's largest beef-producing area.

For visitors, the Naletale and Dhlodhlo ruins between Gweru and Bulawayo are of interest. KweKwe, the steel and gold mining

BUFFALO, SURVIVORS OF THE SAVANNA

Zimbabwe's savanna buffalo have had a precarious life. Like many other animals, they were once prevalent all over the country, but with the emergence of commercial cattle ranches and as buffalo were believed to be one of the main carriers of foot and mouth disease, they were systematically shot, a policy that is now seen to have been short-sighted and hideously destructive. Fortunately, preceptions have changed and cattle ranches today are re-converting to game conservancies.

These 800kg (1 764 pound) beasts that stand up to 1.4m (5ft) at the shoulder and have wicked curved horns are not docile African varieties of the Bovidae family, in spite of the name. Related to Asiatic buffalo and domestic cattle they may be, but Zimbabwe's buffalo, the black, dusty and bad-tempered *Syncerus caffer*, is the most dangerous animal in the bush. Legions of fireside tales are told about its sudden attacks and hunters' miraculous escapes. A lion, even an elephant, can be turned with a clap or a shout, but if a buffalo comes for you, run for the nearest tree – fast. A buffalo will crash through bush and saplings like a tank, sneak in a wide circle to emerge from nowhere and attack you from behind.

Both males and females will hook horns in hierarchy squabbles but the pecking order among bulls is based on an order of precedence. Buffalo will take on lion who occasionally stampede them; the outcome usually depends on weight advantage. They like to drink morning and evening, staying close to water in a well-defined home range, and often eat at night. They are sometimes attacked by crocodiles and inevitably trailed by white egrets, pecking at disturbed insects. A baby buffalo weighs about 40kg (88 pounds) when it is born after an 11 month gestation period.

There are 50 000 buffalo in Zimbabwe, with herds several thousand strong in Hwange.

town, was originally a frontier fort on the KweKwe River, not far from the Sebakwe Dam and the Great Dyke, a range of mineral-rich mountains that cuts right through the highveld. The road at Battlefields leads off to Ngezi Dam, home of a crocodile research centre in *Brachystegia* woodlands.

Kadoma, north of Gweru, was a mining camp a hundred years ago. Today it is a cotton-growing area with weaving mills and textile factories. Cotton, a major cash crop second only to tobacco, has made Zimbabwe the largest producer of cotton south of the Sahara. Chegutu, the last town before Harare, is an important maize, wheat, cattle and cotton-growing area. It is a small, one-street town, rather like a set from a western movie.

Apart from Masvingo near Great Zimbabwe, Chiredzi in the cane-growing Lowveld, and Mutare and Chipinge in the Eastern Highlands, there is a circle of Highveld towns that fan out from Harare. On the road to Kariba is the farming centre of Chinhoyi, famed for its mysterious caves and copper mines nearby. Karoi, further north, is a major tobacco area in what was formerly tsetse fly country. Karoi takes its name and logo from the Shona word 'karoyi' or 'little witch'. Local witches were once tossed into the nearby Angwa River, presumably for having gotten their spells mixed up. Both Chinhoyi and Karoi often have rain when the rest of the country has very little and their commercial farms are known for their extent, profitability and woodland beauty.

Game-ranching, flowers for export and a host of sophisticated farming pursuits are followed on the Highveld where farming is a carefully monitored, hi-tech science requiring huge financial outlays. The rewards are such, however, that relatively young farmers are soon millionaires. The Highveld crescent from Bulawayo to Harare and then east to the mountains is inter-connected by good road and rail communications but in the main has insufficient population to justify scheduled air services. Many farmers, however, keep their own small aircraft and private operators help fill some of the gaps.

Msasa trees quilt a Burma Valley hillside.

VEGETATION

Zimbabwe is largely a dry miombo woodland of msasa and munondo trees, recognized by their rough fire-resistant trunks and tiny filigree leaves. This is particularly so on the central Mashonaland plateau which has a good summer rainfall. Here you will see open stands of trees averaging 6m (20ft) high, divided by a continuous carpet of grasses.

In Matabeleland in the west where it is lower, hotter and drier, the dominant tree of the woodlands is the mopane. The drought-resistant *Adansonia digitata*, or baobab tree, grows in the Lowveld. It has large white flowers that are much loved by bees. Animals often shelter in its easy-to-hollow-out trunk when it hasn't been gnawed at by elephants. The Kalahari sandveld in the west, particularly near Hwange, produces lovely stretches of *Baikiaea* (Zimbabwean teak) woodlands, while in the eastern mountains, forestry is based on exotics such as wattle, eucalyptus and particularly pines. Nowadays, National Parks are making considerable effort to keep these trees at bay so as to allow the indigenous acacia flat-tops, grasses and wild flowers, including mountain proteas, to survive.

Almost impenetrable gorges of beautiful montane forest occur in the Highlands, and the banks of the Zambezi are a wonderland of giant albidas and riverine tree types. The typical view in rural Zimbabwe is a mosaic of

TOP: *Wild proteas grow on many windswept slopes in the Eastern Highlands.*
ABOVE: *The dungbeetle, indefatigable worker.*

small cultivated fields or large commercial farmlands, interspersed with tumbled *koppies* (small hills) and msasa or mopane woodlands, with thatching grasses in the *vleis* dividing the copses of trees. Using wood fires for cooking and heating is still a common practice. One of the features of the winter landscape is the dust and smoke caused by natural or man-made fires which clear the lands to allow for new growth and for ploughing before the summer rains.

Virtually anything can be grown in Zimbabwe, from aloes, roses and macadamias to bananas, grapes and hops; in the urban areas, all types of imported shrubs and trees flourish. There are no deserts and seldom any snow, but thunder and hail storms in summer dramatically light up the *koppies* with their balancing boulders and candelabra trees.

ANIMALS, BIRDS AND FISH

In Zimbabwe, as elsewhere in Africa, there is a real threat that man's rapid population growth, urbanization and indifference to his habitat will replicate the history of Europe whose forests of bears, wolves and stags were decimated in recent centuries. In Zimbabwe, however, there are still vast areas where the animals of the wild take precedence: a total of nearly 300 mammals, of which 32 are carnivores, range from elephant, lion, buffalo and leopard, to bat-eared fox, wild dog, hyaena, mongoose, shrew, bat, porcupine and pangolin. The larger animals are mainly concentrated in Hwange and Gonarezhou National Parks and along the Zambezi Valley, but there are some 40 wildlife parks and safari areas in Zimbabwe, as well as many private santuaries, former cattle ranches.

It is also true that Zimbabwe's wildlife is threatened by a reluctance on the part of government to financially support and adequately manage the wilderness areas, leaving it in many cases to private agencies with inadequate resources. The first casualty has been the rhino, all but poached out by international crime syndicates determined to monopolize the black market for its horn, perceived in the Far East to have medicinal properties. How to deal with elephant is also a controversial issue. Zimbabwe believes in managing these animals as is done with domesticated cattle and sheep in European countries: selling the ivory and meat for the benefit of local communities. This, however, has met with determined resistance in the west and trading in ivory is still restricted.

Zimbabwe is fortunate that, within the ranks of its National Parks staff, it has some superb ecologists and conservationists, professionals, who, despite political chicanery and inadequate funding, refuse to abandon their posts and their defence of Zimbabwe's wildlife. Thanks to them, the remaining rhino are now protected, elephant, up to 200 at a time, are translocated, wildebeest now browse on the slopes of Mount Inyangani, and baby elephant can be seen in Harare's suburban Mukuvisi woodlands.

Some 153 reptile species are found in the country, including snakes, tortoises, terrapins, chameleons, lizards and crocodiles. Although there are 76 species of snake alone, you can live in Zimbabwe all your life and only come across a few. There are several crocodile farms in the country; especially notable are the ones at Victoria Falls and Kariba with populations of up to 10 000 each, and every sunny Zambezi island crawls with them.

Zimbabwe is a huge aviary, its sunny skies, river banks and woodlands alive with approximately 640 of the worlds 9 000 species of birds, including 40 specially protected large birds. Five hundred species breed locally while 75 species, including 14 birds of prey, are periodic visitors who migrate south from Europe and Asia. About 60 species, including cuckoos, also fly in from neighbouring African territories. The largest single family of bird species in Zimbabwe is the warbler, 53 varieties of these reed bank songsters. Fortunately no species of bird has ever become extinct in Zimbabwe; the Natural History Museum in Bulawayo has Africa's largest collection(92 000) of bird skins.

Zimbabwe has 17 species of eagle and the highest concentration of black eagles in Africa is found in the Matobo Hills, while one of its most prolific fish eagle populations

VICTORIA FALLS ON THE MOVE

The Victoria Falls on the Zambezi River is 1 708m (5 604ft) wide and 100m (328ft) high. Up to 500 000 million m^3 (17.6 million ft^3) of water pours over it in times of flood, and it is historically the last of eight identical avalanches on the Zambezi. Although an extension of the Great Rift Valley, it was the erosive power of the Zambezi that made the Falls, not any cataclysmic tearing of the earth's crust.

The Zambezi flows over a slab of black basalt which rose to the surface 150 million years ago when the fires in the bowels of the earth raged in a volcanic continent-shifting inferno. Gradually this basalt was covered with softer sediments, filling the cracks and crevices and smoothing out the land. The river, however, worked away at both sediments and basalt, carving out the 40km-long (25 miles) Batoka Gorge. Near the Falls itself, the basalt is crisscrossed with giant zigzag cracks, or faults, cutting across its flow. These were filled with sediment but the river scoured out one after the other over thousands of years, creating a series of waterfalls, one replacing the other.

It was half a million years ago that the river attacked the first fault to form a giant ravine for the river to cascade into. Its work complete, it backed up, concentrating its power on the next weakest link diagonal to the existing waterfall, and rubbed away there. This process has been repeated eight times, a waterfall like Victoria Falls created each time. The river is now working at Devils' Cataract where the brink is already 30m (100ft) lower than the rest of the Falls. Fortunately, the 45° angle cut will once again create a new fall, a mere 100m (328ft) behind the existing drop. Where the brink is today, will probably evolve a new rain forest. When the new Falls emerges it will not be the highest, widest or largest waterfall in the world, but still the most awe-inspiring amphitheatre of smoking thunder ever.

Thundering into the chasm, Victoria Falls.

Brooding rain clouds over Mana Pools.

lives on Lake Kariba. Twelve owl species live in Zimbabwe, as well as trogons, hornbills, woodpeckers, lily trotters and 14 species of colourful sunbirds for which Zimbabwe is renowned. Surprisingly, there are even two types of seagull found in this inland country.

Insects also abound in Zimbabwe, plus several hundred species of spider. The fastest, the sun or rain spider (nicknamed Kalahari Ferrari), is found on the banks of the Zambezi. After mating, the male runs for its life to avoid being eaten by the female who has a penchant for radical divorce.

There are 131 fish species in Zimbabwe's 10 000 dams and rivers, including the fighting tigerfish of Lake Kariba, which can reach a weight of up to 15kg (33 pounds).

CLIMATE

The most pleasant time of the year to visit Zimbabwe is in the winter months of June and July which promise sunny days and cold nights. Although lying between the tropics of Cancer and Capricorn, Zimbabwe's high central plateau results in a temperate climate, drier, cooler and much more comfortable than you would expect in Africa. Seven to nine hours of sunshine daily is normal for Zimbabwe except during the rainy summer months of December to February. Lake Kariba recorded the world's hottest resort temperature of 57°C (130°F) in November 1994. Frost and hail does occur in Zimbabwe and very occasionally a touch of snow in remote areas. Winter lasts from mid-May to mid-August when the night temperatures can drop by 25 °C (77 °F). It is much hotter in the game areas but very cold at night on the low-lying *vleis* that animals love.

Zimbabwe also boasts spectacular thunderstorms and cloud formations in summer, the downside being a fairly high incidence of deaths by lightning. Droughts occur periodically but there are no hurricanes or tornadoes, although the wind can blow the waters of Lake Kariba into a stormy seascape.

Low and high pressure systems moving in a southeasterly direction past the South African coast, the nearness of the inter-tropical convergence zone and the Nino phenomenon, all affect Zimbabwe's weather where rain, or the lack of it, is paramount. It often does not get enough during the rainy season, making life for the rural people exceptionally tough and occasionally life-threatening. Dams and boreholes are thus common.

THE PEOPLE

The first Zimbabweans were undoubtedly Stone Age San, some of whom probably settled as iron-making herdsmen; they were possibly joined some 2 000 years ago by African-speaking migrants from the north and later, others from the south to form the ancestors of today's Shona, the largest group of people in Zimbabwe. In the main, the Shona-speaking people inhabit the north, centre and east of the country. The Ndebele-speaking people, who entered the country in 1837, occupy western Zimbabwe. Europeans and Asians and those with both African and European parentage have never comprised more than 6% of the population.

A third of the population lives in the cities, the rest in rural villages and communal farming areas. There is an estimated 80 000 strong population of European descent, mainly business people and commercial farmers, a few Zimbabweans of Indian and Chinese extraction, and a substantial number of Afro-European descent, who in southern Africa, refer to themselves as Coloureds. Urban drift to Harare is, at the rate of 60 000 people per annum, a phenomenon that is not replicated in Bulawayo, the second-largest city.

Apart from the language difference, both Shona and Ndebele have much in common. City dwellers are constantly nostalgic for and return at weekends to the traditional rural thatched homesteads. Both groups are African-speaking, eat the same food, consult the same ancestors, dress similarly and in the rural areas, both are anxious to find schools for their first-born and jobs in the city for themselves. But there are cultural differences, mainly historical.

It is politically incorrect to define people ethnically in Zimbabwe though, for example, the terms blacks and whites are often used. There is little inter-racial tension, and seldom at street level. It rears its head occasionally during economically difficult times or during elections, and then only in some sections of an excitable Sunday press. The control of businesses and the ownership of land are on-going subjects of debate, and occasionally acrimony, as they have been for 15 years.

The Europeans arrived in 1890 although the occasional Portuguese or Scots missionary arrived much earlier. By 1961, 35% of whites were Zimbabwean-born but now there are only some 60-80 000 in the country with twice that number of ex-Rhodesians, as many prefer to call themselves, in Australia and South Africa. Many would like to return but have neither the skill nor capital that government requires. Eighty per cent of today's whites live in towns, 40% in Harare, 20% in Bulawayo. The average Zimbabwean family has five children. Infant and child mortality is low in comparison with other so-called developing countries, life expectancy 58 years. Half the population is under 15.

Zimbabwe's population (estimated at 700 000 in 1901) with a growth rate exceeding 3% per annum is increasing at nearly 450 000 per year, one of the highest rates in the world. Harare has doubled its population in recent years and accounts for 50% of the urban total.

LANGUAGE

Nearly all of Zimbabwe's almost 13 million people speak English, but 67% speak mainly Shona, particularly at home, while 16% speak Zulu-derived Ndebele.

Shona is one of the few southern African languages that did not take on any of the click speech of the Bushmen-San and only very few words of their Arab, Swahili and Portuguese trading partners. Apart from Kalanga around Hwange in the far west, Shona speakers in the centre and east include the Karanga, Zezuru, Manyika, Ndau in the mountainous east and the Korekore in the north. All can understand the other's dialects, the differences being rather like those between Glasgow, London and Dublin.

Town Shona, or *chiHarare*, is a delightful street-slick, free-wheeling mix of dialect, English and jargon. Many Zimbabweans espouse a mix of all three main languages and often do in the course of one conversation.

Ndebele is the second most widely spoken language. It comes from Zulu, although the San click is not as pronounced, and is spoken in Bulawayo and throughout Matabeleland. Singing in this language is particularly evocative. *Chilapalapa* is a politically incorrect patois, based on Ndebele, and these days only used with discretion on commercial farms between farmer and worker.

English is exceptionally widely spoken, due largely to intensive school expansion and the local English colonials' apparent inability to acquire other languages. It has some amusing consequences: to speak English with a Shona accent is good for politics, but to speak with a private school accent is better for business. Urban fast talkers who went to St George's, Peterhouse or Arundel Girl's High are called 'Nose' or stuck-up, while those with a pronounced accent suffer, it is said, from SRB, or Severe Rural Background.

People of mixed descent in Zimbabwe refer to themselves as Coloured; it contains no pejorative connotations. They have an accent and wry jargon of their own, similar to that of the so-called Coloureds of Cape Town, but unlike them, use very little Afrikaans, a language that is only spoken in tiny farming pockets such as coffee-growing Chipinge in the mountains.

In the rural areas whites are *Varungu*, an old 19th-century word for English-speaker, as opposed to *Vazungu* for Portuguese-speaker.

Vapestore, or apostles, pray in an open vlei in Harare. Even the children wear biblical gowns.

All the street signs and practically every newspaper is in English. English is the medium for teaching, TV news, taxi-drivers, petrol attendants, hoteliers and policemen. Very few continental European languages are spoken in Zimbabwe, and to the dismay of Kenyans, no Swahili. American-English is increasingly spoken by young city blacks.

RELIGION

The practice of a faith is more widely spread in Africa than in Europe, perhaps because the people still live closer to the reality of soil and seasons. Ancestral worship and Christianity live side by side in Zimbabwe. Many follow a mix of traditional belief and Christianity, and the hospitality and humility of a people, of whom 70% live in rural areas, fits easily with the heartland of Christian spirituality. Traditional *midzimu* ancestors are consulted to bring relief, particularly from worries, via a *zvikiro* spirit medium. Baba Jesus is also called *Mwari*, the 17th-century Kame and Rozvi term for God.

The San (Bushman) soul force as reflected in their mystical cave paintings and trance dances, possibly played its part in the development of the Shona and Ndebele spirituality. The belief in one supreme *Mwari*-God came in part from the Mbire Shoko people who originated in East Africa around Lake Tanganyika and migrated to Zimbabwe over the last 1 000 years. This faith took root in Great Zimbabwe hundreds of years ago and later manifested itself in the shrine-caves of the Matobo Hills.

Probably some 25% of the population are 100% Christian, the main groupings being Roman Catholic, Anglican and Methodist. The Apostolic faith, which is an indigenous Christian faith, is widespread and white-robed apostles with their shepherd crooks open-air prayer meetings and exuberant weekend dancing can often be seen.

In the eastern mountains the tiny Anglican churches are exquisite replicas of English country churches. Islam also has quite a few adherents and you will easily notice the lacy skull cap of the devout and the handsome mosques, particularly in the smaller midland towns. The impact of Islam in Africa goes back some 1 300 years. Jewish and Hindu communities also form part of the religious make-up of Zimbabwe.

A NATION OF CRAFTSMEN AND ENTREPRENEURS

Iron-smelting, riverside gold-panning and underground tunnelling are ancient Shona crafts, the latter widely and often illicitly practised even today, while the standard farming tool, a narrow hoe, is universally used. In the rural areas many a man carries a wedge-shaped axe fixed into a knob of wood over his shoulder, not for fighting but for farm and forest chores. Drums and *mbiras* (thumb pianos in huge pumpkin gourds) are still made and widely played in the rural areas and in domestic workers' houses.

Ochre and black clay cooking and water pots (copied from ancient Kame designs, among others) are still crafted and used. You will see them on sale on the highway from South Africa, together with walking sticks, stone carvings and more recently, wooden hippos and giraffe, all in colourful open-air stalls by the road. Cloth was made in Zimbabwe from wild cotton 700 years ago and 'Zambia' wraparounds are all the rage, although ironically often made in Malawi. Like other nations, many small Zimbabwean entrepreneurs trade in big neighbouring South Africa, often illegally, particularly in the city of gold, Johannesburg. Some 15 000 Zimbabwean hopefuls are extradited annually from South Africa, but many more wrangle permits, identification and passports and stay in the big city to make their fortune.

Msasa bark hats, bags and particularly rugs can still be bought in Nyanga and Chimanimani, while rugs from baobab bark fibre are common in the Lowveld near Birchenough Bridge. Women today display lovely crocheted table cloths of cotton and rugs of wool. The Venda in the south are specialist basket-makers, while the Ndebele are makers of fine straw hats and inexpensive multicoloured sisal bangles.

A nation well-known for its friendliness (top) and for its artistic skills (above).

THE ZIMBABWEAN WAY OF LIFE

Zimbabweans are crazy about soccer, beer and books. Crowds of up to 45 000 are drawn to big football games, and in township streets and dusty rural roads you will see impromptu games with home-made balls of plastic tied with string. Horse-racing, or rather, betting, attracts many punters, the Castle and OK Challenges being annual excitements. Many schools play rugby, while cricket and golf are also popular. One of the world's top golfers, Zimbabwean Nick Price, occasionally comes home to grace one of the country's 70 courses on big-play occasions. Tennis is gaining popularity throughout the country.

Stella Chiweshe, who plays the *mbira,* is the soul of Zimbabwe, while Oliver Mtukudzi is one of several superb folk singers. Ndebele chant-singing is magnificent. Music is heard and is played boisterously everywhere, often to a Chaucerian street listenership of basket-makers, packers of fruit, instant garages, food vending 'tuckshops' and other small entrepreneurs. Many Zimbabweans are without jobs and partial employment is the norm. Were it not for the extended family mutual help system, life for many would be tough in a country subject to droughts, bureaucratic indecision, inflation, economic uncertainty and topsy-turvy international export markets.

Doris Lessing, Wilbur Smith and John Gordon-Davis all originally hail from Zimbabwe, and there are many excellent Shona writers and poets, some with a substantial following among overseas literati. Charles Mungoshi's *Waiting for the Rains* is a Zimbabwe classic; so is Dambudzo Marechera's *House of Hunger* or *Bones* by Chenjerai Hove. Local magazines, such as *Horizon* and *Moto*, and the capital's daily paper, *The Herald*, display penmanship of a high quality. The good opposition press, like the *Financial Gazette*, has a limited banker and northern suburb readership.

Although there are dozens of imported boutique beers these days, Castle is still number one. Brown tubs of Chibuku shake-shake beer with the grains still in it are quaffed in large quantities. Drinking and driving is still, unfortunately, a common practice. Marijuana in Zimbabwe does not carry a death sentence but it is illegal and punishable.

Sadza, a stiff maize meal porridge, is the national dish both in city chophouse and rural *musha* (kraal). It is served with a vegetable relish and when possible, meat. Coca-Cola, buns and cold corn on the cob are the workers' diet. Fast foods flourish wherever there is a pavement, and the Englishman's staple, chips, is favourite fodder. Zimbabweans abroad miss their local margarine spread (never butter) and *Mazowe* orange juice. Every type of local vegetable and fruit can be bought, depending on the season, although grapes are sometimes imported from South Africa and fish from Mozambique, Namibia and South Africa. Zimbabwe makes a wide range of wines drunk by those of Western culture and tolerant palate.

Zimbabwe's cities are much safer than many elsewhere in the world and there is only the occasional, rather ham-fisted armed robbery. Car theft remains an art form with a devout following. The police force is becoming increasingly thorough and individual policemen are inevitably courteous to strangers. The judiciary is probably without equal in a developing country.

To own any car that starts, even if it's 30 years old, and a small house in one of the high-density suburbs, is the aim of the urban dweller in Zimbabwe. There is a big backlog for houses, but surprisingly few shanties, although many families have to sleep in one room, while some of the rural areas near the borders are seeing more and more refugee homesteads. Owners of plush houses call their homes lodges, decorate them with brass plaques, satellite dishes and 4 x 4's, and surround the lot with high walls, uniformed guards and black electronic gates.

Zimbabweans are used to a high standard of medical care with some 300 hospitals and 500 clinics countrywide. Private medicine is excellent. Aids is a major killer of men, women and children, death from which is inevitably hidden behind journalistic euphemism when the afflicted is well-known.

The majority of Zimbabweans travel by rural bus packed high with higgeldy-piggeldy goods. In the cities, the 'commuter omnibus', minibuses that seat a dozen people, are a law unto themselves. The poorer man has a bicycle, firewood strapped to the back with lengths of inner tube rubber. Second-hand clothing marts flourish while wealthier suburbs boast multi-boutique shopping villages with restaurants, cinemas and exhibitions.

Family and friendships interlock importantly in Zimbabwe society, resulting at times in rampant nepotism. Bribery and corruption have not reached Kenyan or Nigerian proportions, but 'favours' are fashionable and the temptation to jump the bureaucratic or business queue with a backhander is all too often expected and guiltily given. But you will still meet many hard-working and honest civil servants, particularly in the rural areas.

ABOVE: *Beautiful Naletale was modelled on the design of Great Zimbabwe (top right).*

HISTORICAL BACKGROUND

Zimbabwe's many rock caves, overhangs and clusters of balancing boulders contain a wealth of rock paintings, an estimated 30 000 sites, legacy of stone implement-using and nomadic hunter-gatherers that a later civilization would refer to first as Bushmen, then as San. Neither name was ever known to these little folk who peopled the great spaces of Zimbabwe, living in total harmony with nature and the creatures of the wild, and who reached their god through a ritual trance-dance, the focus of much of their art. In the far west of Zimbabwe, in the Makulela area near Plumtree, is a small 300-strong remnant community of San. Known as Masili, or Tshwa, they originated in Botswana, but no longer follow the old, simple lifestyle.

At roughly the beginning of the Christian era and over several centuries, some San may have settled down to a more sedentary sheep-herding and grain-planting life, others developing iron-smelting and pottery skills. They possibly imitated and joined the African-speaking herdsmen and agriculturalists who some historians believe began to appear in Zimbabwe, having migrated over the centuries, it would seem, from the far north.

MAKERS OF IRON, BUILDERS OF STONE

Around 800 AD, at about the time Alfred the Great was battling the Danish Norsemen, Zimbabwe's central plateau was populated by cattlemen and farmers, ancestors of today's Shona people. It was on the Highveld around the area of modern Masvingo, halfway between Harare and South Africa, that was to become one of Africa's greatest towns, Great Zimbabwe. Geographically, the area was perfect for both summer and winter grazing.

Surplus wealth from cattle herds and control of the east coast gold and ivory trade enabled the powerful to cast their eyes around the many granite hills surrounding them and build *musha* of mud and timber surrounded by walls made of granite blocks. Soon it became a highly sophisticated art form and over the period 1100 to 1450, signified the wealth of dynasties under whom textiles, weaving, copper-working,iron-smelting, gold-refining and cattle herding were unified into a vast city whose political, economic and cultural influence stretched across much of Zimbabwe and Mozambique.

Great Zimbabwe at its height was a town in which 18 000 people lived, with an army that was able to exact tribute, if not political dominance, far and wide. Trade with the Swahili middlemen of the coast was central to this unusual society that built majestic walls and stone enclosures, possibly for the defence of the royal and spirit-medium hierarchy but equally to demonstrate their wealth and power.

MUTAPA AND PORTUGUESE

Historians still debate as to why the state of Great Zimbabwe collapsed around 1450 AD: economic reasons combined, perhaps, with declining political and civic skills? Other dynasties were already developing on the periphery of this great state. Mutapa in the northeast was one. The Mutapa were originally based at Great Zimbabwe but broke away during its twilight years. These new stars in the political firmament, the *madzimambo*, or rulers, would only later acquire the title of 'owner of the land' or *Mwene-Mutapa*, interpreted as master pillager, the name by which the Portuguese, the first Westerners to visit this part of Africa, would come to know them.

In the year of the Prophet 903 (1498 AD), a historian on the East African coast recorded the arrival of 'the Franks' (Europeans) in Mozambique. It was an era of both Christian and Islamic fundamentalism. Soon al-Mirati (Admiral Vasco da Gama) and those who followed him, attacked, sacked and plundered every ancient coastal Swahili town from Safala to Mombasa. In the latter, 'neither man nor woman, young or old, nor child however small' apparently survived the depredations of the conquistadors. They believed the *monomotapas* of the interior to be dripping with gold and power, source, perhaps, of the King Solomon's Mines tales, and they made many forays into the country. It was these tough, sea-faring people who would bring southern Africa to the attention of Europe. They ventured into the interior, set up *feira* (trading posts) and introduced maize, tobacco and citrus fruit from the Americas. Portuguese pressure and conquest, combined with internal dissension, eventually caused the collapse of the Mutapa State.

DYNASTIES OF THE TORWA AND ROZVI

With the Mutapa tucked away in northeast Zimbabwe and battling with the Portuguese filtering up the Zambezi, the Torwa in the southwest were successors to Zimbabwe's cultural empire, building beautiful structures at Kame, others at Danangombe (or Dhlodhlo), and the magnificent chevron, herringbone and checked pattern walls of Naletale. This dynasty lasted from 1480 to 1684, extending over part of the Highveld and western Zimbabwe. It in turn succumbed in the 1680s to the warlike Changamire of the central Shona Rozvi dynasty who destroyed neither their state nor culture, but chose to preserve it as they continued their wars with the Mutapa in the Zambezi Valley and the Portuguese in the east. By 1840 a new, even more militaristic and ferocious dynasty was emerging from the south: the Zulus.

ZULU DAWN

Shaka's rise to power resulted in tribes being scattered throughout southern Africa, even as far north as Lake Victoria. Soshangane left his mark on southeast Zimbabwe, the Lowveld area where the people still speak Shangaan. Zwangendaba, too, fought his way across the country, but the most successful tribe was Mzilikazi's Zulu clan, the Khumalo, named the Ndebele by their victims as 'those who disappear behind long shields'.

Mzilikazi, 'great bull elephant', king of kings, was born around 1795. He defied Shaka, escaped with his life and with a handful of followers settled in South Africa's Magaliesberg mountains for many years. He befriended the great missionary Robert Moffat at Kuruman in the far west, but plagued by advancing Boers, hightailed it to north of the Limpopo, where in the area around the Matobo Hills he settled his people and finally destroyed the last of Changamire-Rozvi hegemony on the high plateau. He never succeeded in subjugating the Shona who largely kept a wary distance from his impis, but occasionally emerged to make rather daring raids of their own on the invaders.

ENTER THE ENGLISH

The first Portuguese explorer to enter Zimbabwe was Antonio Fernandes in 1513. Scottish missionary Robert Moffat arrived in 1854, followed by his son-in-law, Dr Livingstone. The latter, along with earlier Scottish

Harare's Heroes' Acre, a monument to liberation.

medic, Mungo Park in West Africa, brought the continent to the attention of English-speaking Europe and America through their dramatic travels, maps and writings on Africa. Adam Renders, who lived at Great Zimbabwe, ivory hunter Frederick Courteney Selous, artist Thomas Baines and American journalist Henry Stanley's heroic tales of darkest Africa soon had young Englishmen clamouring for adventure. With the arrival of imperialist and diamond magnate Cecil John Rhodes, this mix of jingoistic military adventure, lust for land and gold, and well-meaning missionary zeal, translated itself into the brutal colonial conquest of Zimbabwe.

By 1895 Zimbabwe was known outside Africa as Rhodesia with Salisbury the capital. In spite of revolts and uprisings, the English who came to settle on the high plateau with its lush farming lands and perfect climate, were not to relinquish control for 85 years.

THE RISE OF ZIMBABWE

Taxes, forced labour and appropriation of land were the sparks for a war of liberation, a *chimurenga*. After a defeat in 1893, the Shona and Ndebele, traditional enemies, combined to attack Rhodes' European settlers. They were led by spirit mediums Mbuya Nehanda and Sekuru Kaguvi (the terms of respect mean Auntie and Grandfather). With the exception of Major Wilson's platoon wiped out on the Shangani River (his monument still stands atop World's View in the Matobo Hills) and many a lonely farmstead and mining camp over-run (the names of some can be seen on old-fashioned plaques inside Harare's Anglican Cathedral), horses and modern firepower prevailed. For the next 85 years the whites ruled.

In Rhodesia the early years were tough. The Rhodesians – laid-back, convinced of their superiority and their civilizing mission – regarded themselves as frontier folk, the rugged fringes of the Empire. They believed they had a natural right to the best government, land, jobs and privileges. 1957 saw the emergence of the Southern Rhodesian African National Congress with Joshua Nkomo as president. In 1963, this movement split into the Zimbabwe African National Union (ZANU) and the Zimbabwe African People's Union (ZAPU). Furious rivalry developed.

Meanwhile, the white Rhodesians pressed the British government to give them independence on their narrow terms. Ian Smith, a farmer, became prime minister of Southern Rhodesia in 1964. He was determined to grab independence, unilaterally if necessary, which he did on 11 November 1965. The British government deliberated, the United Nations imposed mandatory sanctions, and the Shona and Ndebele took to the gun. But the Zimbabweans were ineffectual until the 1970s when rural infiltration on classic guerrilla lines was combined with the support of a Mozambique free of Portuguese control.

Gradually the war approached the cities. A million rural farmers were forced into PV's (protected villages) to cut off food and supplies to the guerrillas. The Rhodesian military launched attacks into Mozambique, killing thousands at a time. Eventually, the pressure became too much. An all-party conference was called in London and signed on 21 December 1979. Free elections followed in February 1980 and Robert Mugabe became Zimbabwe's first Prime Minister. Nearly 8 000 people died in the last year of the war, 27 000 in total, while some 150 000 had become refugees. But the rebuilding of a nation could now begin.

ZIMBABWE TODAY

GOVERNMENT

Zimbabwe has been an independent state since 1980, following a long civil war between the majority black population of Shona and Ndebele and the whites of British and South African descent. Politically and culturally the *chimurenga* war years saw the Zimbabwe leaders almost out of necessity embrace Marxist economics and Maoist military tactics. Consequently, many of the present generation of Zimbabwe leaders (or chefs as they are somewhat ironically called), including Mugabe the current President, initially tried to establish one-party politics and a command economy. But the British and Western traditions in the country, where Parliament is modelled on Westminister and where the legal system is totally Western, proved durable.

Today Zimbabwe is a multi-party democracy with a one-house parliament elected by universal sufferage. Instead of a Prime Minister, however, there is an Executive President. His terms of office are unlimited, and thus a weak link in an otherwise democratic constitution. The President is chairman of the cabinet and appoints all ministers. In many ways he holds far greater power than his equivalent in Western countries, as there is a marked tendency in Zimbabwe to give undue reverence to those in authority whether president, policeman, headmaster or civil servant. In Zimbabawe longevity in office, a weak opposition and the presence in Harare of rather too many Westerners bearing gifts, has all but banished this constraint in public affairs. Open criticism is allowed but not often practised and it is not easy to see how political change, vital to true democracy and the avoidance of disillusion, will come about.

LEGAL SYSTEM

The legal system with its magistrates, high and supreme courts, is based on the collected historical decisions of judges; in other words, 'case law' based on precedent. This forms what is known as the common law of Zimbabwe. But this common law, based upon principles evolved over a long period, is being progressively taken over by laws enacted in parliament. The courts, since independence, have lost some of their authority to politicians keen to exercise more control.

Oral tradition preserved customary law. Shona chiefs prior to 1890 tended to exercise effective authority in their own areas. This was more centralized under the King among the Ndebele. Customary law largely applies through village and community courts to folk living in rural areas and covers such matters as marriage and *lobola*, custody of children, adultery and seduction.

Statute law is embodied in Acts of Parliament with the Chief Justice being the senior legal officer. There is no trial by jury in Zimbabwe. The Ministry of Justice provides the necessary expertise and manpower for the independent court system, together with the Attorney-General and a Director of Public Prosecutions. Legal aid is available for those without funds to pay for a lawyer, and a Law Department at the University provides education for law students. The Zimbabwe Republic Police Force, with its inherited British formalities, ranks and procedures, enforces the law.

THE ECONOMY

Zimbabwe, with export earnings around $US1.9 billion, has always had a diversified economy with industry a major factor. Zisco, one of the few steel works in Africa, was launched in 1955. Tobacco has been the main crop since the 1920s and all the country's food requirements for a population of 13 million are locally produced, although recently, and for the first time in 25 years, a wide variety of luxury imported foodstuffs and other goods began appearing on the nation's shelves.

When farming exports collapsed in the worldwide Great Depression 60 years ago, many farmers took to the hills with pickaxe, *badza* (hoe) and wheelbarrow to mine gold, the country's third largest earner of forex

Coffee on the bush. Soaked in water, the fruit releases its familiar black bean.

after tobacco and tourism. Zimbabwe has never been King Solomon's Mines but in the hills there has always been a nugget or two, and prospecting is deeply ingrained in the national psyche and has been for 1 500 years. To this day in remote villages a smiling salesman will sidle up to you and offer a spent cartridge or porcupine quill of gold for sale.

When the Zimbabwe African National Union (Patriotic Front) – ZANU (PF) came to power in 1980, it aimed to revolutionize the imbalance of land, health and education, and jerk its people up by the bootstraps of a command economy, promising political paradise. But Robert Mugabe inherited a largely Western and British system – and an economically sophisticated country that was the envy of many in Africa. The new government moved fast to establish its control of the economy, thus creating only partially competent parastatals, state-purchased enterprises, red tape, price controls and draconic currency exchange. The government reached the point where they controlled 60% of exports, 100% of imports and employed 25% of the national workforce.

Having stretched itself on education, defence and health, the government has, for the past few years been trying to turn it around in co-operation with the World Bank and the IMF, a decidedly mixed blessing. Zimbabwe's economy is based on tobacco, tourism, gold, ferro-alloys, nickel, asbestos, agricultural products that include meat, cut flowers, coffee, tea, maize, sugar and lumber, and a variety of manufactured goods including machinery, leathers, radios, furniture, clothes, shoes, fertilizer, medicines, plastics and $40 million worth of stone works of art. It is a bustling and energetic economy with some of the world's most innovative farmers and industrialists, both large and sidewalk.

Sanctions in 1965 after Ian Smith's UDI stimulated local industry but also brought in excessive and habit-forming government controls. Since 1990 there have been real efforts to improve these bureaucratic yokes but it's a huge task as so much of the economy is government-owned. Even more difficult has been the task of cutting the government budget deficit. Zimbabwe is one of the most highly taxed countries in the world and inflation often exceeds 25% per annum. Despite high taxes the government budget deficit has run at 10% of GDP (the total value of goods and services produced by the economy annually) for most years since the early 1980s, an unusually high rate.

Zimbabwe has one of the largest armies on the continent, which places a considerable strain on the country's hard-pressed economy. Partially trained by the British, it is favoured by the U.S. military for peace-keeping missions in Africa.

AGRICULTURE

'Thank you for smoking' could easily be the motto of Zimbabwe where tobacco is king. The country is the world's largest exporter and one person in 12 is dependent on its vast receipts. (But you are not allowed to smoke on the national carrier's internal flights.)

Farming in Zimbabwe is of two types: small-scale farming (which is partially subsistence and partially profit-driven) and large-scale commercial farming. During rare good years, the small farmers can even produce as much and sometimes more maize, cotton and foodcrops than the big commercial farmers. Some 6 000 large-scale farmers using massive inputs of capital and high-tech expertise form the economic backbone of Zimbabwe. Only mining and tourism can compete with the massive surpluses of maize, cattle, coffee, sugar, wattle, flowers, vegetables, milk, tea and fruit that are produced on the vast plateau farms, using irrigation, fertilizers, computer technology and innovative management skills. Zimbabwe, except in bad drought years, feeds itself and usually has a surplus to export to neighbours and abroad.

Wherever you travel along the plateau in Zimbabwe you will see high brick tobacco barns where tobacco is cured, seas of green maize, white cotton fields, ridges of lush-leafed tobacco plants and well-fed cattle herds. Sugar cane is grown in the Lowveld and used in the country's blended fuel. Triangle in the Lowveld, Africa's first ethanol plant, produces 40 million litres (8.8m gallons) annually. Hops, granadillas, grapes, apples, peaches, flowers (particularly proteas which are of a particularly high standard) are all grown in Zimbabwe. Agriculture accounts for 40% of Zimbabwe's exports so when the rain does not fall, it is disastrous.

The rains only arrive once a year, from November to March, and everyone, farmer and urbanite, anxiously looks to the skies, praying for rain. It can wipe out a huge farm or send a poor rural family scurrying to the city in search of non-existent work. Many rural families have to walk 30km (20 miles) daily to find water in years of drought.

MINING

Iron, copper and gold have probably been mined in Zimbabwe for over 2 000 years, certainly since the 11th century. Zimbabwe is one of the world's largest producers of gold and its long list of minerals not only includes beautiful diamonds, emeralds, sapphires and rubies, but also much sought-after platinum, asbestos, copper, chrome, nickel, coal, iron ore, silver, cobalt, tin and a total of 40 minerals and metals. The country has every precious and practically all the semi-precious stones. Gold panners operate legally and illegally along riverbeds. In rural areas you will quietly be offered the chance to buy; resist

Burley tobacco grows in the lush Burma Valley.

it, it is illegal. Most mining is done by huge international companies but there are still quite a few small registered prospectors.

It was, in fact, Zimbabwe's gold that attracted Cecil Rhodes and his settlers 100 years ago. Ironically, they found very little among the 6 000 deposits that had been worked by the Shona and that had produced 150 tonnes up until they arrived. But the gold was there alright, only deeper and more difficult to access.

Some 450 smallish gold mines exist in Zimbabwe. Coal is mined, underground and opencast, at Hwange near the country's giant game park. The largest asbestos mine is at Zvishavane (near where the emeralds come from), west of Great Zimbabwe. The country is also one of the world's top three producers of asbestos (the non-dangerous-to-health chrysolite variety), and Zimbabwe has over 80% of the world's high grade chromium ore which is used in such industries as stainless steel manufacturing.

INDUSTRY

South of the Sahara desert, only South Africa with its vast industries and mines, produces more manufactured goods than Zimbabwe. From 1965 and the imposition of sanctions and for the first 10 years of independence, Zimbabwe hardly imported any manufactured goods and certainly no consumer goods. Almost everything was made locally. This caused great difficulties with items such as car spares, light bulbs, matches, books and practically anything approaching a choice of goods in a consumer world, but it made Zimbabweans exceptionally innovative, self-reliant, and necessarily, patient.

Harare is the industrial centre, four times as big as Bulawayo, but there are car assembly plants and oil refining facilities in Mutare, Bata Shoes in Gweru and textiles in Kadoma. Zimbabwe exports fertilizers, medical and pharmaceutical goods, piping, paper-board, yarns, fabrics, blankets, hardware, furnishings, TV's, trailers, railway trucks, batteries and furniture, among many others.

The country produces practically all its own foodstuffs, canned goods and drinks, although boutique beers, fruit juices and Coca-Cola in cans (cans are still relatively new to Zimbabwe) can now be seen on supermarket shelves. Plus, for some strange reason, an incredible range of Scotch whisky. Rubber tyres, cement, construction materials and chemicals are all made in Zimbabwe. Industry contributes some 30% to Zimbabwe's export revenues. The country's chief trading partners are South Africa, United Kingdom, Germany, America, Japan, most E.U. countries and all its neighbours, plus China, Australia and Hong Kong.

ENERGY, CONSTRUCTION, BANKING AND TRANSPORT

Zimbabwe's coal reserves stand at 30 000 million tonnes, sufficient to last, some say, until the next Ice Age 17 000 years hence. Thermal power stations operate from the Hwange coalfields with hydroelectricity generated at Lake Kariba. Hwange supplies three times the energy of Lake Kariba. Most urban households have electricity but there are still small villages without. Solar energy units are increasingly evident, particularly in smaller centres. Coal supplies the bulk of Zimbabwe's electricity, although wood fuel is common in rural areas. At Triangle ethanol from sugar cane is blended with imported fuel to provide for the country's petroleum needs. About 10 000 dams are found in Zimbabwe, and 25 of these are situated in recreational wilderness areas. Bulawayo, the second largest city, is always in danger of running out of water but there is hope of diverting water from the Zambezi River for its needs.

In 1993, half a billion dollars worth of construction plans were approved for Harare where new skyscrapers seem to shoot up each day, $133M for Bulawayo and $900M for the whole country. Harare's new Reserve Bank is the latest and largest construction. Schools and clinics form the main rural buildings, with a good deal of private shops, mills and bottle stores built at growth points. Forty per cent of Zimbabwe's construction is residential. Despite the fact that about 18 000 low-cost houses have been built and some 20 000 other houses in the last 10 years, there is still a dire need for more low-cost housing. Nevertheless, there are few shanty towns.

Zimbabwe's excellent rail network of 3 400km (2 113 miles) carries an average of 13 million tonnes of goods annually and some 2.5 million passengers. Air Zimbabwe, another parastatal, transports some 750 000 passengers annually in its fleet of 737 aircraft regionally and 767's to Europe. Both companies have clever advertising; both are short on profitability.

Zimbabwe has a good system of roads, linking all the main centres and tourism areas. But be careful when travelling at night as the road markings are poor and you will come across cattle, vehicles with only one light and diesel-belching buses that totally blind. Game, particularly on the road from South Africa, is another night-time hazard. The national vehicle fleet is possibly approaching a million vehicles. In rural areas one third of all households have a bicycle although there are not that many in the cities. People prefer to pack into an E.T. (Emergency Taxi), Peugeot station wagons held together with bubble gum and reggae music. There are some 250 rural bus operators each with a bus or two. Up to 120 million passengers use these buses annually. Visitors who want to experience the colour and life of real Zimbabwe should ride in one of these jolly people-packed road-runners.

Victoria Falls airport may soon be too small for the growing number of visitors it receives.

GETTING AROUND ZIMBABWE

For the traveller keen to see all that Zimbabwe has to offer, such as the game parks, Victoria Falls, Eastern Highlands and Great Zimbabwe Ruins, Zimbabwe could not be easier. No part of the country is further than a day's drive on good metal roads; even travelling from Nyanga in the east to Hwange in the west is only about 1 000km (621 miles). The central part of the country and all the major towns sit on a high crescent-shaped plateau rich in maize, cattle and tobacco farmlands. As this plateau tumbles down through Zambezi River escarpment, Matobo Hills or soaring Nyanga mountains, there lies the country's wildlife and scenic splendour.

HOW TO GET THERE

BY AIR

Direct flights are available to Zimbabwe from Europe, the Far East, Australia and many countries in Africa, including direct flights from Johannesburg and Cape Town, some straight to the Victoria Falls. From the USA there are good connections via the UK, Europe and South Africa.

Internally the country's three main attractions, Lake Kariba, Hwange and Victoria Falls, are linked with the capital and each other by daily flights. No scheduled Air Zimbabwe services exist to Masvingo (Great Zimbabwe) and the Eastern Highlands resorts, but United Air operates smaller aircraft departures to Masvingo several times weekly. Harare and Bulawayo (Matobo National Park) are linked by air and numerous charter operators exist. Zimbabwe has commercial airports, including one in the Lowveld at Chiredzi, and dozens of airstrips in game reserves, holiday resorts and on private farms.

BY RAIL

Train services operate to the Victoria Falls and Hwange game reserve, to Bulawayo, Harare and Mutare, the capital of the Eastern Highlands, but not to Kariba or direct to Masvingo. Good services link Zimbabwe to South Africa, the port of Beira in Mozambique, Francistown in Botswana and Lusaka in Zambia via the Victoria Falls.

BY ROAD

It is possible to travel the whole of southern Africa south of the Zambezi, covering Zimbabwe, Namibia, Botswana and South Africa, on good, well-maintained metal roads. The roads inter-connect, the driving is on the left, the service stations well-spaced, the rest spots convenient. In Zimbabwe in particular there is seldom need for a four-wheel-drive vehicle.

Access from South Africa is via Beitbridge on the Limpopo River, from Botswana at Plumtree in Matabeleland, from Namibia at the Caprivi Strip Kazangula border post near the Victoria Falls, from Zambia at the Falls and at Chirundu on the Zambezi, from Mozambique at Mutare and from Malawi via Mozambique at Nyamapanda.

The only gravel access road is the one via Caprivi but it can be done in an ordinary car with care (200km; 125 miles from Katima Mulilo to Victoria Falls). The road from Malawi is full tar. The metal roads in Zambia can be potholed but are continually improving. The route south from Kenya (4x4) can be along the coast from Mombasa to Morogoro in Tanzania, then inland through to Mbeya and Zambia. A reasonable road runs from Beira on the Indian Ocean to Mutare.

TRAVEL WITHIN ZIMBABWE

ON ARRIVAL

There is usually an airport bus or minibus run by your hotel or safari operator to meet you at the airport. Taxis are available at Harare and Bulawayo and can be called at the holiday resorts. Car hire facilities (Europcar, Avis, Hertz) are available at every airport and holiday destination. At the railway stations, there are taxis and E.T.'s: Emergency Taxis. Take one if you care to sample the local colour and some people-packed and rather abandoned driving. They are actually good fun and you'll get a great reception.

The two worst roads in Zimbabwe are, of course, the most heavily used: Beitbridge to Harare and Bulawayo to Harare. But even these are well-maintained metal roads but with no shoulders for overtaking, equivalent to regional roads in South Africa. At night the road markings are poor – beware of game between Beitbridge and Masvingo, Victoria Falls and Hwange, and Chirundu-Makuti-Kariba. The maximum speed limit of 120km p/h (75 miles p/h) is rigidly enforced.

Long-haul carriers are usually good drivers, everyone else is potentially suspect. Defensive, alert driving is needed in Zimbabwe, especially at weekends. Drinking while driving is not unheard of and some buying of licences has been known.

The roads from Harare to Mutare, Harare to Kariba and from Bulawayo to Victoria Falls are excellent. All Zimbabwe's fuel, refreshment and roadside facilities are of a reasonable standard, some really excellent.

VISITING VICTORIA FALLS

Zimbabwe's top resort is served by many flights from a variety of carriers. It lies 439km (273 miles) north of Bulawayo, 758km (471 miles) from Beitbridge and 1 312km (815 miles) from Johannesburg. Visitors could go by road directly to the Falls from Etosha Park via the Caprivi Strip and from the Okavango via Nata and Kasane. The Victoria Falls is often combined, not only with trips to Hwange Game Reserve and Lake Kariba, but also with safaris in Botswana (Chobe), Namibia (Caprivi) and Zambia (Luangwa Valley). Victoria Falls also sits astride the great rail system linking South Africa with Zaire (Congo), Zambia and Tanzania. And one of the best ways to travel the route is by train, particularly old-fashioned and luxurious steam train rail safari.

An air safari over Lake Kariba is a visual feast.

At the other end of the scale there are rural buses for the adventurous. The roads leading off the main Bulawayo-Victoria Falls route access Hwange game reserve (which is often done en route) and the western basin of Lake Kariba. It is possible to travel to Victoria Falls via the scenic rural route from Harare and Karoi, the length of Lake Kariba but some 50km (30 miles) inland. Half the 600km (375 miles) is on a gravel road.

ON SAFARI

Harare hosts a major safari travel fair each February. Most visitors who come to Zimbabwe, come from densely populated urban western cities where truly fresh water is a rarity, solitude is difficult and there are no high skies by day or stars at night. They come to see game and the vast open spaces, and to touch, if only briefly, the wild. For many their only contact with nature before coming to Africa is perhaps to have sympathised with animal transport or fox-hunting protests and for them the thought of someone actually hunting game is appalling. This is understandable. The conservationists, however, will say that it is only high hunting trophy fees that guarantee the value of the animals and the survival of their wilderness habitat, while at the same time providing an income for peasant communal area villagers near whose lands some hunting takes place. A concept known as Campfire in Zimbabwe and one that, by encouraging rural families to protect their now valuable animals, may just be the answer to conserving Africa's wildlife which to date has always lost out to human population pressure.

There are about 120 big game, plains game, and ranch hunt operators in Zimbabwe and 35 species of game can be hunted. One elephant can bring in tens of thousands of dollars to a rural village whose annual cash income is often insufficient to pay clinic and school fees. Zimbabwe is well known for its fabulous herds of elephant (in fact, far more than the country's habitat can withstand), buffalo and practically all of Africa's game with the exception of the gorilla.

Eighty photographic safari operators exist. A photographic safari covers a touring, game-watching and resort-visiting trip. The top photographic game areas are Hwange and Mana Pools National Parks and Matusadona National Park on Lake Kariba, but there are many others including the wide, wild and lovely Gonarezhou in the southeast where the Runde and Save rivers meet. The best time of the year for Hwange is in winter and the best viewing is probably in the south of the park and near Dete Vlei.

Specialist photographic safaris in Zimbabwe include week-long canoeing safaris on the Zambezi, sailing safaris on Lake Kariba, walking safaris in the Chizarira wilderness,

Elephants cross regularly between Hwange National Park and the nearby Dete Vlei.

houseboat, elephant-back safaris, birding, horseback, fly-in and practically every combination of these. Zimbabwe's wilderness guides are considered to be the best trained in Africa and need a minimum of three years experience before getting their licence.

Some 20 luxury lodges are found in or near Hwange including tree lodges, tented camps and thatched chalets. All are superb. Along the Zambezi, nothing can beat Ruckomechi Safari Lodge's location in Mana Pools beneath giant albida trees. But others with chalets, canoes and mobile camps both on the Zambian and Zimbabwe shores give excellent service. On the shores and islands of Lake Kariba and high in the Chizarira massif are more delightful safari camps, many with swimming pools and huge double-storey thatched booze 'n view platforms. Fothergill Island was the first safari camp and is still difficult to beat. Mahenye Safari Lodge at the confluence of the Save and Runde rivers in Gonarezhou is great with lovely forest and sandriver walks and there is good game at Lone Star Ranch. Many private game ranch reserves operate in Zimbabwe, some up to 344 000ha (850 000 acres) in extent and many offering the 'big five' (lion, rhino, leopard, elephant and buffalo) to visitors. Both Great Zimbabwe Ruins and the Matobo Hills have excellent safari lodges and there are even a clutch of them within striking distance of Harare and Bulawayo.

Hotels range from five-star CNN TV to rural swat-the-mozzies. Some of the best are the small log fire and candlelit dinner inns that dot the Bvumba and Nyanga mountains and the delightful Hot Springs south of Mutare. They outclass the large hotels when it comes to cuisine and personal service. Accommodation at the Falls tends to be in the form of big hotels with the venerable Victoria Falls Hotel as the all-Africa choice.

En route to the holiday resorts, many will enjoy such Bwana Game hideaways as Three Way Safaris near Bubi River, Cloud's End Motel at Makuti near Kariba, Gwaai River Hotel near Hwange and Mlibizi Hotel en route to the Victoria Falls. In the mountains

The luxurious Elephant Hills Hotel at Victoria Falls also boasts a casino and golf course.

there are many cottages for hire; backpacker crashpads are inexpensive and often with homely bed and breakfast service. Rustic National Parks chalets, fully equipped and serviced, exist in practically every wildlife area of Zimbabwe, including Nyanga (the best), Victoria Falls, Matobo Hills, Gonarezhou, Matusadona (Lake Kariba), Mana Pools and Hwange National Park. There are many camping facilities in Chimanimani, Bvumba, Gonarezhou and practically everywhere else. Due to lack of funding the facilities in the parks are not as good as they once were.

Big safari hotels are similar to ones in the city except for the thatch, drum music, warthogs chomping the grass and colourfully dressed waiters. The best safari locations in Zimbabwe include Dete Vlei in Hwange, National Parks lodges above the Falls, anything in Matusadona, Chizarira, Kuburi Camp, Kariba, Ruckomechi in Mana Pools and Chikwenya along the Zambezi. But check the less well-known places such as Imire near Harare, Save Conservancy in the Lowveld, the Mavuradonha mountains and the ranches west of Bulawayo.

If your guide carries a powerful rifle while walking with you in the bush, you know he or she is fully qualified. Really up-market and exclusive mobile 'Out of Africa' safaris where you and your party are taken through Zimbabwe's wilderness sancturies for a week or longer and treated like kings and to the best Africa can offer, are also available.

PART TWO

EXPLORING ZIMBABWE

The mighty Victoria Falls is Zimbabwe's premier attraction. But the one million visitors that come to Zimbabwe, a sunny, high-plateau country between the Zambezi and Limpopo rivers, also delight in its spacious woodlands and valleys of mopane and msasa trees which, in turn, lead to trout pools and cool mountains, ideal for hiking, the fabulous ruins of Great Zimbabwe, Lake Kariba's vast tigerfishing lake, the Zambezi River and its canoeing safaris, and the Matobo Hills, burial eyrie of Cecil John Rhodes. Above all, they come to see the great herds of wild game: elephant, lion, buffalo, giraffe, rhino, impala, leopard, baboon, even the tiny honey badger. And there are enough colourful songbirds to exhaust any birder. All of Zimbabwe's scenic attractions offer good, inexpensive accommodation.

LEFT: *Regiments of fiery aloes guard the ancient walls of Great Zimbabwe.*
ABOVE: *Considering the options, Mana Pools.*

VICTORIA FALLS AND SURROUNDS

The Victoria Falls area, in Zimbabwe's north-western corner, stretches from Kazungula where Zambia, Botswana, Namibia and Zimbabwe meet, back along 60km (37.5 miles) of the Zambezi River to the Falls, and then for 130km (80 miles) down the mountain-hemmed Batoka Gorge and Devil's Gorge to where the river opens out into Lake Kariba. To the south is Hwange game reserve; to the north, the 1905 Edwardian bridge links Zambia with Zimbabwe.

Within earshot of the Falls is the town of Victoria Falls itself and two national parks: one is the Victoria Falls National Park (often called the Victoria Falls Rainforest National Park), the other the Zambezi National Park. The former covers 23km^2 (9 miles^2) and includes the Victoria Falls, the rain forest opposite it and the 1km-wide (⅝ mile) stretch of rugged bush on the southern edge of the Zambezi River which flows through the great white-water rafting gorges. Like the waterfall itself, the river is heavily protected, fragile and vulnerable to big money exploitation. Not much game occurs in this park but you will be rewarded with sights of lovely birds.

THE VICTORIA FALLS NATIONAL PARK

Entering through the thatched archway of the Victoria Falls National Park and walking along the paved path through the woods, you could be in any national park in Africa. But with one exception: a rumbling in the distance. It gets louder as you move on, and the excitement builds. Through the trees, a flash of white, then more trees, lianas, orchids and tangled vines. The noise is powerful now as everything is drawn magnetically to the great throb of the Falls and the primeval shuddering of the seething cauldron. On the jungle canopy above you, it is like a sudden squall of rain, then sunlight appears through the dappled rain forest. The noise builds. And suddenly you break through the tree line and stop still, catching your breath. All that you have heard does not prepare you for this horizon-to-horizon cavalry charge of white and green thundering, tumbling, dancing, leaping water. It stretches ahead as far as the eye can see. Although divided by the giant rock canyon below, you feel you can reach out and touch this wonder, only 60m (200ft) beyond the strategically placed thorn bush and fireball lilies, the spray updraughts, drenching the trees and the red-spangled flowers. To the left is the mighty Devil's Cataract, directly in front of you Cataract Island, then Main Falls. This is the Victoria Falls, in the local Leya-Tonga language, *mosi-oa-tunya*, 'the waters which rise in the air' or more dramatically, 'smoking thunder', the greatest tapestry of falling water in the world.

OPPOSITE: *The flight of angels – a microlight flip offers unparalleled views of the Falls.*

Haemanthus multiflorus*: rain forest fireballs.*

Shongwe was the name the Tokaleya people, who still live there, gave the Falls. Mzilikazi's wandering Zulu-Ndebele referred to them as *amanza thunquayo* or 'water rising as smoke', while the Kololo, on the run from other impis, called them *mosi-oa-tunya* the name we use today. A huge bronze statue of Dr David Livingstone atop a plinth of chiselled granite reads 'Missionary, Liberator, Explorer'. It stares boldly across Devil's Cataract and was sculpted by Sir William Reid-Dick of London in 1933 as a tribute to 'a great Christian gentleman'. Livingstone,

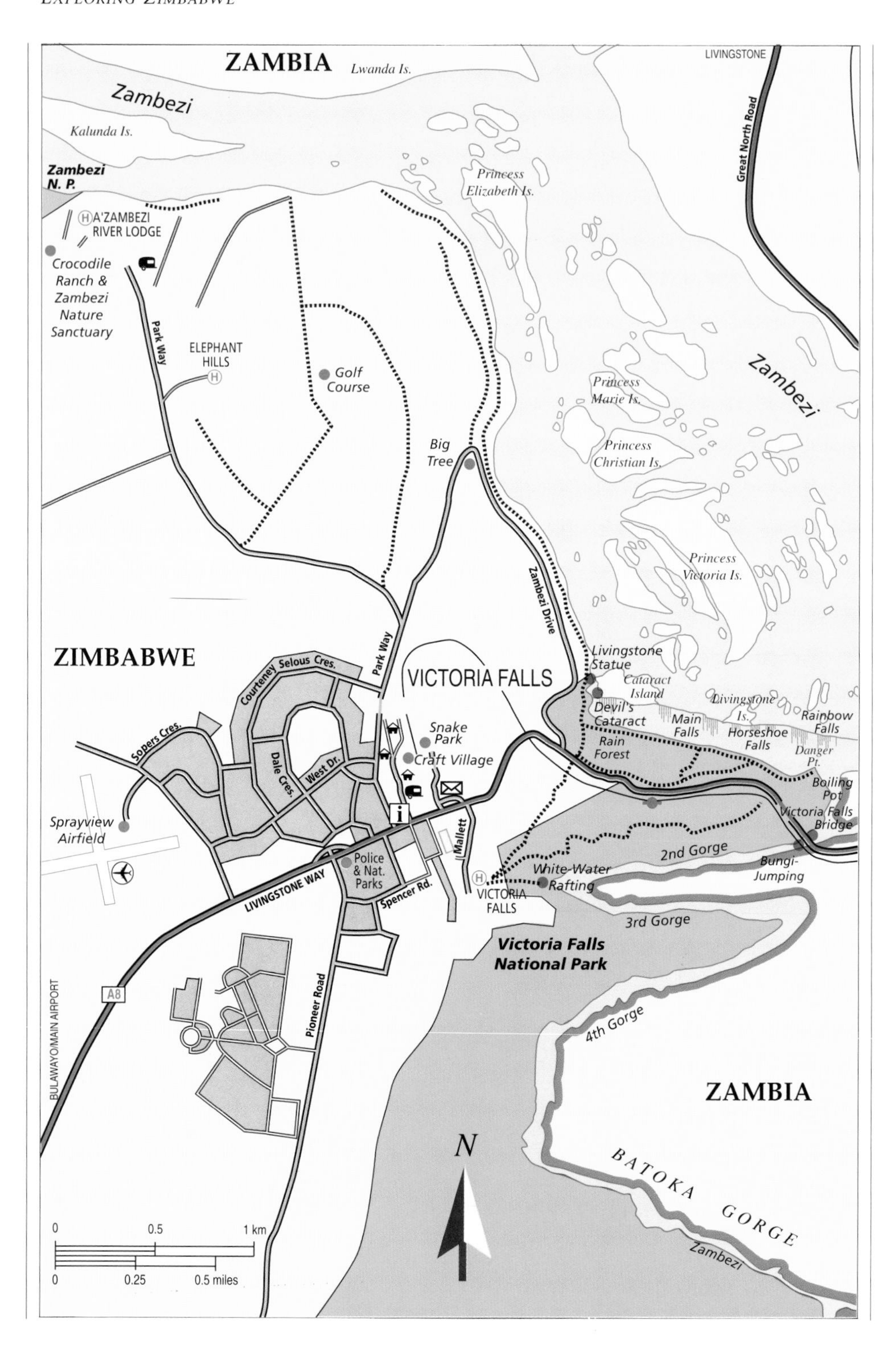
ZAMBIA
Lwanda Is.
Zambezi
Kalunda Is.
Zambezi N. P.
A'ZAMBEZI RIVER LODGE
Crocodile Ranch & Zambezi Nature Sanctuary
Park Way
ELEPHANT HILLS
Golf Course
Princess Elizabeth Is.
LIVINGSTONE
Great North Road
Zambezi
Princess Marie Is.
Princess Christian Is.
Princess Victoria Is.
Big Tree
Zambezi Drive
ZIMBABWE
Selous Cres.
Courteney
Park Way
VICTORIA FALLS
Livingstone Statue
Cataract Island
Devil's Cataract
Livingstone Is.
Rainbow Falls
Main Falls
Horseshoe Falls
Danger Pt.
Rain Forest
Boiling Pot
Victoria Falls Bridge
Sopers Cres.
Dale Cres.
West Dr.
Snake Park
Craft Village
Sprayview Airfield
Mallett
2nd Gorge
Bungi-Jumping
Police & Nat. Parks
LIVINGSTONE WAY
Spencer Rd.
VICTORIA FALLS
White-Water Rafting
3rd Gorge
Victoria Falls National Park
A8
Pioneer Road
BULAWAYO/MAIN AIRPORT
4th Gorge
ZAMBIA
N
BATOKA GORGE
Zambezi
0
0.5
1 km
0
0.25
0.5 miles

A Zambian youngster pauses awhile near the impressive Eastern Cataract.

despite his failings, was indeed a man of enormous stature, integrity and selfless dedication, a man who can justifiably claim to have done more than anyone else to rid Africa of the scourge of slavery. He was the first European to record the Falls, but Arab slavers, if not geographers, were very probably there before the Scottish missionary.

DEVIL'S CATARACT AND CATARACT ISLAND

Admission to the park is along Livingstone Way, opposite the car park and through the thatched National Parks display. After walking along the path through the woods, the visitors' first view of the Falls is Devil's Cataract. In monstrous green and white churned turmoil, the Zambezi River boils through the Devil's Cataract in awesome savage fury, power and thunder. Devil's Cataract lies right at your feet, and is the first and lowest of the five falls that make up this horizon-wide waterfall. It represents a fault in the underlying rock structure through which the Zambezi cuts a channel. Looking from here upriver, the wide, palm-lined shores seem to urge the great river on until, fretful and turbulent, it harnesses its massive strength for its final, frenzied leap over the Falls.

Beyond the flimsy barrier of thorn bush and across the frenzy of cavorting water, is Cataract Island where smaller flows of the river twist through the dense vegetation to join the huge flow of the Devil. It was more appropriately known as Boaruka Island by the local Toka folk, meaning 'divider of waters'. Early European visitors also called it by the pedestrian name of 'three-rilled cliff'. Francis Coillard of the Paris Missionary Society visited the Falls in 1878. The island, he said, was believed to 'be haunted by a malevolent and cruel divinity'. California's Bridal Veils Falls is the world's longest, Angel Falls in Venezuela the highest, Khone in Laos the widest, but what makes Victoria Falls different is its immense visible curtain of water.

THE RAIN FOREST AND FALLS

In the gossamer spray that hovers as high as 300m (1 000ft) over the Falls are the river's rainbows. At full moon, the lunar rainbow is a ghostly, ethereal experience. It is often seen in the chasm below Devil's Cataract.

The Victoria Falls is the most flamboyantly panoramic curtain of falling water in the world. And it is from the lovely rain forest opposite the Falls only 60m (200ft) away, that it is best seen: the billowing updraughts and spray-drenched jungle of twisted lianas, orchids, mosses and ferns; the thunder of its smoking waters rumbling day and night as a mile-wide avalanche of water falls ceaselessly 100m (330ft) over the basalt brink. Do not take a camera for your first visit; rather absorb the many moods of this rainbow-sparkled wonder and the delicate forest that overlooks it. Every new vista is more dramatic than the last. Go down the chain walk where steps are cut into the steep side of the cliff parallel to Devil's Cataract, and from there up again into the tangled, forest. Remember your raincoat and be prepared for the whoosh of the spray and sudden 'rain'.

The first six vantage points concentrate on Devil's Cataract and Cataract Island, offering long views the length of the chasm. In the rain forest behind you are strangler figs, African mangosteen, climbing acacias and the Cape fig bush, noted for its black berries and yellow flowers which, in the evening, smell like potatoes. You will see plenty of dragonflies near Devil's Cataract and in the dark-light depths, blackeyed bulbuls and, if you are lucky, the Livingstone lourie winging scarlet and emerald across the gorge. In November, 20 000 m^3 (26 161 ft^3) of water per minute hurtles over the 1 708m-long (5 604ft) Falls but it has been known to reach 500 000 m^3 (17.6 million ft^3) per minute at full flow. At the Victoria Falls, the Zambezi is 1 000km (621 miles) from its source.

WHITE-WATER RAFTING

Suddenly you are in the maelstrom, a suction of swirling green water and an explosion of spray. The Batoka Canyon, 22km (13 miles) of the surging Zambezi forged into 19 rapids, some only 12m (39ft) wide and with 400m (1 312ft) high cliffs to left and right, is the wildest river-rodeo one-day white-water run in the world, and after the waterfall itself, the greatest single attraction at the Victoria Falls. The young and not so young come from all over the world to experience this heart-stopping rubber-raft ride on Africa's great river.

It was started by Sobec, an American company who have pioneered rivers all over the world. Shearwater and Frontiers are the other big local operators of this exhilarating, big-river action. The inflatable Avon rafts bounce and twist in the surging water, navigated by a daring skilled oarsman and seven passengers who shift their body weight to manoeuvre the ducking craft. Several rafts do the run together which can be run only during July through to mid-March. Those who have done it will tell you that nothing can beat the 24km (15 mile) low-water option from mid-August to December. This counts as a grade 5 run (rapids are graded 1-6); 6 is non-runnable.

The rapids all have nicknames: Morning Glory, Muncher, Devil's Toilet Bowl, Jaws of Death, Overland Truck Eater and Rapid 13, 'the mother', with its huge waves. Thousands of people have shot them. Very occasionally the great whirlpools claim a victim, three in 13 years. Each year teams, professional and amateur, compete in the Zambezi River Festival, watched by 30 million viewers worldwide.

Ride the Zambezi once and you will certainly be back – it's like a fever in the blood.

Swallowtail, swordtail and numerous other butterflies can be seen in the forest, while the spoor of leopard, banded mongoose, waterbuck, baboon, monkey and bushbuck can be spotted by the observant. Hippo are seldom seen here these days, while the buffalo in Baines's famous painting can today only be seen up or downriver. Black and white trumpeter hornbills, paradise flycatchers, sunbirds, apalis and Heuglin's robins are some of the birds found in the forest that weaves between viewpoints.

In the rainy season, the local brown and green flame lily is seen in the forest. Aloes grow in cracks in the cliffs of the waterfall islands, while the pincushion flower that grows on the forest floor from October to December looks like red candyfloss. A necklace of thorn bush frames the viewpoints; in the old days there was nothing to stop you slipping off the muddy edge onto the rocks far below in the vertical chasm.

The water is not normally very deep in the chasm but in 1958 when the Zambezi River reached an all time flow of 700 000 m³ per minute (14.3 million ft³), the water in the gorge rose to a dramatic 18m (60ft) higher than any other previous flood, the sort of immense power responsible for the zigzag gorges that have been cut into the riverbed downstream of the Falls.

The sequence of the Falls, beginning at Devil's Cataract, is Main Falls, divided by a projecting coxcomb of rock and 821m (2 694ft) wide, Livingstone Island, Horseshoe Falls, Rainbow Falls, and finally, Danger Point which overlooks the Boiling Pot, Zambia and the river's escape route to the next of many zigzagging gorges.

In the year-round spray area across from Horseshoe Falls to Rainbow Falls and Danger Point, wild date palms, Cape figs and waterberry trees are more widespread. Near Danger Point it is open grassland and rock. A pool here has freshwater crabs which the hornbills fancy. At times during the dry season, the Falls pause and the vast reef of water practically disappears, leaving only filigree ribbons to lace the great face of the basalt.

TOP: *The Heuglin's robin, a rain forest resident.*
ABOVE: *The big baobab tree in Zambezi Drive is an easy walk from Victoria Falls hotels.*

The return route runs closer to the spidery steel bridge from which the bungi-jumpers leap and which leads to Zambia, with a main-arch span of 152m (500ft); it carries one rail and one road track and was opened on 12 September 1905 by Charles Darwin's son, Francis. It was built close to the Falls because Cecil Rhodes wanted train passengers to feel the soft touch of the spray as they crossed. When it was completed, it was the highest bridge in the world, utilizing 2 000 tonnes of steel and was assembled in England before being sent out by ship and train; the two spans finally touched at 06h00 on the morning of 1 April 1905.

The long-serving, medal-bedecked concierge, Oddwell, at the Victoria Falls Hotel.

Victoria Falls Hotel

The Victoria Falls Hotel, dowager empress of the Zambezi, is chunky, colonial and orange-tiled. Surrounded by giant mango trees filled with chattering monkeys, she sits regally within earshot of steam trains arriving from Bulawayo and the thunder of the world's greatest waterfall.

The hotel was built in 1904 when a room was a guinea a day: corrugated tin roofs, wooden steps up to the verandah, raised to fend off the white ants and other undesirables of the African night, and roll-down blinds to keep m'lady's complexion pale. Rickshaws were the first transport to the Falls and were later replaced by hand-worked rail trollies, one of which today forms a decorative seat in the lily pond gardens.

By 1910 the hotel had sanitation, electricity, fans, an Italian manager, a French chef, an American barman and Arabian waiters. At this time the *Victoria Falls Advertiser* of 3 October 1910 informed readers that meals at Tommy's Restaurant nearby were 2/-. Today the hotel with its white-gloved, parasol and pink gin atmosphere, elegance and green and white decor, its gardens and views over the Falls, has become one of the 25 most famous hotels in the world. At the entrance, a short, treed walk from the Edwardian railway station, hangs a filigreed name-sign, a memento from a TV series filmed there.

A regular Zambezi river festival of white-water rafting and canoeing is held at the Falls each year. This goes back to the first River Regatta of 1909; then, a thousand people wanted accommodation in the hotel that had rooms for only a 100. The Victoria Falls soon became a popular destination for visitors from as far away as Cape Town who travelled there by train, so in 1913 the hotel was rebuilt in brick. Today there are direct flights from Cape Town to Victoria Falls, unfortunately not by flying boat as was the custom after World War II. But there is still a flying boat operating on the Zambezi and the guide

INTERESTING PLACES EN ROUTE

- Hwange's Robin's and Nantwich camps can be reached by turning left off the Bulawayo road, 390km (242 miles) from that city and 48km (30 miles) from Victoria Falls. It is then 68km (42 miles) to Robin's.
- Mlibizi is a fishing and birding resort at the headwaters of Kariba. Turn right at the cross-roads 281km (175 miles) from Bulawayo, sign-posted Kamativi. It is then about 95km (60 miles) on a metal road.
- Deka Drum Fishing Resort on the Zambezi River. Turn right off the Bulawayo road at Hwange town and drive for 47km (29 miles) on a narrow tar road. Furnished cabins are available. Msuna fishing area is a little further.
- Stop for tea at the Baobab Hotel perched on a bluff amongst palms high over and opposite the entrance to Hwange town.
- If you are arriving from Namibia or Botswana, the village of Katima Mulilo, capital of the Caprivi Strip on the Zambezi, is a comfortable riverside stopover (200km or 125 miles and four immigration posts) from Victoria Falls, mainly on rough gravel roads.

ABOVE: *Even tiny crocodiles have sharp teeth, Victoria Falls Nature Sanctuary.*
RIGHT: *Canoeists, dwarfed by the Batoka Gorge.*

will point out the Imperial Airways 'Jungle Junction' mooring point. Bicycle hire companies flourish at the Falls, a grand way of exploring the area.

The best place to eat at the Falls (today there is a choice of at least 20 restaurants) is the elegant claret-and-cream Livingstone Room at the Victoria Falls Hotel. Colonially formal, it features *kapenta* tartare and crocodile tails, high ceiling fans, and the *Debvu* ('beards') ensemble. Book well in advance. Outside on the patio are barbecues, marimba music and high-stick Makishi dancers.

When Dr Livingstone arrived at the Falls, slavery was rampant and the East African slavers are believed to have imported the ilala palm that now graces the Falls. The seats of the old chairs in the Hotel's chapel of St Mary Magdalene are made of palm weave.

ZAMBEZI NATIONAL PARK

The Zambezi National Park stretches 40km (25 miles) west from the Victoria Falls village halfway to the Kazangula border post with Botswana, Namibia and Zambia, and 24km (15 miles) south to the Matetsi Safari Game Area. Interspersed with lovely ilala palms, ebonies, figs and acacias, the park, with its 25 fishing, camping and picnic sites and rustic chalets, faces the Zambezi where warthog snuffle, African fish eagles cry, hippo snort, and the sunsets are perfect.

Tributaries of the Zambezi run into the river, including the Mpala Jena, Siamunungu and Chomunzi, all good fishing sites. Elephant, lion and particularly sable can be seen in the well-wooded park which covers an area of 56 000ha (138 408 acres). Chamabonda Drive leads to Kaliankuo Pan and Njoko Pan's game-viewing platform. Lion have regularly been seen on the golf course at Victoria Falls.

ZAMBEZI NATURE SANCTUARY

Twenty-seven crocodile and caiman species occur worldwide, but none seem quite as lethal as the 10 000 at the Crocodile Ranch and Zambezi Nature Sanctuary. Yet they are vital to the ecology of rivers and Africa.

About 5km (3 miles) upstream of the Victoria Falls just outside the Zambezi National Parks gates, the Crocodile Ranch is set amongst shady trees, pools and walkways where you stroll past long pools of crocodiles, graded by age and size. Some of the larger crocodiles, a breeding group, can be seen along the banks of the sanctuary stream, creamy orange mouths open to the sun. Crocodiles have remained unchanged for 140 million years. They can stay submerged for hours and swallow 1% of their body weight in stones to help digestion, although broken glass or earthenware pots will suffice, and crocs will travel a long way to get their quota.

Crocodiles see and hear exceptionally well on land and underwater. Being cold-blooded creatures, they need to bask in the sun, especially after the night's chill; this is when whitecrowned plovers unconcernedly eat the parasites on the crocodiles' gums and tongues. Fish is their staple diet, with mammals a popular option for larger specimens. They prefer fresh to decomposed or rotten food as this can cause gastroenteritis.

Contrary to popular belief, they hide their catch under riverbanks for fear of theft by other crocodiles, not to decompose it. Ironically, crocodiles cannot swallow underwater. Ninety-eight per cent of baby crocodiles do not survive in the wild. Pneumonia is a major killer while leguans, working in pairs, regularly invade the crocodile nests. There is thus a need for the 15 or so crocodile ranches which are found throughout Zimbabwe.

In the Zambezi Nature Sanctuary there is a crocodile walk, leather workshop, wild cat orphanage with caraculs and leopards, a 50-seat auditorium, an animal farm where children can enjoy tractor rides, a tea garden, the 'Old Crocarosity Shop' and an open 'vulture restaurant' where these huge birds arrive to fight over take-aways.

BUNGI-JUMPING

The world's highest bungi-jump.

Jack Soper, the toll-keeper of the bridge when it opened in 1905, was the first person to bungi-jump at Victoria Falls. He had himself lowered 30m (100ft) down into the chasm oposite the Falls to capture an unusual camera angle. Today African Extreme operates this sensational bungi-jump off the Victoria Falls bridge, with the dark green gorge of the Zambezi below, and the thundering spray of the Falls as backdrop. People crowd the rails on the bridge to watch the fun. Only 40% of the fall is free-fall, the rest is slowed down by the stretch in the rubber rope, not terribly comforting although being strapped into the extra safety harness helps. Six different bungi cords for different weights are hand-made by the New Zealanders who run African Extreme.

First they weigh you on a bathroom scale, then wrap your ankles in thick towelling as you sit on a carved African stool. Next your ankles get tied together with webbing used by mountain climbers in a knot that hasn't slipped in a half a million jumps, and they smile again. You have to be mad, of course, to have a rubber rope wrapped around your ankles, edge to the lip of the bridge, try not to look, listen to the count-down, wish you had taken a river cruise instead, then at the massed shout of 'BUNGI-I-I-I-I-I-', hurl yourself in a swallow dive into 111m (364ft) of mist-blown air with the raging, boiling whirlpools and rocks of the mighty Zambezi below and your own screaming in your ears. The cruelest cut is that they video you all the while. Bookings can be made through Shearwater in Zimbabwe or Valley Ventures in Zambia (*see* p. 51).

ABOVE: *A crocodile feeds mainly on fish but will lunge the length of its body for an antelope.* RIGHT AND BOTTOM: *The Craft Village illustrates the lifestyles of the different ethnic groups.*

VICTORIA FALLS TOWN

Victoria Falls town specializes in super-sell: curio shops, white-water rafting, aircraft flips over the Falls, traditional African dancing. Even its street signs are bold. Despite this, Victoria Falls is still a gorgeously sleepy village, the man-made hinterland of one of the world's most dramatic, awe-inspiring and beautiful sites. Neither the bungi-jumping, art gallery, snake park, bicycle hire nor frenetic pubs affect this charming image. Old-fashioned steam trains still chug past low-level crossings en route to the bridge, Zambia and Tanzania.

The *Debvu* band still plays 50-year-old reprises at the Victoria Falls Hotel, the hippo grunt in the Zambezi, warthogs eat the A'Zambezi Hotel lawns, the National Park's chalets look like rustic 1930s prints, the little Catholic church is tucked away in West Drive, and the Edwardian Railway Station is truly something out of Africa. There is a supermarket, chemist, shoe shop, craft shops behind the post office, a bookstore, two garages, car hire and the interesting Chinotimba township. There are canoe wine route trips upriver, horse trails, a tiny arboretum on the corner of Courteney Selous Crescent, restaurants, take-aways and a dozen hotels, even splat ball. But none of it is near the Falls and it all has a refreshingly amateur touch.

Traditional Living and Dancing

Fred Forrest is actually a woman. Tough, self-made and artistic, she brought African dancing as a performing art to the Victoria Falls 25 years ago, and today it is imitated not only at the Falls but in many parts of the country. Seventy-five dancers and drummers perform a dozen different traditional routines nightly at the Victoria Falls Craft Village and Victoria Falls Hotel. These include the Chibububu Shangaan air turns and high jumps, the intricate footwork of the Nyau dance, paced by drums, and the circumcision dance performed by the Mwaro Makishi, a combination of several tribal groups. In the Chikuza dance, visitors watch as fathers symbolically pass onto their sons the technique of the Kaluwe tradition. The multi-beaded, colourfully striped body costumes, masks (with iron-like beards) and headgear, the drumming, shouting, stilt-climbing and leaping dancers seen in the flashing light of fires is an exciting, fiery display. Besides the evening performances which are announced by kudu-horn blowing and drumming, there are daytime performances at the Falls Craft Village, a colourful Venda-walled *kraal* with Ndebele-Zulu warriors dancing and singing to entice visitors inside.

As Shona women perform their inimitable shake-shake routine to the music of *mbiras* (thumb pianos in gourds), wander around and see the San (Bushman) beehive shelters, the lion-proof doors of the Tonga people of the Zambezi River, the highly decorated grain bins of the Venda, an Ndebele kitchen, the Nyanga stone-walled platform enclosures with their underground circular stock pits, and much more.

There are also fish traps, iron smelting furnaces, burial huts, a Shona meeting place, or *dare*, maize driers, bird traps, a fall trap, a *kraal* for cattle, sheep and goats and even a diviner-herbalist, or *n'anga*, in case you'd like your future told. And at the exit of this 'living museum', Cokes and curios to jerk you back to reality.

TOP: *Curio sellers display their many wares near the Snake Park.*
LEFT: *A barrel-shaped hippo jealously guards its territory on the Zambezi above the Falls where ilala palms line the river (below).*

A relaxing sunset cruise on the Zambezi, Africa's fourth largest river, begins above the Falls .

ZAMBEZI CRUISE

Man has been sailing up the Zambezi ever since he learned to hollow out a canoe, and certainly long before Arabian and Portuguese explorers ventured forth 1 300 years ago in search of gold, iron and slaves. Due to the Cahora Bassa rapids and the Victoria Falls, however, it has never been really navigable.

The Zambezi is very wide at the Falls and there are some large islands upstream and, at Katombora and Sansimba, exciting rapids. Today, you can even visit them by float plane. The Zambezi, 2 740km (1 703 miles) long, is the fourth largest river in Africa. It rises in Zambia and always, especially at boat level seems hemmed in with lush green trees, the grunt of hippo close by.

The best way to explore the Zambezi is in a small boat with a small outboard that you can switch off and cruise into shore to see birds and game. Or try a canoe 'wine cruise'. Best of all is a three-day canoeing safari starting at Kazangula 80km (50 miles) upstream. The choice includes kayaks, 3m-long (10ft) two-man, rubber 'crocodils' that look like large inflatable lilos or two-man klepper canoes, all ideal for exploration of the hidden waterways and over-grown channels. The sundowner booze cruise is often rather noisy, crowded and not ideal if you really want to see game and birds.

THE EASTERN BANK

The eastern bank of the Zambezi is worth a visit. One-day passes to cross into Zambia are easy to obtain but involve some queuing, and a good way to explore the area is to hire a bicycle. Apart from the National Museum in Livingstone with its Tonga collection, the Zambian Falls themselves at Knife Edge Point, Boiling Pot and Eastern Cataract are particularly powerful views of the giant gorge into which the river falls. The Eastern Cataract is a dozen rushing streams glinting gold and green among the palms before the final leap over the basalt brink. The edge, spray-filled and deafening, is only metres in front of you. At the craft village, backpackers bargain T-shirts for decorated wooden guineafowls and local hand-made baskets.

ADVISORY: VICTORIA FALLS

CLIMATE

The weather is exceptionally hot here for most of the year. In winter (June and July) the days are warm but nights cool. November brings the rain; at this time, and the weeks preceeding it, even the nights are hot and humid. Victoria Falls lies at an altitude of 880m (2 887ft), twice as high as Kariba.

BEST TIMES TO VISIT

The Falls are magical throughout the year, but their flow is lowest in November and December. The end of the rains from February and March onwards see the heaviest flow and volume of spray.

MAIN ATTRACTIONS

Devil's Cataract, followed by a walk through the rain forest, should not be missed as this encompasses all the views of the Falls. White-water rafting, bungi-jumping, a flight over the Falls, traditional African dancing at the Craft Village or Victoria Falls Hotel, canoe game-viewing, a visit to Zambia's Eastern Cataract, and a walk across the bridge, are all highly recommended. Picnic and fishing spots are found along the river and a game drive through the Zambezi National Park is usually rewarding. The crocodile ranch makes an interesting outing.

TRAVEL

By air Direct flights to Victoria Falls leave from Harare, Bulawayo, Cape Town, Johannesburg, Hwange, Kariba and Gabarone. Call Air Zimbabwe, tel (263) 13-4316 or Harare (263) 4-575021.

By road Good access roads run from Zambia, Botswana, Namibia and South Africa. Victoria Falls is 2 900km (1 802 miles) from Cape Town on metal roads. Luxury coach services are available twice weekly between Harare, Bulawayo and Victoria Falls. Tel *Blue Arrow* (263) 4-729514 (Harare) or (263) 9-65548 (Bulawayo).

By rail Steam train safaris operate from Bulawayo, tel (263) 9-75575, and a daily overnight passenger train, NRZ tel (263) 9-322210.

By ferry A good route is to take the overnight car ferry from Kariba to Mlibizi which is two hours from the Falls, tel Harare (263) 4-614162/7.

GETTING AROUND

The best way to tour the Falls is by bicycle (*Bushtrackers*, Parkway, tel (263) 13-4348) or on foot. Also try the *Victoria Falls Rambler*, a tractor-pulled trailer that tours the village. Hire a car (*Europcar*, tel (263) 13-4598; *Avis*, tel (263) 13-4532; *Hertz*, tel (263) 13-4267), or catch a *UTC* or hotel bus. You can also join a four-wheel-drive safari or hire a scooter (tel *Scoot Selfdrive*, Pumula Centre, (263) 13-4402).

TOURS AND EXCURSIONS

Elephant Safaris Elephant Back Safaris, tel *Wild Horizons* (263) 13-2004, fax (263) 13-4349.

Zambezi Canoe Wine Route *Zambezi Canoe and Safari Co* tel (263) 13-2059, fax (263) 13-2058.

Local Culture Tours *Touch the Wild*, tel (263) 13-4694, fax (263) 13-4676. P O Box 122, Victoria Falls.

Traditional Dancing At the *Falls Craft Village* or *Victoria Falls Hotel* nightly. Tel (263) 13-4309.

Crocodile Ranch (Zambezi Nature Sanctuary) 5km (3 miles) along Parkway. Tel (263) 13-4637.

Snake Park Behind the Post Office, near curio shops. Tel (263) 13-5801.

Bungi-Jumping *African Extreme*, c/o Shearwater, tel (263) 13-4471, *Valley Ventures*, Livingstone, Zambia, tel (260) 3-320742, or book at the bridge.

Canoeing Upper Zambezi above the Falls. Canoe, kayak, inflatable rafts. *Frontiers*, tel (263) 13-4772; *Kandahar Safaris*, Sopers Centre, tel (263) 13-4502, fax (263) 13-4556; *Shearwater*, Sopers Centre, Parkway. Tel (263) 13-4471, fax (263) 13-4341; *Zambezi Canoe Company*, Sopers Centre, Parkway, tel (263) 13-4298, fax (263) 13-4683; *Zambezi Odyssey* Pumula Centre, Parkway. *Safari par Excellence*, tel (263) 13-4424, fax (263) 13-4510.

Horse Trails Contact *Zambezi Horse Trails*. Full day or overnight. Parkway, tel (263) 13-4471.

River Cruising: *Mosi-oa-Tunya Cruises*, 299 Rumsey Road, tel (263) 13-4780; *UTC*, Zimbank Building, Livingstone Way, tel (263) 13-4267; *Zambezi River Cruises*, the Croc Farm people, tel (263) 13-4637.

White-Water Rafting High water run June/July and December/January. Low water run August to December (or longer). *Frontiers*, 306 Parkway, tel (263) 13-5800, fax (263) 13-5801 (same office as Abercrombie and Kent); *Shearwater*, Sopers Centre, tel (263) 13-4471, fax (263) 13-4341; *Sobek*, tel Zambia (260) 3-321432, fax (260) 3-323542; *Safari par Excellence*, tel (263) 13-4424, fax (263) 13-4510.

Sea Plane Converted Cessna 185. Four passengers. See 'tkts' at Parkway, tel (263) 13-3300, fax (263) 13-3299. *Abercrombie and Kent*, tel (263) 13-4780; *Shearwater*, tel (263) 13-4471; *Kalambeza Safaris*, tel (263) 13-4480.

Flight of the Angels Aircraft and helicopter flips over the Falls. *United Air*, tel (263) 13-4530; *Southern Cross Aviation*, tel (263) 13-4453. For **microlight flights**, tel *Batoka Sky*, c/o tel (263) 13-4424.

Night Drives Game-viewing. Tel (263) 13-4614, fax (263) 13-4614.

Sky-Diving Contact *Zambezi Vultures*. Jump same day in tandem with instructor, tel (263) 13-4424.

Game-Viewing Any Victoria Falls safari operator.

Walking Safaris *Back Packers Africa*, tel (263) 13-4424, fax (263) 13-4510; *Khangela Safaris* Sopers Arcade, tel (263) 13-4502, fax (263) 13-4556.

Golf *Elephant Hills Hotel*. Tel (263) 13-4503/4793.

ACCOMMODATION

Victoria Falls Hotel The original hotel overlooking the Victoria Falls bridge; colonial, lush setting. Call the Zimbabwe Sun Group, tel (263) 13-4203, fax (263) 13-4586. P O Box 10, Victoria Falls.

Victoria Falls Safari Lodge Seven-storey, Balinese thatched dining area and chalets overlooking game pan. 4km (2.5 miles) from the Falls. Tel (263) 13-3201, fax (263) 13-3205. P O Box 29, Victoria Falls.

Ilala Lodge Independently owned hotel, centrally situated, open breakfast patio. 16 rooms. Video venue for rafters. Pool bar. Disco. Tel (113) 4737/6, fax (263) 13-4417. P O Box 18, Victoria Falls.

A'Zambezi River Lodge Semi-circular lodge at riverside location, quiet, good for bird-watching; warthog roam on lawns by the pool. Tel (263) 13-4561, fax (263) 13-4536. P O Box 130, Victoria Falls.

Matetsi Safari Camp Conservation Corporation Africa. Huge private game reserve with Zambezi River frontage. 40km (25 miles) west of Victoria Falls. Tel Johannesburg, South Africa on (27) 11-8038421, fax (27) 11-8031810.

Elephant Hills Enormous conference hotel with 18-hole golf course and panoramic views of the Zambezi; call Zimbabwe Sun Group, tel (263) 13-4793, fax (263) 13-4655. P O Box 300, Victoria Falls.

Elephant Camp Safari on elephant back. Four new chalets, four elephants. 15km (9.5 miles) southwest of Victoria Falls on the Chamabonda border of the Zambezi National Park. Tel (263) 13-2004/4219, fax (263) 13-4349. P O Box 159, Victoria Falls.

Rainbow Good mid-range choice, arched Arabic architecture overlooking lawns. Tel (263) 13-4585, fax (263) 13-4653. P O Box 150, Victoria Falls.

Makasa Sun Casino Hotel Most attractive pool in town, lovely open air breakfast boma, tel (263) 13-4275, fax (263) 13-4782. P O Box 90, Victoria Falls.

Spray View Hotel Recently refurbished, owner-run. Good value. Tel (263) 13-4344, fax (263) 13-4713. P O Box 70, Victoria Falls.

Masuwe Lodge Award-winning tent and thatch safari lodge. Game platform. Tel (263) 13-426512, fax (263) 13-750785. P O Box 257, Victoria Falls.

Acacia Palm Lodge Four roomy, luxury lodge suites on a 6 069ha (15 000 acre) private game conservancy 45 minutes south of the Falls. Tel (263) 13-4527, fax (263) 13-4224. P O Box 335, Hwange.

Tongabezi (Zambia) Built literally over the river, luxurious safari lodge. Tel (260) 3-323296, fax (260) 3-323224. Private Bag 31, Livingstone, Zambia.

BUDGET ACCOMMODATION

National Parks Lodges and nine riverside game-viewing and fishing camps; write well in advance to National Parks, P O Box CY826, Causeway, Harare, tel (263) 4-706077, or call Victoria Falls on tel (263) 13-4222.

Town Council Rest Camp Town centre. Chalets, camping and caravaning. Tel (263) 13-4210, fax (263) 13-4308. P O Box 41, Victoria Falls.

Zambezi Camp Site Along Parkway on the Zambezi River, not far from A'Zambezi River Lodge.

WHERE TO EAT

Livingstone Room, Victoria Falls Hotel, recently refurbished: elegant dining; offers evening patio buffet. Tel (263) 13-4203.

The Pizza Bistro, Sopers Centre: Crêpes, pasta and pizzas; small, homely, good food. Tel (263) 13-4396.

Explorers Pub, Sopers Centre: Pub food, music; no rafter under 25 would be seen anywhere else. Tel (263) 13-4298.

Boma Restaurant Open-air restaurant serving game meat and *potjiekos*, tel (263) 13-3201.

Wimpy, cnr. Parkway/Livingstone Way: Burgers and breakfasts. Tel (263) 13-4470.

The Cattleman, Pumula Mall: Good, clean steakhouse. Tel (263) 13-4767.

Ilala Hotel Restaurant has good vegetarian meals. Tel (263) 13-4738.

HEALTH HAZARDS

Remember to take precautions against malaria. Bilharzia can also be a problem. Be warned: wild animals can appear anywhere in the Falls area.

ANNUAL EVENTS

Zambezi River Festival White-water rafting and canoeing competition in October. Contact *Frontiers*, tel (263) 13-5800, fax (263) 13-5801. P O Box 117, Victoria Falls.

Elephant Hills Golf Open October. Contact *Elephant Hills Hotel*, tel (263) 13-4793/4503, fax (263) 13-4655. P O Box 300, Victoria Falls.

USEFUL ADDRESSES AND TELEPHONE NUMBERS

Please note: Add an extra 1 before local telephone codes if you are ringing within Zimbabwe.

AA c/o Jays Bookshop, CABS Building. Tel (263) 13-4223.

Air Zimbabwe Livingstone Way, near Post Office. Tel (263) 13-4518/4316 (4255 is the airport).

Banks: *Barclays*, tel (263) 13-4272; *Standard Chartered*, tel (263) 13-4248.

Doctor Tel (263) 13-3356/423121.

Medical Air Rescue Service (MARS) Tel (263) 13-4764/4646 (in Victoria Falls ring only 4764/4646).

National Parks Livingstone Way. Tel (263) 13-4558/4222/4310.

Pharmacy Pumula Centre. Tel (263) 13-4403.

Post Office Tel (263) 13-4302.

Victoria Falls Publicity Association Corner Parkway/Livingstone Way. Tel (263) 13-4202.

HWANGE NATIONAL PARK

The park is divided into three main sections: Main Camp, Sinamatella and Robins'-Nantwich, spread over 170km (105 miles). There are nearly 500km (300 miles) of drives, loops and game-viewing roads in the park; although there are limited access roads, you never get the impression of crowding except occasionally in the evenings around the large elephant pans near and south of Main Camp where the luxury safari tour operators are mainly concentrated.

Hwange (pronounced Hwaang-geh) can be reached by daily air service from Harare and Victoria Falls (direct connections to Cape Town), by full tar roads, train and bus. A private car is needed to tour the park unless you are with a tour operator. Facilities include one hotel, luxury private lodges, and a variety of camp sites and rustic cottages run by the National Parks Board.

Hwange National Park has a special affection in the hearts of all Zimbabweans. Set aside in 1929 from former uneconomic ranching land, and in order to arrest irresponsible hunting, this 14 620km^2 (5 645 miles^2) chunk of dry and beautifully mixed woodland in the northwest corner of Zimbabwe, not far from the Victoria Falls, is Zimbabwe's first and largest national park.

The park supports 107 species of game, including all the big animals: 15 000 buffalo, 3 000 zebra, 6 000 impala, 17 000 elephant (possibly more; this, the world's largest concentration, is apparently too many for the park's carrying capacity), 2 000 sable, hyaena, rhino, 3 000 giraffe, wildebeest, baboon, cheetah, lion, leopard, packs of endangered wild dogs, right down to tiny, perky banded mongooses – these delightful animals move in packs of up to 40, skipping, purring and chuckling as they bob up in unison on hind legs to make sure they miss nothing, then drop down again before scampering away.

OPPOSITE: *In the golden late afternoon, elephant and buffalo churn up the dust at a Hwange pan.*

The bird life is a constant pleasure as you drive through the park. Of Zimbabwe's checklist of 640 species, at least 400 can be seen in Hwange. Near Manzi Cheesa, a small riverbed with a low-level bridge, blacksmith plovers strut about, making an irritated klink-klink noise for disturbing their bath.

Some 230 trees and shrubs species occur in Hwange. In the south on the Kalahari sands are the grasslands, open pans, and huge teak and bastard mopane trees that drain away on ancient wooded dunes and fossil rivers into the wastes of the Makgadikgadi Salt Pans of Botswana. The northern half is more broken, hilly and heavily wooded with mopane forests. Various rivers, often sandy and dry, flow north from here into the Zambezi.

Mzilikazi, one of the many truant warlords to flee from the domination of Shaka Zulu, came to Hwange in 1838 to escape from the predations of advancing Boer nomads in South Africa. For a while it became his private hunting domain, but white hunters followed during the reign of his successor Lobengula and all but denuded the area of its game. By the time Ted Davison, the first warden, walked the park in 1929, there were only 1 000 elephant left, and the white rhino had been totally eliminated. It was he who launched the construction of 60 pans that attracted and saved the animals.

A total of 64 black rhino were dehorned in the Sinamatella area to protect them against poachers. Of Zimbabwe's once 3 000 strong herd, only 300 remain in intensive protection areas such as Hwange and Matusadona national parks. Dehorning did not work, but radio tagging and the presence of armed game rangers has kept the poachers at bay.

A DRIVE THROUGH HWANGE

There are three access routes into Hwange National Park. From Bulawayo, turn left at the 261km (162 miles) crossroads, or from the Kariba car ferry at Mlibizi this entry point is 135km (84 miles). Another route lies in the middle of the park at Sinamatella which is off the 330.5km-peg (196.5 mile) from Bulawayo

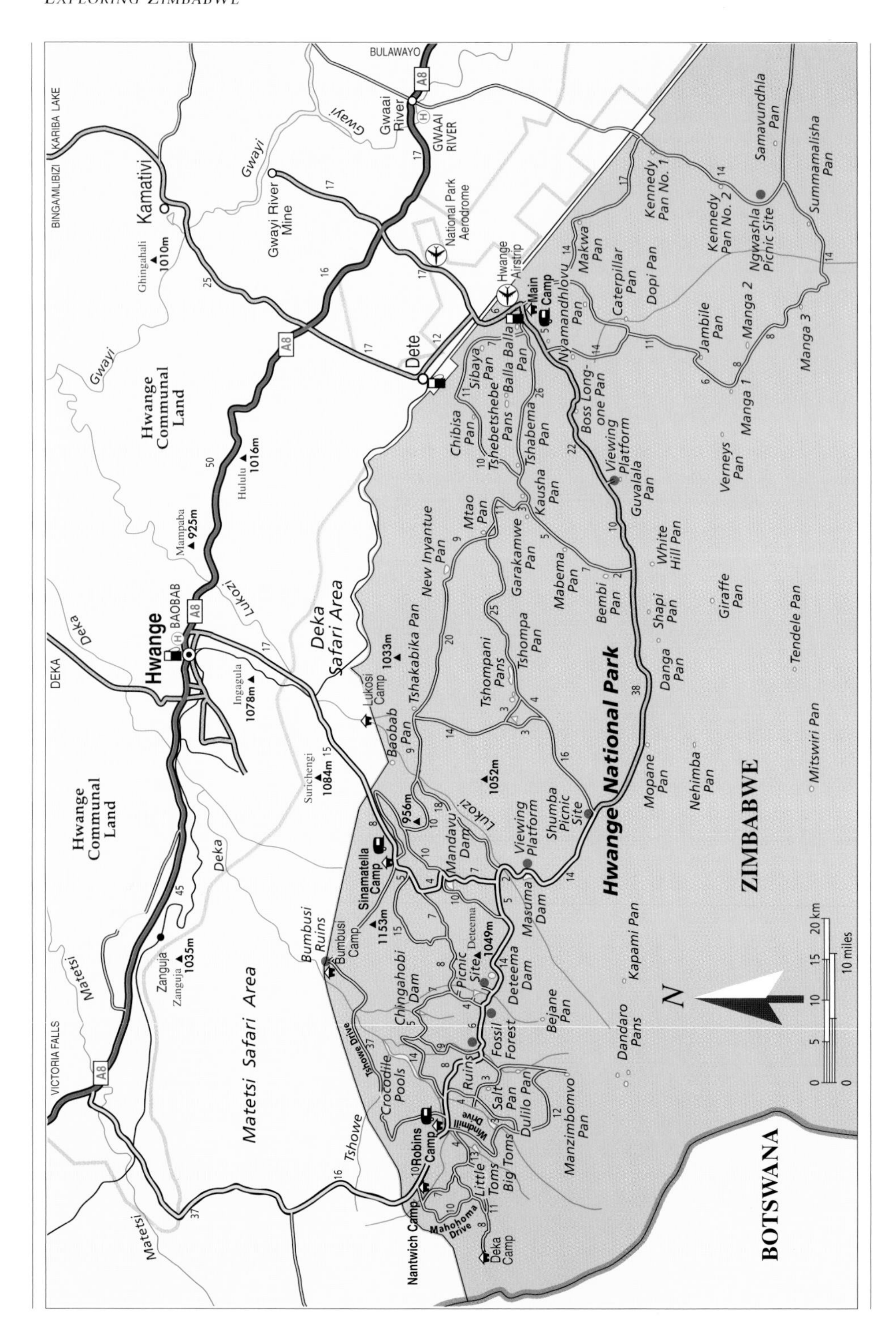

BULAWAYO
A8
Gwaai River
GWAAI RIVER
KARIBA LAKE
BINGA/MLIBIZI
Kamativi
Gwayi
Gwayi River Mine
National Park Aerodrome
Hwange Airstrip
Main Camp
Ghingahali 1010m
Hwange Communal Land
Dete
Mampaba 925m
Hululu 1016m
Hwange
BAOBAB
DEKA
Deka
Lukozi
Ingagula 1078m
Deka Safari Area
Lukosi Camp
1033m
Surichengi 1084m
Hwange Communal Land
Sinamatella Camp
1153m
Bumbusi Ruins
Bumbusi Camp
Zanguja
Zanguja 1035m
Matetsi
Matetsi Safari Area
VICTORIA FALLS
Tshowe
Tshowe Drive
Crocodile Pools
Robins Camp
Nantwich Camp
Mahohoma Drive
Deka Camp
Little Toms
Big Toms
Windmill Drive
Salt Pan
Dululo Pan
Manzimbomvo Pan
Ruins
Fossil Forest
Chingahobi Dam
Picnic Site
Deteema 1049m
Deteema Dam
Bejane Pan
Dandaro Pans
Kapami Pan
Masuma Dam
Mandavu Dam
956m
Viewing Platform
Shumba Picnic Site
1052m
Baobab Pan
Tshakabika Pan
Tshompani Pans
Tshompa Pan
New Inyantue Pan
Mtao Pan
Garakamwe Pan
Mabema Pan
Bembi Pan
Kausha Pan
Tshabema Pan
Chibisa Pan
Tshebetshebe Pans
Sibaya Pan
Balla Balla Pan
Nyamandhlovu Pan
Boss Long-one Pan
Viewing Platform
Guvalala Pan
White Hill Pan
Shapi Pan
Danga Pan
Mopane Pan
Nehimba Pan
Giraffe Pan
Verneys Pan
Tendele Pan
Mitswiri Pan
Hwange National Park
Makwa Pan
Caterpillar Pan
Dopi Pan
Kennedy Pan No. 1
Kennedy Pan No. 2
Ngwashla Picnic Site
Jambile Pan
Manga 1
Manga 2
Manga 3
Samavundhla Pan
Summamalisha Pan
ZIMBABWE
BOTSWANA
N
0 5 10 15 20 km
0 10 miles

with a further 40km (25 miles) mainly on gravel. Possibly the most interesting route, however, if travelling south from Victoria Falls, is to come into the park at Robins' Camp, the turn-off being 48km (30 miles) from the Falls. It is then a 68km-drive (42 miles) to Robins' Camp. This gravel road has to be negotiated carefully as it is rather like driving on a beach of ball bearings.

Be aware that particularly in the evening, you may encounter game, especially elephant and kudu, along the tarred or gravel roads from Victoria Falls to and past Hwange National Park. You will need to check in at Robins' Camp before proceeding to nearby Nantwich or on to Sinamatella. The gravel roads in the park at this point are good and you are immediately on a network of game loops running parallel with the usually dry Deka River or west into the Little Toms and Big Toms hides. The main route through the Park goes via Deteema Dam, its open waters and *vlei* leading into thick woods favoured by spurwing geese, waders and elephants. The turn off to Sinamatella is another 20km on (12.5 miles), with Mandavu Dam, 6km (4 miles) along this turn off, a highlight. It holds water year-round and is home to game that include about 14 hippo and a clutch of crocodiles. Sinamatella sits atop a cliff overlooking a huge *vlei*, riverbed and expanse of mixed woodland savanna that stretches as far as the eye can see. It will take three to four hours of game-viewing driving to get from here to Main Camp, either back via the road you came on for 22km (14 miles) or on the much longer Lukosi game-viewing loop. With a further 110km (68 miles) to Main Camp, Masuma Dam is a worthwhile stop with its ilala palms and observation platform.

It is then a long, hot but game-rewarding run to the remote White Hill Pan, a 2km-detour (1.25 mile), where hornbills swoop down from overhead trees, elephants gather

PAINTED HUNTING DOGS

These beautiful honey, white and black mottled creatures, wild dogs as they were recently known, use complicated greeting rituals, calls and body language to communicate with each other.

Working in co-ordinated packs in open country to take maximum advantage of their superb sight, a wild dog's method of hunting is to select a weak or sick animal and chase it down until it is exhausted, a type of hunting that requires a very large range. A pack of perhaps 15 dogs running at 50kmph (30 mph) go into synchronized action as they take turns to tire and run down an antelope or wildebeest, snapping and savaging the buck, tearing pieces from it on the move, even disembowelling their prey before it collapses. Then events take an unexpected turn: these hungry dogs will hold back and deliberately allow the young to move in and feed before them. Pups are boisterous and pampered, not only by the mothers, in tightknit *Lycaon pictus* families.

There is hardly any aggression between packs but any hyaena foolish enough to approach a kill is in for trouble and leopards

Wild dogs, Africa's most imperilled carnivore.

observe only from a distance. Man has killed wild dogs in the past but now along the road fringing Hwange National Park, there are signs advising motorists: Wild dogs crossing place.

And when a pack of these hunting dogs does cross in front of your car, it's quite an event. Long-legged, inquisitive and playful as domestic dogs, these creatures sniff your wheels, skitter away, dart back again, then as if on signal, lope off into the trees, occasionally hooo-hoooing to locate a lost member.

TOP LEFT: *Main Camp Hwange, where the Waterbuck's Head Restaurant (left) sits beneath shady camel thorn trees, is home to many giraffe and zebra (above).*

to drink, swifts dive-bomb everyone and crowned cranes flock. Gubalala Pan – it means an elephant washing off dust – has a view platform. In 1995 its three pools were a rather sorry sight with cracked mud, cracked pipes, blackened generator site and a shaky, dry rot timber platform, but nonetheless rich in birds. The closer you get to Main Camp, however, the more evident is the recent work that has been done on the pans and water facilities; the game-viewing is always excellent near Main Camp, particularly elephant.

You could drive through Hwange in a day, but a night each at Robins', Nantwich, Sinamatella and Main is by far the best way to maximize the ideal early morning and late evening game-viewing times.

MAIN CAMP

The turn off to Main Camp lies 261km (162 miles) along the main Bulawayo to Victoria Falls highway, a boulevard of huge bloodwoods, *Baikiaea plurijuga* teaks, dappled false mopane and camel thorn trees. Here, as your introduction to the park, you are quite likely to see buffalo close to the road, browsing giraffe or possibly even a lion kill.

Main Camp is the administrative headquarters and principal entry point into Hwange. Unlike other sections of the park, its surrounding roads are tarred, albeit badly potholed. Luxury safari operators have access through Main Camp to the game-rich southern pans of Makwa, Kennedy One and Ngwashla. The facilities at the Camp are rustic but good. They include cottages run by National Parks with welcome overhead fans, and the Waterbuck's Head restaurant beneath camel thorn and *umtshibi* trees filled with masked weavers' nests. There is a camp site with clean ablutions, night game walks and accompanied walks three times daily to Sedina Platform Hide and the big Nyamandhlovu ('elephant head' in Ndebele) Pan.

Solar panels discreetly tucked behind mopane scrub provide the electricity at a series of borehole-fed pans surrounding Main Camp. In the dry October to May season, in particular, the pans are vital for the 100-strong families of elephant that come trundling out of the tree line, trunks waving, to drink and splash in the waters. Adult elephants can drink up to 160 litres (35 gallons) a day. As the young frolic in the pan,

ABOVE: *Wildebeest at Nyamandhlovu Pan, a favourite viewing platform near Main Camp.* RIGHT: *At nearby Dete Vlei, these big pachyderms indulge in a welcome mud bath.*

weaving in and out of adult legs, the aunties of the breeding herd will trumpet and patrol the perimeter, neither man nor beast allowed too close. Male elephants are relegated to bachelor groups by the females and old bulls wander off on their own except when invited to call during the mating season.

The Kalahari sands of Hwange only retain water in seasonal pans and water holes for short periods during the rains. The boreholes supplement this, thus ensuring the presence of game and their survival in reasonably large numbers, but it also affects migratory patterns. Elephant would normally migrate through Hwange and, ignoring man's borders, into Botswana across the Caprivi in Namibia and deep into Angola as well, an area of a hoped-for sanctuary of 246 000km^2 (94 984 miles^2). The boreholes also enable a far larger number of elephant to breed, putting considerable pressure on the availability of tree cover, particularly near water holes, as one elephant can consume as much as 250kg (551 pounds) of green fodder daily.

Hwange probably has the world's largest concentration of elephant. Estimates vary between 17 000 and 30 000 but the park can only sustain a portion of these. A few will be translocated and many will probably be shot in culling exercises. Until such times as other African countries can afford translocation costs in order to replenish their own herds, or the elephants' territory can be extended in competition with man's needs to plant subsistence crops, conservationists do not see any way round this unfortunate practice.

Apart from elephant, the game in the area includes many giraffe, zebra, wildebeest, buffalo and fairly substantial lion prides. The birdlife throughout forested Main Camp is excellent and flocks of tall white and grey crowned cranes with their helmets of golden fans are common after the rains.

Be a little wary of some of the more remote dirt roads as they can end in heavy sand, while some of the viewing platforms are in need of maintenance.

DETE VLEI

The word *vlei*, from the Afrikaans language, is used in East and southern Africa to describe a marshy, low-lying drainage area where grass but not much else grows. It is usually surrounded by a wealth of trees such as camel thorn, teak and sweet-tasting terminalia in a variety of habitats or ecozones that make it very attractive to game. Such is the 15km-long (9.5 miles) Dete Vlei that flanks Hwange Main Camp's boundary. Famous for its spectacular sunsets and moon rises, it was here that the Victorian adventurer Frederick Courteney Selous (after whom the world's largest game reserve, the Selous in Tanzania, is named) hunted.

The game-viewing around the *vlei*, with its necklace of high trees and long vistas, includes the locally named 'presidential herd' of some 300 elephant. The antelope species range from eland, best seen in August after calving, to waterbuck, or *isidumuka*, and skittery, high-jumping impala harems. This area is heavy with teak forests and consequently cheetah, who prefer open grassland, are not common, but there are plenty of lions in prides of up to twelve, particularly towards the southern end of nearby Hwange park. The list of wildlife in this area is extensive: black-backed jackals, warthogs, zebras, hyaenas and kudus, while there is a staggering variety of birds, including wood owls, secretary birds and ground hornbills.

Hidden away on former ranch land around Dete Vlei are some 15 safari lodges. None of these lodges are cheap but the quality and knowledge of their professional guides who take visitors around the game-rich *vlei* and into Hwange National Park itself make them more than good value.

The railway to Victoria Falls runs between Dete Vlei and Hwange Park and game is often seen from the windows. Best of all is the twice monthly rail safari on an old-fashioned steam train. These pass through the little village of Dete itself, a sleepy settlement to the north of the *vlei* with its dusty Game Reserve Hotel on 'Last Hope Estate'.

LEFT: *Crimson water lilies in a quiet loop of the Sinamatella River. Sinamatella Camp sits on a high ridge overlooking a vast plain (below).*

SINAMATELLA

The aloe-strewn rocky ridge of Sinamatella, 46km (29 miles) from Hwange town, sits like the rim of a volcanic crater overlooking a vast and ancient floodplain stretching to dusty, distant hills. Below the daring geckos and lichen-covered drop-off, everything seems obscured in sun-blasted haze, but then you begin to pick out the features and the game. Giraffe emerge from a phalanx of fever trees near a small river; at a water hole, wart-hogs snuffle and a lone elephant approaches. To the right, an army of trees marches across the plain, then abruptly stops at the snaking Mandavu sandriver, merging into grassland where sun-lazy zebra browse. Further away a line of impala move through a swathe of sand. The well-treed ridge, backed up by the Camp's long line of cottages and soaring thatched restaurant, is so placed that you actually look down on birds in flight: glossy starlings, desert cisticolas, and gorgeous lilacbreasted rollers. The rock-hollowed bird-bath in front of the restaurant is tagged 'for animals only' while the visitors' books in the Park's chalets occasionally complain of water pipes damaged by elephant.

The Mandavu Dam, 12.5km (7.8 miles) from Sinamatella, is a large lake with a new thatched viewing platform overlooking hippo, wading herons, egrets, sandpipers and giant saddlebilled storks in the waters. Crocodiles lurk close to shore while hippo grunt in the deepest middle section. Beyond them a huge termite mound marks the furthest shore which flows into green marshland. Financially assisted by the Zimbabwean and British Branch of the Hwange Conservation Society, Mandavu Dam is an ideal, well-shaded picnic spot, as is the newer and smaller Masuma Dam nearby, ploughed out by bulldozers and set in thick mopane woodland. The pan, where ilala palms grace the shore and pygmy geese and blue-billed maccoa ducks swim in the reeds, is a magnet for birds and game.

Were it not for the sixty man-made dams and pans, both the game and birds would largely have deserted Hwange. Although moves are being made to enable parks such

PLEASE SAVE THE TREES

Local carvers favour using hardwood trees.

Zimbabwe is a nation of sculptors. Although plenty of stone is available, much of this carving is done in wood, a process that is posing a major threat to the trees between Hwange and Victoria Falls, in the area south of Masvingo, in the Chimanimani forests and the baobab trees in the Chipinge area where the bark is used for making carpets. The threat to teak, mahogany and mukwa trees in all these areas is a common one: a huge demand for carvings made from hardwood, particularly of hippos.

Traditional carvers have, in the past, only used softwoods, but visitors love the beautiful, deep colours of the indigenous trees and the sculptors have now started using hardwoods, cutting down whole trees instead of just the branches to make huge sculptures. Wood is available from the Forestry Commision, but because it is dead and therefore hard, sculptors prefer to poach softer, growing wood.

If visitors understand the devastation the cutting of indigenous woods is causing and stop buying these admittedly lovely creations, then Zimbabwe's Forestry Commission and conservationists may be able to persuade the carvers to use exotic woods such as pine, or to use stone. If not encouraged to change now, the sculptors will eventually exhaust the trees, the environment and their own livelihood and in 20 years the forests will have gone.

Mopane trees surround secluded Robins' Camp.

as Hwange to retain the monies they earn, a more supportive approach by government will probably be needed if Hwange and its magnificent tourism-attracting wildlife is to survive. Shumba picnic site, where the tarred road between Main Camp and Sinamatella ends, flaunts lovely open grasslands and small groups of elephant, zebra and buffalo. One of Hwange's most appealing features is the constantly changing vistas and habitats, a panorama of different woodlands, rocks, low hills and grassland.

ROBINS' CAMP

To reach Robins' Camp, turn left off the Bulawayo road, 390km (242 miles) from that city and 48km (30 miles) from Victoria Falls. It is then 68km (42 miles) to Robins'.

This northern Zambezi River watershed-drained area of Hwange is largely a woodland of tall mopane, their butterfly leaves turned from the sun, and silvery looking terminalia with yellow bottlebrush flowers in spring. It is a hillier and more broken than the Kalahari sandveld of the south and buffalo seem to prefer this area. En route from Sinamatella to Robins' Camp you will pass great chunks of rock by the side of a rise, the remains of petrified trees frozen by time. Millions of years ago northern Hwange was covered with great swamps and forests, hence the vast underground reserves of coal today, enough to last for many generations.

Robins' Camp was named after Herbert Robins, Fellow of the Royal Geographical Society, a recluse and self-taught astronomer. In 1934 he gave his two game farms, Little Toms and Big Toms, to the government in return for a new house and water supply and both of these are now game-viewing hides. Robins died five years later and is buried, just outside the camp's entrance arch, 100m (330ft) beyond the lily pond. He built a tall, square tower for all-night stargazing; the bottom floor of his observatory is today the Hyaena Restaurant. Round the corner from the restaurant is a clinic and the next floor up is the office of the warden.

Robins' teems with hyaenas; a sign reads 'A hyaena eats anything. Do not leave pots, pans, shoes outside'. They have jaws like guillotines and the first time you hear their eerie evening whoop is enough to make you jump. Guided walking trails are available with plenty of kudu and lions in the area. The camp has chalets with outdoor cooking facilities. Although the swimming pool has long been empty and the camps' generator is often out of order, the game-viewing in the dry winter season is marvellous.

NANTWICH CAMP

Possibly the loveliest of all of Hwange's rustic camps is Nantwich Camp. Three thatched cottages, one with an old wood fire-heated outdoor bath, are situated on a knoll adorned with purple stones, trees and aloes, overlooking a broad *vlei* surrounded by thick woodland. Sit with a pair of binoculars in the early morning or evening and game will traverse the *vlei* in a quiet cavalcade: zebra, warthog, buffalo, impala, wildebeest and if you are very lucky, a glimpse of leopard in the skeletal mopane trees. Eagles ride the high thermals, and when the *vlei* has water, a myriad wading birds come to prance and peck.

Nantwich Camp is so old that the original wood Dover stoves are still used in the kitchens while some of the crockery is stamped 'Federation of Rhodesia and Nyasaland'. Remote, exclusive and 11km (7 miles) from Robins, this hunters' road and tall-story section of the Park is the camp nearest to the Victoria Falls. The exit road passes, on a hill, an unusual granite square. Inside is a lone grave and tombstone: 'Percy Durban Crewe. One of Rhodesia's earliest pioneers. 1931'.

Hwange Town

Stones that burn, coal, had been known to the local Nambya people of Hwange and their Rozvi chief Hwange Rusumbani for generations. Hwange means peace, a state wished for, no doubt, by Rusumbani who was ousted by Mzilikazi, king of the warrior-wanderer Ndebele 170 years ago, who came, saw and declared this lush wilderness to be his private hunting preserve. But he kept the old regime's name. Early European settlers included the German prospector Albert Giese who in 1894 pegged a claim which turned

Lion (top), hyaena (centre) and baboon (above) are often seen in the vicinity of Robins' Camp.

out to be one of the world's largest deposits of coal. This encouraged the Cape to Cairo railway, nine years later, to be re-routed via Hwange town and Victoria Falls.

Much of the coal is mined opencast and is used in Zimbabwe's thermal power stations. It is the country's major power resource and there is enough to last until the next Ice Age. Ironically, it has a high ash content plus unwanted sulphur and phosphorus and thus coal for specialized ferrochrome smelting, for

Distinctive bateleurs favour the open thornveld.

example, has to be imported. Ninety per cent of Hwange Colliery's output is consumed internally and mining is conducted around the clock. In 1972, 427 miners were buried underground in No. 2 Colliery following a huge explosion, an event still sorrowfully etched in the memories of the town's small population. The entrance to Hwange town is marked by a venerable green steam locomotive, while on the steep bluff above the road, the palms, tin roof and colonades of the colonial-style Baobab Hotel dominate both town and Hwange game park with views that stretch to the dusty western horizon.

Coal, copper and tin caused Hwange to boom (names such as Miners Takeaways and Diggers Rugby Football Club bear evidence), and with plenty of water piped from Deka on the Zambezi, its well-treed and flowered Coronation Street reflects this prosperity. If going to Sinamatella and you do not want to drive through the park from Main Camp, then Hwange town is your fill-up point; the Sinamatella access route is 3km (2 miles) south of town off the Bulawayo road.

KAZUMA PAN NATIONAL PARK

Hwange wildlife area stretches south 280km (174 miles) from the Zambezi River halfway to Bulawayo, then across to Botswana and the old hunter-trader Pandamatenga Road. It covers two indigenous forests, the Hwange National Park of 14 620km^2 (5645m^2), the difficult-to-access Kazuma Pan National Park and three safari hunting areas. The open, rolling grasslands of Kazuma are not dissimilar to the plains of East Africa.

Covering 31 300ha (77 342 acres), Kazuma Pan National Park is host to migratory concentrations of elephant and buffalo moving between northwestern Botswana and the borehole-fed pans of Kazuma, particularly during the arid pre-rain months of September to October. Lion are common while the wealth of mammals includes giraffe, oribi, sable and roan antelope, even gemsbok. When the westerly depression has water, waterfowl proliferate in the area, including cormorants, storks, numerous varieties of African duck, kingfishers and the rare wattled crane which breeds here.

Only two groups of up to 10 visitors each in two four-wheel-drive vehicles are allowed to camp in Kazuma at any one time, and day visitors are not allowed. Basic camp sites supplied only with water are available at the natural springs of Kasetsheti and Insiza overlooking the great depression. Victoria Falls-based Backpackers Africa operate three-day walking safaris into Kazuma, but otherwise apply months ahead to the National Parks Central Booking Office in Harare.

INTERESTING PLACES EN ROUTE

- Sentinel Limpopo Safaris. Luxurious private estate 32 793ha (81 000 acres) near Sashe-Limpopo confluence 80km (50 miles) west of Beitbridge. Dinosaur sites, rock art and horseback game-viewing. Access on gravel roads or via Inter-Air from Johannesburg to Messina. Tel/fax (263) 86-351, P O Box 36, Beitbridge.
- Bubiana Conservancy & Barbeton Lodge. Luxury clifftop chalets overlooking river and private game reserve formed from seven former ranches near West Nicholson. One hour on gravel roads. Big game-viewing, fishing, bush walks. P O Box 444 Famona, Bulawayo. Tel (263) 9-64638, fax (263) 9-72870.
- Halfway Halt (halfway to Victoria Falls). 222km-peg (138 mile) from Bulawayo. Restaurant, fuel and new roadside chalets.

DEKA AND MATETSI SAFARI AREAS

Lying between Hwange town and Sinamatella Camp is the mopane, commiphora and combretum woodland of Deka's 51 000ha (126 020 acres) Safari (or sport hunting) Area. A nearby and similar area, the Matetsi Hunting and Safari Area, is split into two sections. One stretches for 30km (20 miles) south of the Zambezi River (with a small section, the Zambezi National Park, set aside for game-viewing) and the other is adjacent to Hwange's northwestern border.

This region of 300 000ha (741 300 acres) is well-known for its game ranching studies and its concentrations of game such as buffalo, eland and particularly the handsome scimitar-horned sable. Half of Zimbabwe's park and wildlife estate is set aside for hunting. Many of the hunters are American and it is an incredibly expensive pastime that brings much money into Zimbabwe. One hunter brings in revenue equivalent to a dozen or more ordinary photo safari tourists. High hunting fees, the theory goes, guarantee the survival of both habitat and game which would otherwise too easily become croplands and meat respectively. Thirty five species of game in Zimbabwe can be hunted under strictly controlled conditions with set quotas.

The Zimbabwe Campfire philosophy, whereby small communal-area farmers adjacent to national parks are encouraged to participate in and benefit from the hunting proceeds and are therefore motivated to conserve the game, is growing in momentum.

MLIBIZI AND DEKA FISHING RESORTS

Flying from Victoria Falls to Harare, the tortured crack of the Zambezi is seen below as it journeys to the headwaters of Lake Kariba at Devil's Gorge some 100km (62 miles) from the Falls. Among high cliffs and the wooded ravines and creeks of this area are a variety of fishing resorts. The Mlibizi Basin, where the car-carrying Kariba ferry ends its lake-long journey, is an area of attractive, thickly wooded bays, gorges and islands where the lake broadens up to 2km (1.25 miles). It is a

Sable and impala drink at Big Toms Pan.

LEFT: *Huge and haughty is the saddlebilled stork.*
ABOVE: *Ivory Lodge, one of many luxury options.*

uniquely tranquil holiday lagoon, which specializes in tigerfishing, and hires out fishing boats, canoes and rafts.

The thatched Mlibizi Hotel has bungalows, shady green lawns, swimming pool and a lakeshore pub, while the nearby Mlibizi Zambezi Resort facing the inlet lagoon channel has petrol for sale. The area is excellent for birding. The tarred road runs from Mlibizi to Hwange, while a gravel road covers the hour and a half drive east to the wild and mountainous Chizarira National Park overlooking the Zambezi Valley and Lake Kariba. Mlibizi is accessed via the Bulawayo/Victoria Falls Road, the best route for South African visitors, or via KweKwe, Gokwe and Binga, a route of which the last portion, some 100km (62 miles), is on gravel.

Various rivers snake north from the Hwange Game Park watershed into the rugged Devil's Gorge section of the Zambezi. They include the Gwaai, Lukozi, Msuna, Matetsi and Deka. All are choice fishing areas. The Deka Drum, at the confluence of the Zambezi and Deka rivers with an island mid-river and 50km (30 miles) from Hwange town on a narrow tar road, boasts of being the spiritual home of the fighting tigerfish, possibly because of the number of these striped 'water dogs' that end their days here at the hands of sportsmen. Also found here are 16 other varieties of fish, including bream, barbel and hunyani salmon. Rustic facilities at Deka include log cabins and a shaded swimming pool beneath trees overlooking the river.

Gwaai

Gwaai means tobacco. This former ranching and now hunting valley, 16km (10 miles) south of the turn-off to Hwange Main Camp, is a railway stop, and lays claim to a unique hotel where the Gwaai River flows under the main Victoria Falls to Bulawayo road.

The Gwaai River Hotel is something out of Hemingway's Africa with a Fawlty Towers overlay. Skins and animal heads adorn the walls, mementos and plants compete for attention, and different styles of furniture live in harmony. Hearty breakfasts are served amid the bougainvillea and trees and the characters at the Gwaai pub would normally only be seen in a Clint Eastwood movie. You will hear about Buck de Vries on whose land several of the luxury Hwange safari camps now operate, about elephant charges, lion kills, baboon thefts, and how Mrs Frick rescued the mailman years ago from the raging Gwaai River when the cage's steel hawser slung across the river collapsed. Don't imagine that you will be able to match the locals drink for drink – tall stories are thirsty work – and take along a musical instrument.

JUMBO SNACKS

Zimbabwe has Africa's largest remaining concentrations of elephant, 17 000 in Hwange and 10 000 in Mana Pools national parks. Elephants run up to 40kmph (25mph) without making a sound on their cushioned legs, but matriarchs will raise their trunks and scream if they think their young are under threat.

At the shoulder, elephant males can stand up to 4m (13ft) high; the elephant world, however, is a matriarchal society in which the lead female in the family group rules. Groups consist of females and their young, which link with others to form herds. Males live in their own herds or alone, and bulls only join the family when the female decides it's time for courting.

Weighing up to six tonnes, the African elephant is a magnificient beast. When confined to a game reserve, its daily intake of 250kg (551 pounds) of leaves and grass and 160 litres (35 gallons) of water unfortunately means it often devastates its narrow environment, pushing down and denuding trees.

Elephants' trunks are used for sniffing as their eyesight is poor. When an elephant's trunk is dangling between its tusks, its ears are fully extended and it's running towards you, beware, for this is usually not a mock charge. Part of aggressive behaviour is pawing the dust with a front foot. Elephant suck up water with their trunks and squirt it into their mouths.

They also pump water over their bodies to cool off. When elephants eat grass, they rip it up, knocking clumps against their legs to shake off the dirt. The name pachyderm refers to the elephants creased and thick skin, but in fact, they are not 'thick-skinned' at all; their twin-tipped trunks are particularly sensitive, their sense of smell superb and they fancy a toilette bath of clay.

On the flood plains of the Mana Pools National Park, the presence of huge *Acacia albida* trees ensures the elephants' survival. The apple-ring pods and leaves of these towering giants are a main source of elephant food in winter. *Albidas* have a reverse foliage cycle, sprouting leaves in the dry season, letting them fall in the rains. In August and September elephant, standing on their hind legs, will reach 14m (45ft) into the tree with their trunks to pick some of the nearly 400kg (882 pounds) of pods each tree produces.

Conservationists are aware that man's political and colonial boundaries in no way define the migratory patterns or natural homelands of elephant. If the boundary fences can be removed, a vast consolidated park covering Hwange, Victoria Falls, Chobe in Botswana, Namibia's Caprivi and the southern Angolan parks of Mucusso, Luenge, Luiana and Longa-Mavinga, would enable the wildlife of this savanna wetland to one day be re-united.

An elephant lives some 65 years, dying when its teeth wear out and it can no longer grind its meals.

ADVISORY: HWANGE

CLIMATE

November through February are the summer rain months in Hwange, bringing life to the grass and water to the pans; it is warm but not uncomfortable (humidity is seldom a problem in Zimbabwe). The June and July winter months are usually dry, sunny and good for game-viewing. Hwange can get very cold at this time, and a jersey or jacket is essential for nights around the campfire.

BEST TIMES TO VISIT

The best time is during the winter from May to October, when the grass is thin and the animals congregate at the pans. Most of the Park's accommodation facilities are open year-round, but some game-viewing roads, particularly in the Robins-Nantwich and Deka camp areas, are closed November to April.

MAIN ATTRACTIONS

The great draw is, of course, the game, particularly the large herds of elephant. Late evening and early morning are the best game-viewing time at the pans, especially near Main Camp.

TRAVEL

By air Air Zimbabwe operates daily flights to Hwange from Harare and Victoria Falls. Tel (263) 4-575021 or locally, Dete (263) 18-393. There is an unlicenced airstrip at Main Camp for those with private aircraft.

By road Other options are to drive by car from Bulawayo to Main Camp or by rural bus from Bulawayo or Victoria Falls. The turn-off to Hwange Main Camp is 580km (360 miles) from Beitbridge and 261km (162 miles) from Bulawayo.

By rail Trains run from Bulaway to Dete Station.

GETTING AROUND

Use your own transport, join a UTC bus tour or make use of Hwange Safari Lodge Landrovers. Hitchhiking is not allowed. Car hire facilities are available at Hwange Safari Lodge; call Hertz on (263) 18-393.

TOURS AND EXCURSIONS

Safari is Swahili for 'walk'. Nowadays not many choose this Dr Livingstone form of exercise; a fully kitted-out land-cruiser seems to be the norm. If you don't have your own and you do have the money, let others show you Hwange, under campfire canvas or even from a perch in a tree. The list of operators and increasingly luxurious thatched lodges grows daily, but well established in Hwange is Touch the Wild with its five Hwange units, among them the superb Sikumi tree lodge. Or *Safari Consultants* in Harare, tel (263) 4-758841, *Kalambeza Safaris*, tel (263) 13-4480 and *Landela*, tel (263) 4-734043.

Bush walks and night walks accompanied by armed rangers are available from *National Parks*. Tel (263) 18-371.

Game drives available at any safari lodge or the many safari operators in the area. Try *Touch the Wild*, tel (263) 9-74589, fax (263) 9-44696, or Kumuna (263) 18-2101, fax (263) 18-295.

Wilderness Walking Trails Three nights. Six people. 18 207ha-private estate (45 000 acre). Tel *Nemba Safaris* (Mzola Trails) (263) 89-271, Lupane (189 8) 03533, fax (263) 18-375. P O Box 4, Gwayi.

Safari operators

Many have their own luxury lodges on the fringes of Hwange National Park and will make all-inclusive safari arrangements for you:

Abercrombie and Kent Tel (263) 4-759930, fax (263) 4-759940. P O Box 2997, Harare.

Safari Par Excellence Tel (263) 4-720527, fax (263) 4-722872. P O Box 5920, Harare.

Touch the Wild Tel (263) 9-74589, fax (263) 9-44696. Private Bag 6, P O Hillside, Bulawayo.

Shearwater Adventures Tel (263) 4-757831, fax (263) 4-757836. P O Box 3961, Harare.

ACCOMMODATION

Safari (luxury) lodges

Note: There are other excellent safari lodges. Every travel agent will have their preference.

Ganda Lodge Sited in a huge teak forest bordering Hwange Park. Luxury thatched lodges overlooking a water pan. Tel *Ngamo Safaris* (263) 9-61495, fax (263) 9-74825. P O Box 467, Bulawayo.

Ivory Lodge Teak and thatch tree houses on a rugged wilderness estate on the northern fringes of Hwange Park. Observation platform. Tel/fax (263) 9-65499. P O Box 9111, Hillside, Bulawayo.

Chokamella Lodge Tented camp overlooking natural game pan. Guided bush walks. Tel *Landela Safaris* (263) 4-734043, fax (263) 4-750785. P O Box 66293, Kopje, Harare.

Makololo Camp Large, two-person tents under thatch with *en suite* solar-heated ablutions. Built around huge camelthorn tree overlooking lion country. Tel *Touch the Wild* (263) 9-44566/7/9, fax (263) 9-44696. Private Bag 6, P O Hillside, Bulawayo.

Jijima Safari Camp Tents under thatch. Central dining under-the-stars boma. Swimming pool. Tel (263) 13-4219, fax (263) 13-4349. P O Box 159, Victoria Falls.

Detema Safari Lodge Lovely hilltop views. Thatched chalets and tree houses. Tel (263) 18-256, fax (263) 18-269. P O Box 69, Dete. Or Tel (263) 4-735995, fax (263) 4-735994.

Sikumi Tree Lodge Thatched tree-top units in exquisite woodland bordering Hwange Park's Dete Vlei. Tel *Touch the Wild* (263) 9-44566/7/9, fax (263) 9-44696. Private Bag 6, P O Hillside, Bulawayo.

Finot's Lodge Sited on a 12 138ha (30 000 acre) private game ranch adjacent to Hwange overlooking Gwaai River. Tel (263) 18-2107. P O Box 28, Gwaai. Or Tel (263) 4-793999, fax (263) 4-791188.

Chimwara Camp Located on Chimwara Wildlife Ranch in the Gwaai River Valley. Luxury walk-in tents. Hot spring. New. Tel *Dabula Safaris* (263) 13-4453, fax (263) 13-4453. P O Box 210, Victoria Falls.

Umkombo Safari Lodge In a hardwood forest overlooking Gwaai River near Hwange Park. Thatched A-frame units. Tel/fax *Kingdon Safaris* (263) 61-2777. P O Box 255, Kariba.

Linkwasha Wilderness Camp Twin-bedded safari tents under thatch in remote area of Hwange Park. Tel *Nemba Safaris*, Lupane (263) 89-271, fax (263) 18-375. P O Box 4, Gwaai.

Kumuna Lodge Children welcome in this gracious lodge run by old Africa hands in the heart of big game country. *En suite* safari luxury. Tel (263) 18-2101/2308. Fax (263) 18-295. Telex 51612. P O Box 19, Gwaai.

The Hide Safari Camp. A photographic, game and birding haven. Tel (263) 4-498548, fax (263) 4-498265. P O Box GD305, Greendale, Harare.

Malindi Station Lodge. Accommodation in two restored vintage railway carriages under thatch. Pool. Tel (263) 4-705551, fax (263) 4-705554.

Kalambeza Lodge. Romantic A-frame chalets overlooking Gwaai River with excellent game- and birdwatching and game walks. Tel (263) 13-4480, fax (263) 13-4644, P O Box 217, Victoria Falls.

Hotels and other accommodation

Hwange Safari Lodge 90 room, cresent-shaped hotel overlooking trees and water hole. It is situated some 12km (7.5 miles) from Main Camp. Hub of safari operators. Tel (263) 18-331, fax (263) 18-337. Private Bag DT5792, Dete. Zimbabwe Sun Hotel Group.

Baobab Hotel On a high bluff overlooking Hwange town. Palms and tea in the gardens. Tel (263) 81-2323, fax (263) 81-3481. P O Box 120, Hwange.

Deka Drum Fishing Resort 50km (31 miles) from Hwange town on tar road. On the Zambezi River. Rustic haunt of serious tiger fishermen. Tel (263) 81-250524. P O Box 2, Hwange.

Game Reserve Hotel Rustic, inexpensive, friendly and situated in Dete village. Tel (263) 28-366. P O Box 32, Dete.

Gwaai River Hotel Colourful, eccentric, gorgeous old-style hotel covered with beautiful bougainvillea. Just off the road approximately 34km (20 miles) from Main Camp. Tel (263) 18-355, fax (263) 18-375. P O Box 9, Gwaai.

National Parks and camping

Rustic, inexpensive lodges and camping available at Main Camp, Sinamatella, Robins' and Nantwich. All are self-catering. There are one-party (maximum 12) 'exclusive' camps with lodges at Bumbusi and Lukosi (both near Sinamatella) and Deka Camp 25km (15 miles) west of Robins. Tel Central Reservations (263) 4-706077. P O Box CY826, Causeway, Harare. For one-night stops you can often find a vacant chalet at Main, Sinamatella and Robins' camps.

There are two basic water-supplied camping sites, Insiza and Kasetsheti, in Kazuma Pan National Park near Hwange National Park. Pre-booking essential. It is only accessible by 4 x 4 vehicles and is closed during January and February.

Lions' Den Enterprises Caravan and Camping Site 9km (5.5 miles) north of Gwaai River Hotel on Main Road. Fax (263) 18-295.

WHERE TO EAT

Main, Sinamatella and Robins' camps all have restaurants, as does the Baobab Hotel overlooking Hwange Town. All safari lodges offer excellent meals. A limited range of foodstuffs can be purchased at the three largest National Park camps (Main, Sinamatella and Robins'), but visitors staying in the National Park lodges and camp sites are advised to come fully provisioned.

HEALTH HAZARDS

Malaria, bilharzia and dehydration. Always carry plenty of water in your car and a spare wheel. Make sure it is inflated. Always be careful of wild animals. Never go too close, and never leave your car. (And please remember, if you annoy an elephant, your car is not much protection.)

USEFUL ADDRESSES AND TELEPHONE NUMBERS

AA Wankie Motors, Hwange town. Tel (263) 81-2275.

Medical Air Rescue Service (MARS) Tel Bulawayo (263) 9-60351, fax (263) 9-78959, Victoria Falls (263) 13-4764, fax (263) 13-4609.

National Parks, Central reservations. Tel (263) 4-706077. P O Box CY826, Causeway, Harare.

National Parks, *Main Camp:* Tel (263) 18-371; *Robins':* Tel (263) 81-270220; *Sinamatella:* Tel (263) 81-244522.

Rent-a-Camper Harare. Tel (263) 4-570459 or 752411, fax (263) 4-791188. P O Box H226, Hatfield, Harare.

BULAWAYO AND THE MATOBO NATIONAL PARK

The city of Bulawayo has a history of being three separate towns. The first was the royal town of the Ndebele King, Lobengula. When his father Mzilikazi died in 1868, a civil war broke out over the succession and was settled by a ferocious battle near Inyati Mission. So many warriors were slain in this encounter that the victorious Lobengula exclaimed 'My people have killed me. I shall call my town guBulawayo', the place of slaughter. This original town, 20km (12.5 miles) south of today's city, was built in traditional Zulu style with beehive-shaped huts inside a 1 000m-long (3 281ft) wooden palisade .

Lobengula and his people left old Bulawayo in 1881 as the available grazing and firewood could no longer sustain the royal court. He moved north to a point near the Umgusa River overlooking the flat-topped hill of N'tabazinduna. Two brick houses, huts for his harem, an indaba tree and a goat kraal for 'rain-making' distinguished the second Bulawayo. It was surrounded on all sides by 200m (660ft) of open plain for military drill, and beyond that, traditional massed huts and the wooden stockade. This, then, was the state residence where Lobengula held court and received visitors, including an increasing stream of white men, hunters, traders, missionaries and more ominously, seekers of gold. His weekend retreat was at Umvutcha Kraal a few kilometres from the capital and it was this kraal, together with the official Bulawayo, which were burnt down when Cecil Rhodes's conquistadors arrived in 1893.

Today's Bulawayo near the Matsheumhlope River and where the Ndebele king had vegetable gardens, was declared a town on 1 June 1894. The grid system drawn up then separating business from residential suburbs is still in use today. Plans are going ahead to reconstruct old Bulawayo as a historical park.

OPPOSITE: *Nswatugi Cave's San paintings in the Matobos hold deep spiritual significance.*

BULAWAYO

To the Western eye, Bulawayo is a more attractive city than Zimbabwe's capital, Harare. Many of its old colonial buildings still stand in uncertain pride and, together with its long railway station, elegant blue lamp-posts and lovely parks, a fleet of almost vintage cars and air of déjà vu, it makes a perfect setting for film-makers. *Cry Freedom*, the prestigious *A World Apart* and *The Power of One* were all partly filmed in Bulawayo.

Steeped in history, its attractions include the ancient ruins of Kame, second only to Great Zimbabwe, and the fascinating wilderness of the Matobo Hills where Cecil Rhodes is buried. Within the city limits are the country's Natural History Museum and main railway junction that includes steam locomotive yards and a museum of trains and coaches dating back to 1896. Animal lovers can visit the Tshabalala Game Sanctuary and the Chipangali Wildlife Orphanage, where sick and abandoned animals are cared for.

Bulawayo is an industrial city but retains much of its old-world flavour. Its streets are famously wide to enable a full team of oxen, 24 pairs, to turn 180 degrees. Its first newspaper, *The Chronicle*, first appeared in October 1894 and is still being published today.

Bulawayo still has many of its old buildings, the most interesting being the City Hall, Bulawayo Club, High Court and Railway Station. The City Hall stands on the site of the 1896 laager that Rhodes' settlers retreated behind when the Matabele rose to throw them back beyond the Limpopo. The Old Well was the beleaguered township's only water supply. It was sunk during the uprising in what are now the City Hall Gardens. The well was later filled in and it effectively vanished, only to be rediscovered in 1951 after a long search.

Natural History Museum

Expanding our understanding of Africa's bio-diversity is Bulawayo Natural History Museum's main research activity. The lowveld wildlife scene hall, the first you walk

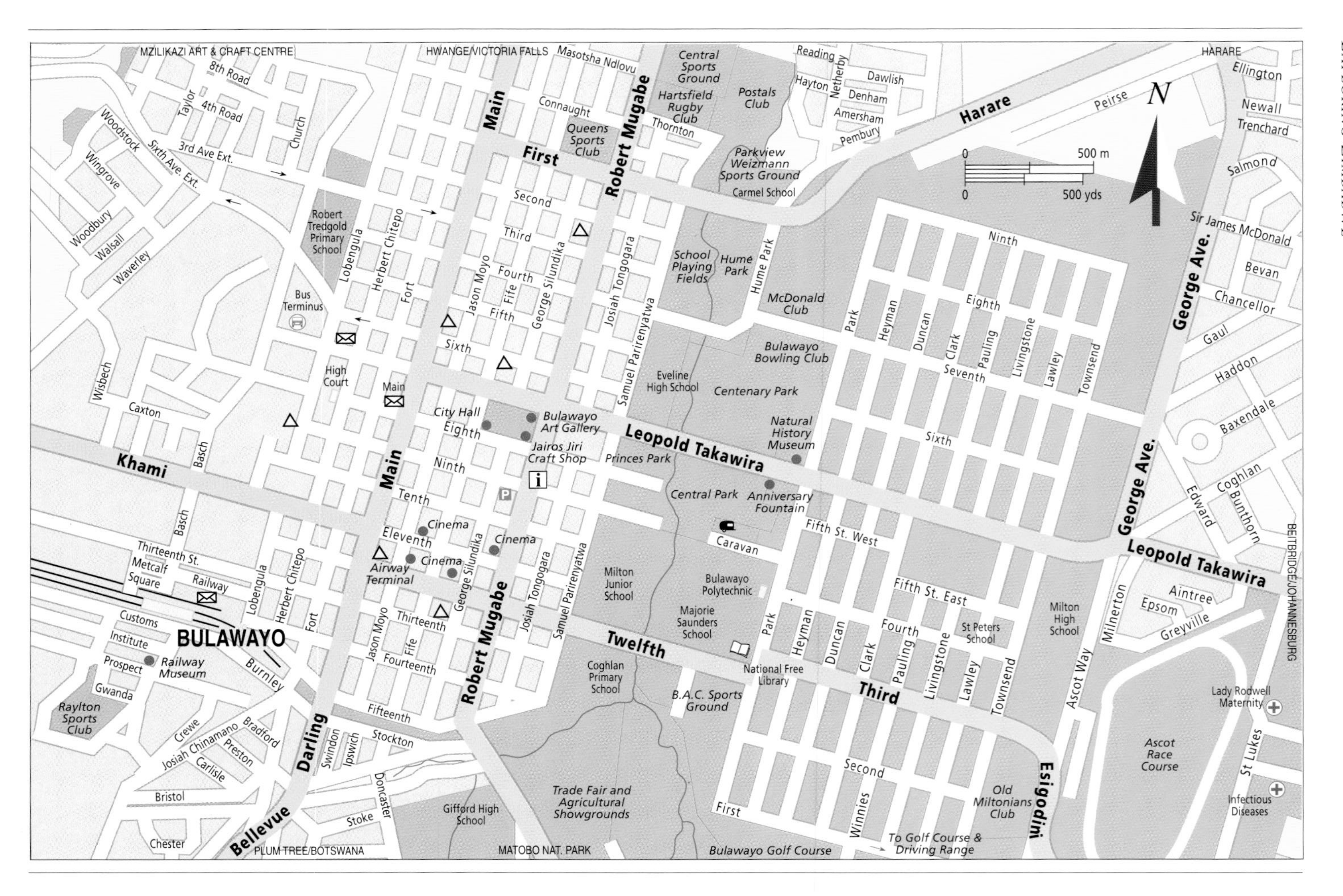
BEITBRIDGE/JOHANNESBURG
HARARE
HWANGE/VICTORIA FALLS
MZILIKAZI ART & CRAFT CENTRE
MATOBO NAT. PARK
PLUM TREE/BOTSWANA
BULAWAYO
500 m
500 yds
George Ave.
Leopold Takawira
Robert Mugabe
Main
Harare
First
Third
Twelfth
Khami
Darling
Bellevue
Esigodini
Ellington
Newall
Trenchard
Salmond
Sir James McDonald
Bevan
Chancellor
Gaul
Haddon
Baxendale
Coghlan
Bunthorn
Edward
Aintree
Epsom
Greyville
Milnerton
Ascot Way
Lady Rodwell Maternity
St Lukes
Infectious Diseases
Ascot Race Course
Milton High School
Old Miltonians Club
To Golf Course & Driving Range
Peirse
Townsend
Lawley
Livingstone
Pauling
Clark
Duncan
Heyman
Park
Ninth
Eighth
Seventh
Sixth
Fifth St. East
Fifth St. West
Fourth
Second
Winnies
St Peters School
National Free Library
Bulawayo Golf Course
Dawlish
Denham
Amersham
Pembury
Reading
Netherby
Hayton
Postals Club
Parkview Weizmann Sports Ground
Carmel School
Hume Park
McDonald Club
Bulawayo Bowling Club
Centenary Park
Natural History Museum
Anniversary Fountain
Central Park
Caravan
Bulawayo Polytechnic
Majorie Saunders School
B.A.C. Sports Ground
Central Sports Ground
Hartsfield Rugby Club
Thornton
School Playing Fields
Eveline High School
Princes Park
Milton Junior School
Coghlan Primary School
Trade Fair and Agricultural Showgrounds
Gifford High School
Samuel Parirenyatwa
Josiah Tongogara
George Silundika
Jason Moyo
Fife
Fort
Herbert Chitepo
Lobengula
Masotsha Ndlovu
Connaught
Queens Sports Club
Bulawayo Art Gallery
Jairos Jiri Craft Shop
City Hall
Cinema
Airway Terminal
Tenth
Eleventh
Thirteenth
Fourteenth
Fifteenth
Stockton
Doncaster
Ipswich
Swindon
Stoke
Robert Tredgold Primary School
Bus Terminus
High Court
Church
8th Road
4th Road
Taylor
3rd Ave Ext.
Sixth Ave. Ext.
Woodstock
Wingrove
Woodbury
Walsall
Waverley
Wisbech
Caxton
Basch
Thirteenth St.
Metcalf Square
Railway
Customs
Institute
Prospect
Gwanda
Railway Museum
Raylton Sports Club
Burnley
Bradford
Preston
Josiah Chinamano
Crewe
Carlisle
Bristol
Chester

into in the giant Colosseum-like museum, is so realistic that you wonder if you shouldn't be running for the nearest mopane tree: recorded sounds of birds, cicadas and animals; life-like scenes of elephant, lion and antelope set among shady trees and rocks; a bubbling brook and spoor track marks at your feet. A sign by artist Terry Donnelly over the entrance to this lowveld hall advises visitors to please keep to the game path.

The mounted elephant, known as the Dodieburn, the second largest mounted elephant in the world, stands 3.53m (12ft) at the shoulder with tusks weighing 40kg (88 pounds) each. There are mounted buffalo, giraffe, eland and zebra, and in a variety of other panels, msasa and mopane woodland, one with four lion at a kill.

Man's art, culture and creative genius reflected in daily living at the Natural History Museum.

HISTORICAL TREASURES

On the high granite hill 105km (65 miles) east of Bulawayo stands the remaining wall of Naletale, one of the most beautifully sculpted *zimbabwes*. The intricate geometric patterning in chevron, herringbone, check, dentil and chord of the 50m-diameter (165ft) hand-laid stone wall is spectacular. Various decorated small stone towers, surmounted by monoliths, were built atop these walls surrounding the house platforms and courtyards of the Rozvi elite 300 years ago. But the builders never got to finish this work of art as a Swazi invading army forced them to abandon the settlement.

Danangombe, also known as Dhlodhlo, is another example of Kame-like Iron Age ruins in the Great Zimbabwe tradition. They are located 16km (10 miles) west of Naletale and 80km (50 miles) northeast of Bulawayo between Fort Rixon and Shangani.

Built in the 16th century, this series of terraced platform ruins were ransacked by looters, including an American, Burnham, who collected 18kg (40 pounds) of gold ornaments, and two Britons, Neal and Johnson, who dug up five burial sites that included 5.9kg (13 pounds) of gold beads and bangles. They sold these in South Africa for £3 000 and promptly established a company, the Rhodesia Ancient Ruins Company. In their quest for riches, they destroyed much of archaeological value. These 'blanket prospectors', as they were known, looted 43 ruin sites.

Ancient artistry at Naletale.

They were eventually stopped when their activities were brought to the attention of Cecil John Rhodes' British South Africa Company. The finds included a Portuguese cannon, a slave's leg-iron, a priest's seal, a silver chalice, a ring, a bell, a bronze censer and bronze oil lamps. It is thought that Portuguese missionaries may have been held captive here hundreds of years earlier.

The museum boasts a collection of 75 000 animals, the largest in the southern hemisphere, while the colourful bird collection is the most comprehensive in Africa. The hall of chiefs covers Zimbabwe's history from Zulu warrior Mzilikazi, to his successor and founder of Bulawayo, Lobengula, to Cecil Rhodes. The Geology Hall has a reconstructed gold mine complete with underground tunnel, railway and 10 000 rock specimens.

One of the best-preserved dinosaurs in the world, *Syntarsus rhodesiensis*, was apparently discovered by schoolboys in 1963 in the Nyamandhlovu area north of Bulawayo and forms part of the museum's incredibly varied collection. The museum also houses exhibits from Robert Moffat's Inyati Mission begun 150 years ago. The mission still exists 62km (39 miles) north of Bulawayo.

The visually striking circular building amidst the trees of Centenary Park is a mecca for conservationists, zoologists and visitors. It is located in Leopold Takawira Avenue and open daily from 09h00-17h00.

ABOVE: *Mechanics at the steam train workshops, near the Railway Museum (top left).*
LEFT: *Striking flamboyant trees line Bulawayo's famously wide streets.*

Railway Museum

The first train to Zimbabwe arrived in Bulawayo on 4 November 1897, part of the Cape to Cairo line which reached Victoria Falls in 1904. Six years earlier, the line from Beira through the sweltering Pungwe River Flats had reached Umtali, and a year later, Salisbury. George Pauling and Co Ltd simultaneously built the lines from Beira to Salisbury, and Mafiking to Bulawayo, and then on to the Congo Border. All of this information can be gleaned at Bulawayo's unique open-air vintage Railway Museum which includes nine steam locomotives (the earliest, Jack Tar, was built in 1896), a 1904 museum coach and the 1896 Pullman saloon that was used to bring Rhodes' body all the way from Cape Town to be buried in the Matobo Hills.

A 1907 Pickering livestock wagon, a Booth travelling crane first used in Beira in 1913 and a tin-roofed country railway station from 1931, are only a few of the many fascinating exhibits that you can actually climb around. Ask for permission and directions to the steam-loco maintenance sheds, and look out for the delightful notice of yesteryear reading: Prevention of Consumption. Passengers are asked to refrain from 'the dangerous and objectionable habit of expectorating'.

You can still capture the old-world pace and courtesy on a journey either from Johannesburg to Harare, or even better, puffing through the Hwange game park in an old-fashioned steam train to the Victoria Falls. Rail Safaris company offers a twice-monthly Zambezi Express nostalgia excursion utilizing coaches built and decorated decades ago such as the coal-fired 28 wheel Class 15 Garratt, a hooting, puffing giant offering private lounge, library, dining car, Africa's game from your compartment window and a special safari excursion at Dete Vlei.

Until 1962 a mobile Christian mission travelled the whole railway network to bring 'light to the line', a touch of which is needed today to track down the Railway Museum's cofusing whereabouts. Go from Fort Street in Bulawayo's southern industrial area, turning right into Preston, right again into Josiah Chinamano and left into Prospect. The museum is closed on Mondays and Thursdays. For more information call the Railway Historical Committee (*see* Advisory on page 85).

CHIPANGALI WILDLIFE ORPHANAGE

Inshlatu, a strikingly coloured, 4m-long (13ft) African rock python (the rock python is Zimbabwe's only protected snake), sits in the glassed-in warmth of the Python House at Chipangali Wildlife Orphanage, 24km (15 miles) south of Bulawayo on the Johannesburg road. These snakes smell with their flickering tongues and coil around their prey to suffocate them.

Chipangali, with the Matobo Hills a long blue line in the distance, is a wilderness parkland for injured or abandoned animals. Hundreds of animals, ranging from lions and leopards, to aardwolfs, flamingoes, pangolins and banded mongooses, are cared for here. There is also a duiker research and breeding centre which incorporates the 16 species of these small endangered buck found throughout Africa south of the Sahara. They are particularly vulnerable to hunting, snaring and man's urban sprawl. Shady walkways lined with aloes lead past the paddocks at Chipangali, enabling close-up viewing that is seldom possible in the wild. There are baby rhino, soft-treading servals and black-eared caracals in the carnivore section and occasionally a lion grumping for its evening meal.

Black-backed and side-striped jackals tiptoe past while the *ihlosi*, the cheetah, regards you languidly from beneath a shade bush. The spotted hyaena, with its death trap jaws, sleeps and a huge black-maned lion ignores everyone, even if you sit on one of the well-placed shady benches near it. The animals, some born in captivity, cannot in the main, be released into the wild.

Birds of prey are kept in a delightful flight aviary, while flamingoes wade in a water-and-tree wonderland, and nearby, crocodiles bask in reed-lined pools. Tortoises, baboons, distinctive bateleur eagles, bush squirrels, or *ubusinti* in Ndebele, wide-eyed bushbabies, civets and lovely dappled wild dogs, the most endangered of all the carnivores, can all be seen at Chipangali.

Individuals and companies from all over the world 'adopt' animals at Chipangali, providing for their support. Their names are listed on the walls of the Interpretive Centre and Information Gallery and they come from New Zealand, the Netherlands, United Kingdom, Hong Kong, even Texas. Princess Diana, the Princess of Wales, is the patron. Chipangali Wildlife Orphanage is open daily from 10h00-16h30.

Loving care at Chipangali for an orphan lion.

Beautiful Kame, built in the 15th-17th centuries using classic dry-stone building techniques.

KAME RUINS

Like balancing rocks, Zimbabwe's ruins can be seen all over the country, some 150 major sites in all. The magnificent Kame Ruins lie in the lovely valley of the Kame, or slow-flowing river, 20km (12.5 miles) west of Bulawayo. Lobengula would not allow visitors near them. He used to perform rain-making ceremonies on the Hill Ruins here and kept an *impi*, or regiment of warriors, there to warn off intruders. An area marked as 'The King's Reserve' can be seen on early maps.

Built by the Torwa dynasty in the 15th-17th centuries, Kame, meaning 'home of kings', is a national monument. The hilly area beneath monkey thorn and purple pod acacia trees is redolent with history. Because of its tall, well-watered trees, *koppies* and unique riverside beauty, this little valley has been the choice of settlers for millennia. Evidence of Stone Age hunter-gatherers dates back thousands of years, while 1 000 years ago and long before the *zimbabwe* builders arrived, Iron Age dwellers built their village in this beautifully treed oasis.

When Great Zimbabwe collapsed, the Torwa state apparently moved to this site and made it their capital. Classic dry-stone building techniques, common to all the *zimbabwes* in the country, were used. The *mambo* ruler's personal hill complex was accessed via a series of rising walled platforms of chequered design, on which were built pole-and-*daga* huts. Rulers' traditional black-and-red patterned drinking pots have been excavated from what used to be an ivory-tusked passageway; other finds include copper items, spears, ivory charms and soapstone pipe bowls.

The stone structures leading up the hill were built as retaining walls in order to support the earth-filled platforms on which the huts of the wealthy and powerful were built. These were inter-connected with beautiful patterning and paintwork; pottery, too, was decorated with zigzag red haematite and black graphite, the sort displayed in the site museum and much copied by Zimbabwean artists today. The draughts-like game *isafuba*, originally introduced by the Arabs and still played all over Africa, is also on display.

Whorls for spinning cotton indicate that the textile skills of Great Zimbabwe were still in use at Kame, while glass jewellery beads, pieces of Ming porcelain and even an old 17th-century European spoon are pointers to trade with the Swahili on the East Coast and later the Portuguese.

Candelabra-like *euphorbia* trees and sweet-fruit marula trees line the path to the hill ruins, the most sophisticated of Kame's five complexes, as it twists up past walled platforms to what was probably the king's domain. Kame, like Great Zimbabwe, was not built for fortification but for display. The courtly Kame elite developed gracious living behind sculpted walls into an art form.

To get to the Kame Ruins, a World Heritage Site, follow the signs (usually spelt Khami) from Bulawayo west on 11th Avenue.

ARTS AND CRAFTS

Zimbabwe is a nation of artists; crocheted bedspreads, carryalls made of fertilizer bags, briefcases from flattened tin cans, Weya (naïve, boldly coloured) paintings, soapstone carvings, oil lamps welded from oil cans, pots, baskets and sculptures are found on every approach road in the country.

THE MZILIKAZI ART AND CRAFT CENTRE is sited in the colourful Mzilikazi high-density suburb, northwest of the city centre; here you can watch sculptors and artists at work. It is closed on weekends but on all other days arrive by 10h15 and get a free guided tour.

Mzilikazi was started in 1963 to help underprivileged women in the township to earn a living. Here, up to 150 people at a time learn and make a wide range of earthenware and ceramic pottery, utilizing up to 15 designs and all under the careful guidance of a team of trained teachers. Commercial art and the design of advertisements, carpentry, fine art, drawing, iron-sculpting and stone work all flourish here. Children are also trained at Mzilikazi where a skill can mean survival on the streets and perhaps a little cash to send home. Mzilikazi exports to a variety of countries worldwide and profits are ploughed back into the school. Slightly damaged seconds sometimes go for very low prices. Mzilikazi is sited in Mzilikazi Square in Mzilikazi high-density suburb. Travel north along Lobengula Street, turn left at Masotsha Ndlovu Way, and it is then 3.5km (2 miles) to the landmark of Mpilo Hospital.

A nation of artists and entrepreneurs: Bulawayo's pavements are a vibrant display of flower sellers, sculptures, curios and African paintings.

BULAWAYO HOME INDUSTRIES was launched 30 years ago. Its main object has been to assist families in Bulawayo's high-density suburbs to pay their way by part- or full-time piece work. Priority is given to the unemployed, the needy and the young. Traditional skills have been adapted to modern usage and the output includes bags made from cord, embroidered and woven materials, sisal, ilala and banana fibres. Women weave cotton, wool, jute, hemp, sisal, ilala and other indigenous materials into wall hangings, lampshades, wraps, bags and men's ties. Chunky wooden pendants and accessories are hand-crafted from sandalwood, ebony and unusual hardwoods.

Bulawayo Home Industries is located in Mizilikazi Square in Mzilikazi high-density suburb and is closed on weekends.

THE BUHLALUSE PROJECT consists of two women's beadwork co-operatives, The Flame Girls and Marigold. They have adopted the finely detailed Ndebele skill of beadwork which has always been part of traditional dress, particularly on ceremonial occasions. They mostly use old Ndebele patterns adapted for use on modern accessories. Articles include necklaces, headbands, leather skirts decorated with beads, walking sticks, purses

Cyrene Mission Chapel, close to Bulawayo, is decorated with colourful frescoes and murals.

SANCTUARIES AND NATURE RESERVES

Mguza Nature Reserve: Richmond Farm Camp Two, sited 15km (9.5 miles) north of Bulawayo on the Victoria Falls road, became Mguza Nature Reserve in 1988 with the aim of promoting conservation, wildlife education and recreation. The area covers over 650ha (1 607 acres) and incorporates the whole of the Lower Mguza Dam. Animals you might see include kudu, vervet monkey, giraffe, klipspringer, reedbuck, zebra, waterbuck,steenbok and impala.

Tshabalala Sanctuary provides the perfect home for a number of thornveld savanna birds that include the crimson boubou, the marico sunbird and the greater blue-eared glossy starling; a total of 200 bird species. At 1 200ha (297 acres), it is the only game park in the country where the thorny acacia tree is predominant. It is open from 06h00-18h00.

One of King Mzilikazi's numerous wives, a Swazi woman named Fulata from the Tshabalala clan, gave birth to Lobengula, a man destined to be king. One of his daughters married Englishman Fairburn Usher, a sailor who lived as an Ndebele on Tshabalala in 1883. For many years Tshabalala was a dairy farm and provided the only source of milk for Bulawayo, but in 1978 it became a National Parks Game Sanctuary. This lovely wilderness, 11km (7 miles) from Bulawayo on the Matobo Hills road, offers walking and horse trails, picnic sites, game (tsessebe, giraffe, serval and zebra among others) and bird-watching.

The **Hillside Dam Bird Sanctuary** in suburban Valley Fun Farm, 16km (10 miles) along the Johannesburg road, the **Ncema and Mzingwane dams**, the rich birdlife on the municipal sewerage works (just outside the city in Aisleby to the right of the Victoria Falls road), the **Mazwi Nature Reserve** 20km (12.5 miles) from the city off the Kame road, and **Mabukuweni** off the Hillside road with its 12ha (30 acres) of indigenous trees and aloes, all offer good birding.

Fishermen love **Insiza Dam** (formerly Lake Cunningham or Mayfair Dam) for big cat fish and **Inyankuni** for bass. Both dams are located east of the Beitbridge Road.

Jumbled granite castles, typical of the Matobos.

and ceremonial tools. Buhlaluse can be found 5km (3 miles) west of 11th Avenue near the shopping centre in Pelandaba suburb. Turn left after the S.D.A. Church School. **THE JAIROS JIRI CRAFT SHOP** in Robert Mugabe Way is another popular visitor venue with a large variety of African arts and crafts for sale made by handicapped people. **BULAWAYO ART GALLERY** (Main Street/ Takawira Avenue) houses a permanent exhibition of paintings, tapestries and sculpture. **BULAWAYO SHELTER** organization for the destitute has hand-woven carpets at their centre in Station Road, Thorngrove, opposite Mpopoma train station (tel 79983). **SELF-HELP DEVELOPMENT FOUNDATION**, corner Main and First streets (tel 76402), make, among others, solar cookers, trashcans and trays out of paper.

THE MATOBO HILLS

Black eagles fidget in the buffeting winds above the avalanche of tumbled red hills in the Matobo Hills. The *amatobo*, or bald-headed hills as Mzilikazi, Zulu warlord and founder of the amaNdebele nation called them, are over 3 000 million years old, a moonscape of granite humpbacks, an hour's drive south of Bulawayo.

The incessant action of rain and sun, of exposure to heat and frost, has left a cataclysmic landscape of abandoned hills, granite *koppies* and gravity-defying boulder castles, a veritable no-man's land of cosmic conflict. The most spectacular section is the Matobo National Park, famed for its San (Bushman) painted caves, wildlife, dams and the World's View grave of diamond magnate Cecil John Rhodes. The local Matabele call it *Malindidzimu*, the place of ancestor spirits, mysterious, eerie, echoing with thousands of years of history. To Victorian poet Rudyard Kipling these aged, moody hills, where Rhodes rode along, were the 'granite of the ancient north'.

The Matobo Hills have been inhabited for thousands of years, first by San hunter-gatherers, later the Torwa (architects of Kame), and then by Changamire and his Rozvi, who were finally edged out by the Zulus. Mzilikazi

INTERESTING PLACES EN ROUTE

- Plumtree, the southwest border post, was founded in 1897. It lies 100km (62 miles) from Bulawayo. Famous for its 100-year-old school, it is a tiny village rich in hunter-rancher tales. Inexpensive rondavels are offered at Omadu Lodge. Tel (263) 80-256.
- Robert Moffat Memorial, Mangwe Pass and Pioneer Column Fort. Moffat travelled to Matabeleland in 1854 to see Mzilikazi and obtain permission to start his Inyati Mission. Turn southeast just before Marula railway siding for 39km (25 miles) on gravel.
- Cyrene Mission. Colourful murals and frescoes decorate Cyrene Mission Chapel, 68km (42 miles) from Plumtree. Figtree, the village a few kilometres south, is named for the spot and tree where visitors waited for permission to enter Mzilikazi's royal domain.
- Birding, small game and fishing is available at Mzingwane and Ncema dams on either side of the road between Esigodini (where Falcon School has its own wilderness sanctuary) and Mbalabala, the latter 255km (158 miles) from Beitbridge. Ncema lies in the lea of the Mulungwane hills with Inyankuni Dam the other side. The larger, remote Insiza (formerly Lake Cunningham) is accessed east from Mbalabala. After 14km (9 miles) on the Masvingo Road, turn left onto Mayfair at the 199.5km-peg (118 mile) for 15km (9.5 miles).

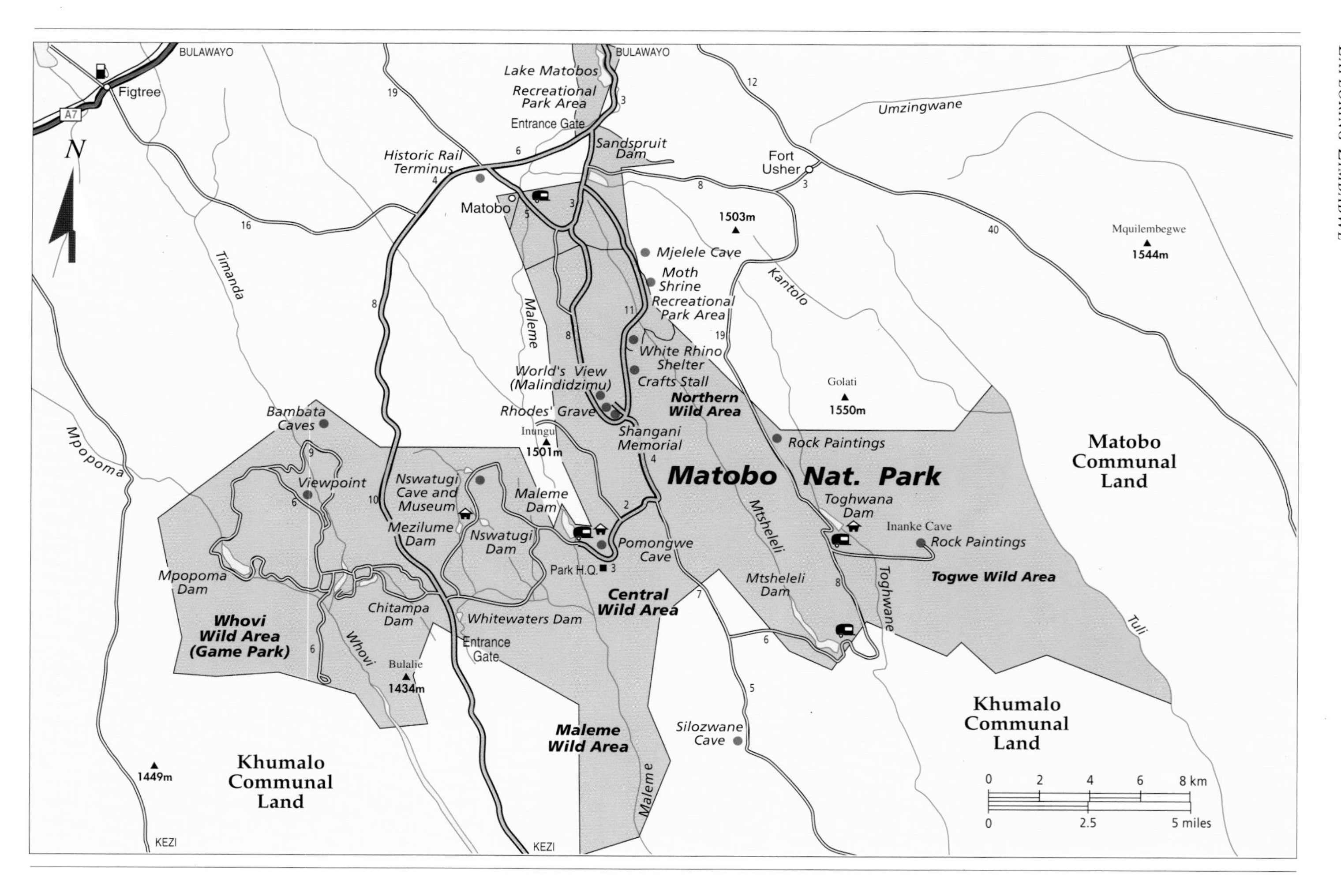

BULAWAYO
Figtree
A7
N
BULAWAYO
Lake Matobos Recreational Park Area
Entrance Gate
Sandspruit Dam
Historic Rail Terminus
Matobo
Fort Usher
Umzingwane
Mquilembegwe
1544m
1503m
Mjelele Cave
Moth Shrine
Recreational Park Area
Kantolo
Timanda
Maleme
White Rhino Shelter
Crafts Stall
World's View (Malindidzimu)
Rhodes' Grave
Northern Wild Area
Golati
1550m
Shangani Memorial
Inungu
1501m
Rock Paintings
Bambata Caves
Mpopoma
Matobo Nat. Park
Matobo Communal Land
Viewpoint
Nswatugi Cave and Museum
Maleme Dam
Toghwana Dam
Inanke Cave
Rock Paintings
Mezilume Dam
Nswatugi Dam
Pomongwe Cave
Mtsheleli
Park H.Q.
Togwe Wild Area
Mpopoma Dam
Central Wild Area
Mtsheleli Dam
Toghwane
Chitampa Dam
Whitewaters Dam
Whovi Wild Area (Game Park)
Entrance Gate
Whovi
Bulalie
1434m
Tuli
Khumalo Communal Land
Maleme Wild Area
Silozwane Cave
1449m
Khumalo Communal Land
Maleme
0 2 4 6 8 km
0 2.5 5 miles
KEZI
KEZI

was one of many fiery warriors who, to escape Shaka, stormed out of Zululand in the early 19th century with 300 Kumalo kinsmen. After being forced north and out of the Magaliesberg mountains in South Africa by Boer trekkers, he crossed the Limpopo.

Eventually he settled at N'tabazinduna, execution hill of his elders not far from Bulawayo and the Matobos, to regroup and divide the conquered land among his *abesanzi* favourites, and build his dynasty. The Rozvi were edged out to ba-Rotse-land (now Zambia) while the Shona in the east were tolerated if not defeated as long as tribute trickled in.

Mzilikazi – lyricized as founder of the Ndebele nation, the great road, bull elephant, lion's paw and warrior king by his praise-singers (who were impaled if they failed) – is buried in the Matobo Hills. His memorial plaque is weathered by time: 'Mzilikazi, son of Mashobane King of the Matabele. A mountain fell on the 5th of September 1868. All nations exclaim: Bayete!' (Hail your majesty!)

The Matobo Hills and surrounding plains, conflict focus of Shona dynasties, Ndebele armies and British colonists, are redolent with history, myth and the memories of a thousand battles. Cecil John Rhodes, born in England, played a major part in this. He made a fortune on the diamond fields of South Africa, became prime minister of the Cape Colony, acquired vast estates in both South Africa and Rhodesia (two of which, Nyanga and the Matobos, are now National Parks) and had two countries – albeit briefly – named after him.

It was his private army, the Pioneer Column, that invaded Zimbabwe in 1890, while his orchestration of the Jameson Raid sparked off the Boer War. Wheeler-dealer of continental proportions, Rhodes never lacked personal courage. His Rhodes Oxford University scholarships are probably academe's most prestigious.

TOP: *Cecil Rhodes' grave, hewn into the living stone, while rainbow-coloured lizards (right) favour the sun-warmed rocks.*

MATOBO NATIONAL PARK

The chaotic weather-cracked hills of the Matobos is the ancestral spiritual home of the Rozvi mediums. It encompasses the national park, a rugged wilderness of soaring black eagles, caves, rain-streaked mountains, San rock paintings, rainbow-coloured lizards and many elusive leopards. The park begins 32km (20 miles) from Bulawayo.

It is divided into five wilderness areas: the southern Maleme Wilderness Area, the northern area encompassing World's View, Togwe in the east with its Inanke Cave paintings, Maleme Dam and holiday chalets in the centre, and further west the actual game park of 43 200ha (106 772 acres) in the Whovi Wilderness Area, all of which can be seen from an excellent network of scenic roads.

Over 50 mammal species are found in the Matobo Park including caracal, sable, rhino, tsessebe, giraffe and possibly the world's greatest concentration of leopard. The park's woodlands and geography varies enormously and supports some 175 species of birds. The Matobo hills are believed to contain Africa's greatest concentration of black eagle (*Aquila verreauxii*), found only in this type of mountainous country. Graceful in flight, fond of cliff-edges and suddenly darting down on unwary prey, it has the ability to make long, vertical climbs, lightning turns and high-speed dives. The black eagle lives mainly on hyraxes (dassies), and being one of the largest eagles, will even dive-bomb leopard.

Surrounding the Matobo Park are a wealth of historical treasures: the Bambata Caves, Cyrene Mission's decorated dwellings, and Fort Usher, where Lord Baden-Powell conceived his idea of the Boy Scout movement. It is also the spot where Rhodes held his peace indaba with the Ndebele elders 100 years ago and where Mzilikazi, founder of the Ndebele nation, is buried. Several luxury safari lodges are hidden among the awesome boulders and hideaway hills of this park.

ABOVE: *White rhino dehorned to deter poachers.* BELOW: *World's View looks over a landscape of endless rocky hills, silent in the sun.*

World's View

Cecil John Rhodes, striving for understatement perhaps, called the Matobos 'one of the world's views'. He is buried here on a bare

granite hill in an amphitheatre of giant balls of stone, with a plain bronze inscription hewn into the granite ground. World's View has a volcanically rugged view as ridge after ridge of hills fall away to the sun-fired horizon. Nearby lies the body of his lifelong friend, medical doctor Leander Starr Jameson, leader of the famous raid that set the Boer War ablaze a hundred years ago. The pantheon includes a gothically heroic frieze of Major Alan Wilson's dramatic last stand on the Shangani River. There is also a pictorial history of Rhodes' life in a thatched shelter at the base of the *dwala*.

The demise of the Ndebele as a warrior nation took place with the arrival of Cecil Rhodes' pioneer corps during the time of Lobengula (Mzilikazi's son). Shield, assegai and rifle were no match for hard-eyed horsemen with machine guns. They had no option but to sue for peace. But like the Shona in the east, their spirit was never crushed. World's View lies 45km (28 miles) south of Bulawayo.

Hunter's vision: San art

Mzilikazi likened these hills to the *matobo*, or bald heads of his *indunas* (elders). But long before the Ndebele settled nearby they were known to man, for here is one of the world's greatest concentrations of hunter-gatherer rock art. The park's numerous caves bear witness to the presence of these spiritually rich and artistically talented people, up to 13 000 and possibly even 16 000 years ago. Here, safe from predators, they could reproduce on the rock faces their trance experiences, the glories of the hunt and the animal wonderland with which they were integrated: 3 000km^2 (1 200 miles^2) of rock overhangs, secret caves and shelters.

Mwari Matonjeni (god of the heavens) was the great spirit of the Matobo Hills. Shrine oracles in caves were consulted by elders, especially when vital rain was needed. The oracles were often older women who spoke as the voice of *Mwari Matonjeni* from the depths of a cave. Mzilikazi had the good sense to allow this Shona *Mwari* cult to continue and to consult the oracles himself. To this day the

Camp Amalinda in the Matobos has its unusual dining room and lounge built into the rock.

Matobos are held in cultural and religious respect by local people. *Mwari* cave shrines in the Matobos include Matonjeni and Mjelele. The paintings in Nswatugi Cave also came to have deep religious significance. It has excellent paintings, particularly of kudu and giraffe, and an interpretive display.

Pomongwe Cave has a site museum where thousands of unearthed Stone Age implements and Iron Age artefacts are on display. In the 1920s, the application of oil and glycerine to the cave's paintings not only failed to preserve them, but came close to destroying the giraffe, zebra, antelope and human figures. Unearthed in the ash, known as the Kame layer, are stone scrapers dating back to 750 BC, as well as other deposits carbon dated to 14 000 BC.

The White Rhino Shelter, so named because of its representation of these handsome creatures, contains outline paintings, Bambata is the most excavated, while the art at Inanke achieves an exquisite harmony of complexity, skill and beauty. Silozwane, just south of the park, contains a fascinating range of domestic scenes. A series of painted arrows leads you to the cave's paintings, one of which depicts a giraffe 2m (6.5ft) high, and a snake that has an antelope's head.

For thousands of years the San lived at peace in the benign boulderland of the Matobos. Then suddenly the dancing hunters, it seemed, vanished, leaving only their art to mourn their passing.

ADVISORY: BULAWAYO AND THE MATOBOS

CLIMATE

Zimbabwe's lowest temperature of -15.6 °C (4 °F) was recorded in the Matobo Hills. Lying close to the Kalahari thirstlands, it is very dry. It has one of the lowest rainfall figures of all Zimbabwe's wilderness areas (excluding Gonarezhou), although the months November through February experience major downpours. Its altitude lessens the worst year-end summer heat.

BEST TIMES TO VISIT

The June to July winter months are always the best times to visit (this applies to Zimbabwe as a whole). April and September are also good months. The Matobo area is drier than much of the country, although February has an average of one day's rain in three.

MAIN ATTRACTIONS

World's View and Cecil Rhodes' grave in the Matobos is everyone's first expedition but you can easily spend a full day in the park, especially if you are interested in hunter-gatherer rock art. And the Matobo Hills are believed to contain Africa's greatest concentration of the magnificent black eagle. Visits to Kame Ruins, the Railways Museum, Natural History Museum, Chipangali and Tshabalala are all rewarding. Bulawayo still has many of its old buildings, some of the most interesting being the City Hall, Bulawayo Club, High Court and Railway Station.

TRAVEL

By air Direct flights are available to Bulawayo from Botswana, Johannesburg, Victoria Falls and Harare.

By road Bulawayo is 322km (200 miles) from Beitbridge, 884km (549 miles) from Johannesburg, 439km (273 miles) from Harare and 439km (273 miles) from Victoria Falls. There are direct road and coach connections to Bulawayo from Botswana, Johannesburg, Victoria Falls and Harare. Coach companies to contact are Blue Arrow/ Greyhound, tel (263) 9-65548, Mini-Zim Travel (luxury minicoach service between South Africa and Zimbabwe), tel (263) 9-76645, or Express Motorways/Translux, tel (263) 9-61402.

By rail There are rail connections to Bulawayo from Botswana, Johannesburg, Victoria Falls and Harare.

GETTING AROUND

Public transport is limited but taxis are usually available. For car hire, try Europcar, tel (263) 9-67925, or Avis, tel (263) 9-68571 or Hertz, tel (263) 9-74701. For bicycle (and car) hire, contact Transit, tel (263) 9-76495. Rural buses from Bulawayo's Mzilikazi Police Station terminus operate to all the small centres in and around Bulawayo. Urban buses depart from the City Hall terminus. You will need your own car for the Matobo National Park, or take a safari company tour.

TOURS AND EXCURSIONS

Rail Safaris By old-fashioned steam train through Hwange Game Park to Victoria Falls. Unbeatable. Tel/fax (263) 9-75575. P O Box 2536, Bulawayo.

Pony Trails Contact *Matobo National Park Office* for trails departing the following day. Tel (183 8) 2504 or ask for Matobo, then (0) 1913.

Walking Trails Try *N'tabazinduna Trails*. Tel (263) 9-62553, fax (263) 9-76658. P O Box 7, Bulawayo.

Photographic Safaris to Matobos. Try *Africa Dawn Safaris*. Tel/fax (263) 9-74941. P O Box 128, Bulawayo.

Hot Air Ballooning Contact *Wildfire Balloon*. Tel/fax (263) 9-42951. P O Box 157, Bulawayo.

City, Matobos, Kame and Other Excursions: *Eddie's Tours and Safaris* Tel (263) 9-66660. *Gemsbok Safaris* Tel (263) 9-63906. *Rhino Safaris* Tel (263) 9-41662. *United Touring Co.* Tel (263) 9-61402.

Mountain Bike Safaris, Matobos. *Ukuthula Safari Agency* Tel (263) 9-78872, fax (263) 9-72427. P O Box 8515, Belmont, Bulawayo.

Chipangali Wildlife Orphanage 24km (15 miles) along Johannesburg road. Tel (263) 9-70764. P O Box 1057, Bulawayo (open Tue-Sun 08h00-17h00).

ACCOMMODATION

Safari Lodges

Camp Amalinda, Matobos. Built into the rock and living hills. Run by ex-Matobos game ranger. *Londa Mela Safaris* Tel (263) 9-41286, fax (263) 9-78319. P O Box 130, Queen's Park, Bulawayo.

Matobo Hills Lodge, Matobos. Attractive. Many lodges plus conference centre. *Touch the Wild* Tel (263) 9-44566/7/9, fax (263) 9-44696. Private Bag 6, P O Hillside, Bulawayo.

Malalangwe Lodge Seven cottages only where the leopards sleeps. Marula area, Western Matobos. *Impi Safaris* Tel (263) 9-74693, fax (263) 9-76197 P O Box 1325, Belmont, Bulawayo.

Jabulani Safaris Shangani area 80 km (50 miles) northeast of Bulawayo. Farm-style hospitality. Near Naletale Ruins. Tel (263) 50-232. P O Box 30, Shangani.

Big Cave Camp Bordering Matobo National Park, owner-managed. Tel (263) 9-64104, fax (263) 9-76854. P O Box 88, Bulawayo.

City and surrounds

Holiday Inn, Bulawayo (Zimbabwe Sun Group). To reach the Inn, take Leopold Takawira Avenue East to Ascot Race Course Area. Tel (263) 9-72464, fax (263) 9-76227.

Induna Lodge Safari in the suburbs. 16 Fortune's Gate Road, Matsheumhlope. Tel (263) 9-45684, fax (263) 9-45627.

The Nesbitt Castle, Hillside suburb. This Macbeth-like fortress has period decor, baronial rooms and sumptuous food. Tel/fax (263) 9-41864. (Johannesburg, tel (27) 11-4422941.)

Churchill Hotel (Best Western Group). Matobo Hills Road, cnr Moffat Avenue Tel (263) 9-41016, fax (263) 9-44551.

McAllister's Lodge Four thatched safari chalets situated in Bulawayo's Burnside suburb. Tel (263) 9-44462.

Budget, backpack, camping and National Parks

Springhaven Rest Resort Farm Camping. 26km (16 miles) south of Bulawayo. Take the Umzingwane Road for 8km (5 miles) off the Johannesburg Road at 18km (11 mile) peg from Bulawayo. Free Bulawayo transport for backpackers 08h00 daily from Railway Station. Tel (263) 88-33515. P O Box 6054, Morningside, Bulawayo.

Municipal Caravan Park Central Park off Park Road. City. Tel (263) 9-63851.

Matobo Ingwe Motel In Matobo National Park. Tel (263) 83-8217. P O Box 8279, Belmont, Bulawayo.

Inungu Guest House Matobo National Park. Sunshine Tours. Tel (263) 9-67791, fax (263) 9-74832. P O Box 447, Bulawayo.

National Parks, Maleme Dam, Matobos. Rustic, scenically placed chalets and camping available. Contact Central Reservations. Tel (263) 9-63646/7. P O Box 2283, Bulawayo. (For Parks Information: Matobos, tel (263) 838-2504 or 0 and ask for Matobos 0-1913).

WHERE TO EAT

There are approximately 26 restaurants (French, Italian, Cypriot, Chinese, Indian), four tea-rooms, 10 take-aways and four night clubs to choose from when visiting Bulawayo. There are no restaurants or shops in the Matobo National Park, although Fryers Store is located 10km (6 miles) from Maleme Dam; call the operator and ask for Matobos, then 0112. The nearby safari lodges all have restaurants, although they are not normally available for guests passing through.

Massimo's Ascot Centre, Leopold Takawira Avenue (Johannesburg road). Italian, the best in Bulawayo (possibly the country). Tel (263) 9-67430.

Cattleman Steakhouse Fast, juicy steaks. Tel (263) 9-76086.

Peking Restaurant Good, occasionally excellent, Chinese meals. Tel (263) 9-60646.

Friar Tuck's Steakhouse Steaks and good gammon grub. 134 Fife Street/14th Avenue, Bulawayo. Tel (263) 9-69265.

New Orleans Chic bayou atmosphere (the owners also run Banff Lodge nearby) and excellent cuisine. Tel (263) 9-43176.

HEALTH HAZARDS

The sun is always a hazard. A hat, sun-block and sunglasses are therefore essential.

ANNUAL EVENTS

The Zimbabwe International Trade Fair. April/May. Tel (263) 9-64911, fax (263) 9-79298. Showgrounds, P O Famona, Bulawayo.

USEFUL ADDRESSES AND TELEPHONE NUMBERS

AA of Zimbabwe Fanum House, Cnr Leopold Takawira/Josiah Tongogara. Tel (263) 9-70063, fax (263) 9-68720.

Air Zimbabwe City Air Terminal. Treger House, Jason Moyo St, between 11/12th Avenues. Tel (263) 9-72051, fax (263) 9-69737.

Banks: Hours: 08h00-15h00 but only to 13h00 on Wednesdays and 11h30 on Saturdays. *Barclays* Main St/8th Ave, tel (263) 9-67811. *Standard Charter* Byo Branch, 84 Fife Street. Tel (263) 9-62395.

Car hire Contact *Europcar* Tel (263) 9-67925. Africa House, Fife St/10th Ave, Bulawayo.

Medical Air Rescue Service (MARS) Tel (263) 9-60351, fax (263) 9-78950.

Mountain bike hire Tel Miles Ahead (263) 9-46503.

National Parks Tel (263) 9-63646. 140a Fife Street, Bulawayo. P O Box 2283, Bulawayo.

Natural History Museum, Centenary Park. Tel (263) 9-60045, fax (263) 9-64019. P O Box 240, Bulawayo.

Pharmacy (after hours). Tel (263) 9-69781/66241.

Post Office Main Street/8th Avenue. Tel (263) 9-62535 (08h30-17h00 Monday-Friday, 08h30-11h00 Saturday).

Publicity Association. Adjacent to Jairos Jiri Craft Shop between Takawira and 8th. Tel (263) 9-60867/72969, fax (263) 9-60868.

Railway Historical Committee Tel (263) 9-363318.

Travel and Safari Shop Gemsbok Safaris, Old Mutual Centre, Jason Moyo/8th Ave, Bulawayo. Tel (263) 9-70009.

Tshabalala Game Sanctuary Tel (263) 9-43411.

Wildlife Society of Zimbabwe Head Office, Harare. Tel (263) 4-700451. P O Box HG996, Highlands, Harare.

GREAT ZIMBABWE AND ENVIRONS

Great Zimbabwe, ruins of Roman proportions and the greatest ancient stone structure south of the Sahara, is sited on an open plain surrounded by hills in the Mutirikwi Valley. The Great Enclosure, a vast boma whose interlocking pieces of hand-trimmed granite are 11m (36ft) high and 243m (797ft) in circumference, contains a chunky, conical tower which looks like a massive African snuff horn. Among the cycads and succulents in the valley lie a myriad other tumbled walls, while on a sheer cliff-face is the Hill Complex ruins, a fairytale castle of interlocking walls and granite boulders. The whole covers an area of 720ha (1 779 acres), and was home to perhaps 18 000 people when it was built in the 13th and 14th centuries.

Great Zimbabwe, a World Heritage site, is one of the great destinations of Africa, for many second only to the Victoria Falls. It is the soul of the nation, the historical heritage of an empire after which Zimbabwe, the 'houses of stone', is named.

THE GREAT ZIMBABWE RUINS

The parkland walk to the huge valley, hill and enclosure of Great Zimbabwe bears several National Monuments and Museums signs at the shady car park entrance. One tells of available guided tours, another that the monkeys should not be fed as they are on a special diet. The path on the approach hill to the little air-conditioned museum displays several easily missed copper plaques. One reads 'Site of Adam Renders' Trading Post c1867-1876', and the other 'Site from where Sir John Willoughby watched an encounter between Mugabi's (sic) forces and those of Nemanhwa. 1892'. Mugabe and Nemanhwa were old rivals in the Masvingo area. Willoughby was Cecil Rhodes' 1890 Pioneer Column's second-in-command, nearby Fort Victoria (now Masvingo, Great Zimbabwe's nearest town) their first permanent laager on the highveld. Renders was possibly the first Westerner to visit Great Zimbabwe and the first to publicize it after Duarte Barbosa reported on this great kingdom in Portugal in 1517. An American of German descent, Renders married a Shona woman. The walk-through museum shows how the edifice was built and how baboons balancing on the walls can cause masonry to fall. Items from the king's treasury which were guarded by the senior wife, or *vahozi*, are in the museum.

OPPOSITE: *The Great Enclosure represents the pinnacle of ancient Shona architecure.*

Looters removed the famous Zimbabwe Birds, slim 40cm-high (16in) soapstone creatures mounted on 1m-high (3ft) columns. Many ended up in Cape Town but were returned 100 years later and are now all in the museum. These fish eagle-like structures graced the walls of the Hill Complex, representing, perhaps, the *Shiri ya Mwari*, the eagle, Bird of God, that formed part of the oracle diviner's pathway to the ancestors.

Earlier this century, amateur excavations undertaken to prove a Phoenician construction did much harm to Great Zimbabwe, one of several ancient sites to suffer at the hands of ignorant and greedy visitors. An American called Burnham at the Dhlodhlo *zimbabwe* looted it of 18kg (40 pounds) of gold artefacts, while two Englishmen, Neal and Johnson made off with 5.9kg (13 pounds) of gold beads from gravels and even set up a professional looters consortium called the Rhodesian Ancient Ruins Co which took away another 14kg (31 pounds) of gold pieces, all of which were melted down. None survived.

Life at Great Zimbabwe

Visualize a wide, sweeping valley decked with hundreds of red shining aloes, msasa, euphorbia and fig trees. On one side lies a giant granite-faced hill, while all over are sinuous, patterned, weaving stone walls surrounding thatched *daga* huts. Great Zimbabwe stretched for 4 km (2.5 miles), most of the 18 000 people living outside the perimeter wall. The valley below the Great Enclosure was probably occupied by the royal

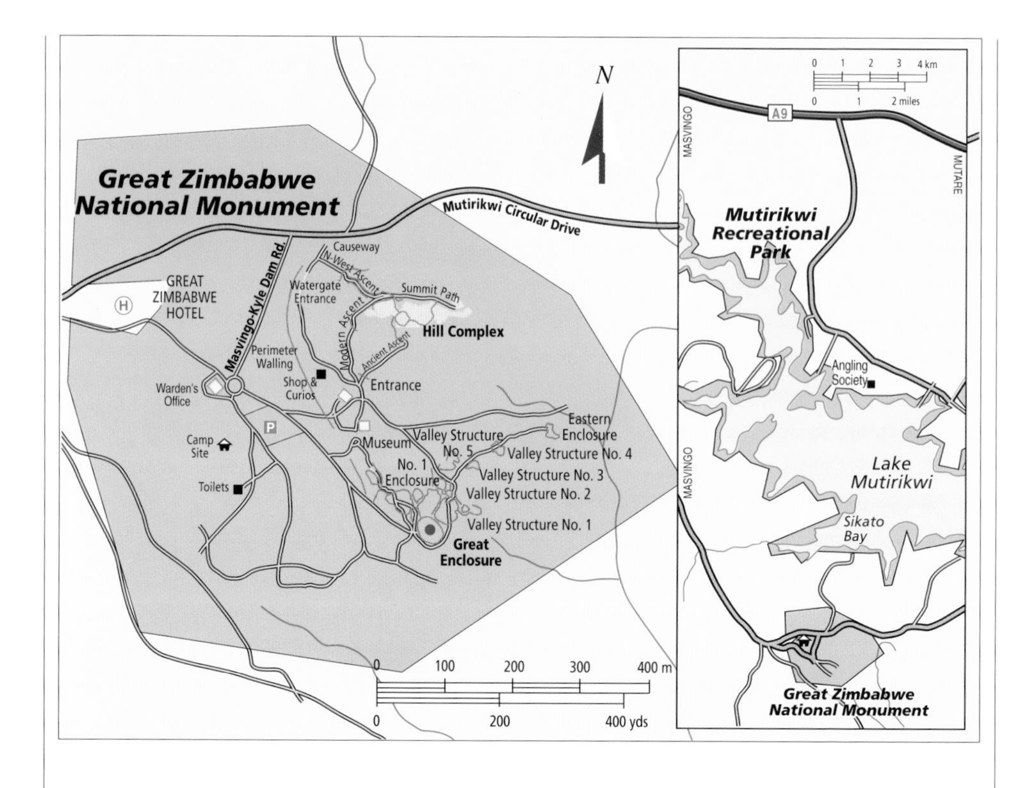

KING SOLOMON'S MINES

The Shona-speaking ancestors of today's Zimbabweans were wealthy cattlemen. They built Great Zimbabwe over a period of 200 years, ending about 1450. The first Europeans to visit Africa, the Portuguese, and the Arabian traders of Sofala and Kilwa before them, knew that Great Zimbabwe was built by Africans, but the Victorians, as they expanded their colonial empire, found this difficult to accept.

A young German geologist, Karl Mauch, started the legend. In 1871 he visited Great Zimbabwe and decided that he had arrived in the Biblical land of Ophir where King Solomon, thousands of years ago, had exported cedarwood for his famous temple.

The Valley Ruins inspired the Dead City in Victorian novelist Rider Haggard's *Elissa or the Doom of Zimbabwe*. Soon every hunter-adventurer who visited Africa had a theory about the mystery of Great Zimbabwe: Romantic speculation included the Arabs, Phoenicians, Indians, even ancient Hebrews.

Zimbabwe, of course, benefitted from the tourism bonanza of all this 'temple of doom' folklore. No brochure, pamphlet or guide failed to whisper about the 'mystery' of Great Zimbabwe. But since 1906 the mystery has been solved. Archaeologist David Randall MacIver, followed by Gertrude Caton-Thompson in 1931, conclusively showed that the scientific, anthropological, archaeological and ethno-historical evidence irrevocably proves that Great Zimbabwe is not King Solomon's mines, Queen Sheba's court, the Valley of the Ancients or even Indiana Jones' hideaway; it is and always was the royal court, the seat or *zimbabwe* of Shona kings. Its very structure replicates normal Shona *musha*, or family homesteads, built in stone.

To this day, however, the old theories die hard. Secretly the Zimbabwe tourist establishment is probably applauding; a little dab of mystery can do wonders when translated into tourism dollars.

wives, while the king and senior diviners lived in splendid isolation on the hill. Great Zimbabwe was the centre of the rich ivory and gold trade with Arabia and India.

Imagine the constant noise of bellowing cattle, sheep and goats, and of children playing, mingling with the industrious sounds of men working on the walls, chiselling stone or hammering at iron hoes. Inside the walls, where the women cook, wash and display their intricately painted pots, are colourful platforms, decorated huts and twisting poles embellished in a hundred different patterns, those very patterns we now associate so much with Africa.

Great Zimbabwe at its height was a symphony of African art, colour and symmetry. The more colours and curves to the huts, their linking passages and balancing rocks, and the higher the walls, the greater the prestige in this vast cattle empire on the well-watered cusp of high- and lowveld grazing in the Mutirikwi River valley.

Zimbabwe also means *dzimba woye*, or venerated house. It was unlikely to have been built for fortification. Protection, privacy and shelter were probably of secondary importance to prestige. The eastern part of the Hill enclosure, where six of the famous Zimbabwe birds were discovered, was probably the national religious shrine, a powerful unifying factor. A land, cattle and trading economy, Great Zimbabwe could probably not have grown or transported sufficient grain to feed itself. Beef was the staple diet. Summer grazing was on the Highveld, in winter, the Lowveld. Throughout the country all the stone *zimbabwes* were built perched on the edge of the high central plateau and all depended on this twin-season cattle-grazing system. Cattle were the property of the ruling class. Even the pottery which was made consisted largely of stone platters for serving meat or pots for beer. Armies were needed to guard the far-flung herds and they doubtless did double duty by building walls.

No natural minerals other than stone were found near Great Zimbabwe, but the capital controlled the trade of an empire stretching for 100 000km^2 (62 000 miles^2) between the Limpopo and Zambezi rivers. Gold and ivory were taken to East Coast trading stations such as Sofala from where dhows shipped them to Arabia, India and possibly China. Internal trade included tin ingots from 600km (375 miles) to the south, and iron bells and cotton from the Zambezi, while copper, salt, soapstone, cattle and grain were probably intrinsic to a tribute system that supported the capital. There was a considerable textile industry at Great Zimbabwe with a host of craftsmen specializing in decorative court crafts.

Fabulous soapstone fish eagles once adorned the walls of Great Zimbabwe.

Ironically, Great Zimbabwe probably did not exercise tight political control throughout its empire. There were too many smaller, competing and independent *zimbabwes*, large towns each guarding their own turf. Great Zimbabwe was abandoned around 1450 AD, the main reason probably being a crucial failure in some aspect of government control of the economy.

TOP LEFT: *The huge conical tower and towering granite walls (above) form part of the impressive Great Enclosure.*

THE GREAT ENCLOSURE

The walls at Great Zimbabwe are huge, built in a series of curves enclosing open spaces, and there are no roofs. The walls are made of granite blocks laid one on the other without mortar. The Great Enclosure, 11m (36ft) high and 243m (797ft) in circumference, probably contains 900 000 blocks of granite, enough, they say, to build 45 houses today. It is the largest ancient structure south of the pyramids, a monument of high walls grey with lichen and echoing with 600 years of history.

The towering majesty, sheer size and symmetry of Great Zimbabwe is awe-inspiring. These great houses of stone were built by the ancestors of today's Shona but only reluctantly ascribed to them by Western visitors. 'I do not think I am far wrong', Karl Mauch wrote in 1871, 'if I suppose that the ruin is a copy of Solomon's Temple on Mount Moriah, and the building in the plain is a copy of the palace where the Queen of Sheba lived during her visit to Solomon.' There was no-one to disprove this and thousands believed this gorgeous piece of thumb-sucking.

The ancient city, whose influence was felt across much of southern Africa, was an incredible feat of architecture, of civic organization and economic sophistication.

Baboons climbing over the chiselled walls and tumbled stones shake the centuries-old work of the masons, and early this century Victorian ladies were regularly photographed on top of the Great Enclosure walls, to the horror of modern archaeologists. At sensitive spots, therefore, each stone has been numbered so that it can be rebuilt.

The outer walls were constructed first. Drains were built through the walls some 6m (20ft) wide, and there were elaborate steps and decorative turrets. One wall that was bulging and in danger of collapse was recently meticulously rebuilt, the ancient lintel entrances re-introduced.

The stone walls enclosed a normal earthen hut complex but the unusual aspect of the Great Enclosure was that it was probably divided into male and female sides and functioned mainly as a premarital initiation school. Groups of young men and women would spend up to a year here learning the correct behaviour for Shona married life. Archaeologists have deduced this from male and female figurines discovered in the Great

Enclosure and from the diving dice (*'hakata'*) symbology such as the chevron 'snake of fertility' patterning on the back wall, and the two senior man and woman conical grain bin towers. Two high walls form a narrow passage, giving direct access to the large tower, and as you walk along it, it is easy to understand the romanticism that gripped both Victorian explorers and modern tourist brochure writers. The Enclosure, with its once sinuous colour-blending domestic interior, represents the pinnacle of Shona architecture and the inspiration for 150 other smaller *zimbabwes* scattered throughout the country.

THE HILL COMPLEX

All the delicate wood carvings, moulded plasterwork and colourful painting that covered much of Great Zimbabwe's structures have been lost, but it is easy to visualize the beauty and opulence of structures such as the Royal Treasury in the valley. Many of these walls have collapsed, some 42 enclosures of circular hut mounds, towers, buttresses, terraces and built-up ridges where the royal wives once lived.

The Hill Ruins, the only part of Great Zimbabwe traditionally known as *dzimbabwe*, or the court of kings, rise 80m (260ft) above the valley. Trelliswork scaffolding on the 30m-high (100ft) and 100m-long (330ft) rock-face occasionally facilitates repairs and research. The original entrance (there are two altogether) is via the narrow, walled series of steps, called the Ancient Ascent.

The whole of the West Wall – 5m-wide (16ft) in places – used to be decked with turrets and pillars, topped, perhaps, with Zimbabwe Birds. The rocky hill is well-treed with euphorbias and *Brachystegia*, and a series of enclosures and platforms are linked by huge snake-and-ladder walls and passageways. The western enclosure was the secluded living area of the king and the oldest of the ruins dating back to 1270AD, although other stone builders were here 900 years earlier. The king, the 'great mountain', ruled by a form of divine right or sacred kingship, a belief common in Europe at this time. His residence was screened at the front by his personal entourage, including the chief messenger and diviner, while his personal chapel, or *chikuva*, was at the back.

Six of the eight existing Zimbabwe Birds were found on the eastern side of the Hill Enclosure, home of diviners and spiritual heartland of Great Zimbabwe. There were possibly hundreds, most made with wood, some enclosed in sheets of beaten gold or copper. On the Hill Enclosure, boulders balance and blend with the intricate patterns of the stonework, while the view across the valley to Lake Mutirikwi is refreshing after the stiff climb up from the curio shop.

TOP: *The oldest of the Zimbabwe Ruins is the Hill Complex.*

RIGHT: *Monkeys scamper on the tumbled walls.*

One of several n'angas, *or diviners, at Great Zimbabwe's reconstructed Shona village.*

Royal Wives and Treasury

Iron hoes were excavated in the Royal Treasury down in the valley that separates the Hill from the Great Enclosure, as well as axes, chisels, an iron gong, copper ingot spearheads, 20kg (44 pounds) of iron wire ready to be made into bangles, and a few imported 'King Solomon's Mines' glass beads, Chinese celadon dishes and various other Eastern trade goods. The treasury was, in fact, the house of the king's senior wife, or *vahozi*, whose job it was to guard such precious items for the king.

The Zimbabwe culture, strangely, originated in present day South Africa at the trading capital of Mapungubwe just south of the Limpopo River, the ancestors of the modern Shona migrating north 200 years before the rise of Zimbabwe.

When Great Zimbabwe was in turn abandoned, most of the people probably moved to Kame in the west (close to Bulawayo) where they continued to build beautiful walls, passageways and hut platforms based on Great Zimbabwe's design.

MASVINGO

Masvingo, halfway between Beitbridge and Harare, is the old Fort Victoria where in 1890, Cecil Rhodes' Pioneer Column went into laager, hourly expecting Ndebele impis to descend on them. They were the first large body of whites to journey into Zimbabwe. Fort Victoria (known as Victoria in the old days), a military earthworks surrounded by barbed wire and thorn brush, was the first 'modern town', some 20km (12.5 miles) from Great Zimbabwe. The pioneers came to this new eldorado in search of gold. The camp's first newspaper was *The Nuggett*, because 'We think of it, dream of it, sigh for the stuff'.

The original lifestyle of tents and mud huts was slowly replaced with bricks. Then came sophistications such as Tattersalls Auctions and the Thatched House Hotel (built by Tom Meikle in 1914). The bell tower of the original fort still stands in Robert Mugabe Street. Masvingo, which means 'walled enclosure', faces palms, post office (early settlers were so poor they got their postage stamps on credit) and wide streets. There is a pioneer cemetery 10km (6 miles) south of town, the remains of the original Fort Victoria at Clipsham Farm and a highway resting place atop what the troopers called Providential Pass.

Masvingo's attractions include Pokoteke Gorge in the Beza Range, Glenlivet Mountain drive, San paintings at Chamavara, the scenic Murray MacDougall drive from Great Zimbabwe around Mutirikwi Dam, tiny St Andrews' Chapel built near the dam wall in memory of the water bailiff's daughter killed in a car accident, a historical tower museum in Masvingo, Mushandike Wildlife Sanctuary, Lake Mutirikwi Recreational Park as well as Morgenster Mission founded in 1891 on Mugabe's Mountain.

The latter has an old red-roofed colonial-towered German church, a lovely 'world's view' overlooking a precipitous drop and dramatic finger rock monoliths guarding the entrance to the mission. A road winds through msasa hills past Great Zimbabwe to the mission. For those who are prepared to travel further afield there is a trio of missions surrounding Masvingo: Bondolfi, famous for its fine leatherwork, Driefontein where many carvings are crafted and sold, and Serima Mission Church. Serima, founded in 1948 by Swiss architect and priest Father John Groeber, was built by the parish community over a period of three years with doors, beams and altar all hand-carved in an exquisite mosaic of African art that has been an inspiration to many a Zimbabwean sculptor.

Chapel of St Francis

The tiny chapel of Saint Francis, just 4km (2.5 miles) from Masvingo on the Birchenough Road, is reminiscent of a Byzantine chapel. Inside, every inch of wall is covered in coloured marble and bronze inlay mosaics. But in fact it is all simulated and everything was hand-painted. The low, multi-angled ceiling inside the tin-roofed building depicts the Nativity scene, crucifixion and the saints. The church is only 15m (50ft) long. Other frescoes and murals picture St Francis himself and St Catherine of Sienna, the patron saint of Italy. The Chapel of St Francis, an incredible gem created inside a humble soldier's hut, is sited inconspicuously alongside an army camp just off the road.

It was built by homesick Italian prisoners of war 50 years ago, men who were captured in the western desert and Abyssinia by British troops and moved south to seven camps in Zimbabwe. It contains the remains of 71 POW's, 46 of whose names are inscribed on plaques in the transepts, and is dedicated to 'our dead brothers who died in captivity'. The incredible wealth of paintings and stained-glass windows were largely the work of one man, a civil engineer in peacetime.

Typical of the area are dome-like granite rocks.

Lake Mutirikwi: bass fishing and game-viewing near Great Zimbabwe.

LAKE MUTIRIKWI AND THE RECREATIONAL PARK

Mutirikwi Dam, formerly called Lake Kyle, was built in 1961 to feed the Lowveld sugar estates. The National Parks game area lies on the north bank of the Y-shaped, 15km-long (9.5 mile) lake, and their chalets are sited on a bluff overlooking the waters. A circular road, starting in Masvingo, travels 120km (75 miles) around the lake and game reserve. After good rains, the lake, in which there are both crocodiles and hippo, is used for sailing, motor-boating and bass fishing.

The scenery through the Mutirikwi communal lands and along forested Glenlivet Drive includes high misty hills overlooking the expanse of blue lake, and on weekends, groups of colourful *Vapostore* dancers and drummers worshsipping beneath shady trees. Most of the leisure resorts are sited on the south bank near Great Zimbabwe.

The Mutirikwi Recreational Park consists of the lake and a substantial game park on its twisting north bank. Here there are many kilometres of game trails and the National Parks cottages. Access is off the Masvingo/Birchenough Bridge road. National Parks provides mooring sites for boats at Sikato Bay not far from Great Zimbabwe. Most of the game in the park was introduced: white rhino, kudu, oribi, wildebeest, nyala, buffalo, giraffe, a checklist of 40 mammals, plus many species of water, woodland and grassland birds. The habitat varies from miombo woodland to acacia thorn scrub and exposed granite *dwalas* (whaleback hills). Rock painting sites, particularly the Chamavara cave, are accessible if you have a guide.

The interpretive centre near the msasa-shaded chalets in the park features the 140 million-year history of the crocodile for which Mutirikwi is famous. There are many game drives along gravel roads in this thickly wooded park with names such as Rhino Peninsula and Buffalo Loop. The narrow dam is 63m (207ft) high and 309m (1 014ft) wide.

The lake, one of the country's largest non border-river lakes, nearly dried out completely in recent droughts, seriously threatening the country's cane fields and sugar-distilled blend petroleum, not to mention the country's most prolific bass fish reservoir. But the waters recovered, as did the cane and the bass; 4kg (9 pound) specimens of the large mouth variety have been caught at Mutirikwi. The best fishing spots for bass are the flooded river entry points such as Pokoteke and Mbebvume. Hooked bass are usually returned by sportsmen to the lake.

The Beza and particularly Glenlivet mountains are a distinctive sight as you drive towards Great Zimbabwe and the lovely lake which fills the valley to the north.

Game-Viewing on Horseback

At Lake Mutirikwi Park, qualified rangers accompany game-viewing groups on horseback. Novice or expert, all are catered for here and children under ten should bring their own riding hats. A horse is able to go where a car cannot and thus enables the rider to draw physically and spiritually much closer to the game. The game park rides last a few hours and the charge is low.

Mutirikwi Park's game was largely introduced, some from Kariba's Operation Noah animal rescue exercise 40 years ago. The white rhino breeding stock came from KwaZulu-Natal. This park, small by Zimbabwean standards, is one of the best-populated wildlife areas in the country.

The first English to come to Zimbabwe travelled in oxwagons. They went into laager near Great Zimbabwe in 1890 to celebrate their escape from the Ndebele *impis*. Later, Cecil John Rhodes brought up a number of black drivers from the Kingdom of Lesotho to help with transport, rewarding them with land where Mutirikwi Park now stands. Many died in the great 'flu epidemic of 1919. Their graves, a few stone huts and a dam, can be seen on a horse trail just off Nyala Drive, 2km (1.25 miles) from the lodges.

THREE LAKES

Three small wildlife sanctuaries are found off the Harare to Masvingo road: Ngezi, Sebakwe and Mushandike, but being off the beaten track, they are not normally visited. Ngezi, in the eastern lea of the Mashava or Great Dyke mountains, 64km (40 miles) from Featherstone on the KweKwe link road, is known for its summer fishing, Cape clawless otters and crocodiles. Solitude is guaranteed as there are only four chalets near the dam wall and jetty, set among rocky *Brachystegia* trees offering lovely sunset views. Further south is Sebakwe Recreational Park, 74km (46 miles) west of Mvuma. It is open for day visitors, especially fishermen in search of Robbie's, or largemouth, bream in the rocky dam.

Mushandike's dam, 26km (16 miles) west of Masvingo, was built in 1938. Here, in this steep *koppie* reserve with its tranquil lake ringed by mountains, you can, in the dry season, lie on the long grassy banks and spot game such as kudu, sable, wildebeest, zebra, waterbuck, even leopard. Camping and caravanning facilities are available on the shores where a panorama of waders and water birds can always be seen in the shallows.

INTERESTING PLACES EN ROUTE

- From Beitbridge, stop for tea and a swim at the Lion and Elephant Motel on the Bubi River, 70km (45 miles) from the border.
- Bulawayo to Masvingo via Mbalabala and the road from Zvishavane links a variety of mines and small mining settlements: Filabusi (gold), Fred Mine (gold), Mberengwa (emeralds), Zvishavane and Mashava (asbestos). There are some lovely mountain ranges along the 280km (174 mile) route.
- Mushandike Sanctuary, 26km (16 miles) west of Masvingo, boasts game, high mountains and a lovely lake.
- Mtao Forest Reserve, 10km (6 miles) south of Mvuma on the Beitbridge road. Look out for the turn-off to Driefontein Mission near the railway crossing and growth point nearby, a distance of 16km (10 miles), with Serima Mission's wood sculpture church another 31km (19 miles) along the same gravel road. Both are worth a visit.
- Chivhu is roughly halfway between Harare and Masvingo. The latter is halfway to Beitbridge and this border town is just over halfway to Johannesburg, a total distance of 1 134km (705 miles). Chivhu used to be Enkeldoorn, or One Thorn Town.
- Denise's Kitchen and Tangenhamo Safaris. Game animals, open-air restaurant, chalets. 156km-peg (97 mile) just south of Chivhu on the Beitbridge road.

ADVISORY: GREAT ZIMBABWE

CLIMATE

Great Zimbabwe, at the edge of the central plateau, is high enough to enjoy cooler temperatures but with a touch of Lowveld warmth. Its rainfall pattern is the same as the Highveld, but it receives less rain. The rainy season occurs November through February while June and July are cold, dry months. A sweater or jacket for the evening is a good idea.

BEST TIMES TO VISIT

May to September are the coolest months. Rain comes in December and January. Game-viewing is best from July to September; October is pleasant but can be very hot.

MAIN ATTRACTIONS

The Great Enclosure and the Hill Complex should not be missed. Set aside half a day at least as the Ruins are huge and spread out. Game-viewing on horseback can be booked with National Parks, Mutirikwi Recreational Park, tel (263) 39-62913, Private Bag 9136, Masvingo. The drive around the lake and into the Glenlivet hills is quiet and scenic. Don't miss the smallest church in Zimbabwe, the 12 person chapel of St Andrews at the top of the picnic site overlooking Mutirikwi Dam wall, nor the equally picturesque Chapel of St Francis.

TRAVEL

By air United Air, in conjunction with Air Zimbabwe, operates three weekly flights between Harare and Masvingo. Tel (263) 4-575021. For package day tours by air from Harare, contact UTC, tel (263) 4-793701, fax (263) 4-792794.

By road If travelling by car, a 21km-tar (13 miles) access road commences opposite Riley's Service Station 5km (3 miles) south of Masvingo. Good tar roads lead to Masvingo from Beitbridge – 288km; 180 miles – and all of Zimbabwe's major centres, including the Lowveld and the Eastern Highlands. An alternate route from Harare is the new metal road from Chivhu south through communal farming areas to Gutu, then west at the main Birchenough Bridge to Masvingo road, for 43km (27 miles).

The following companies operate **bus services** via Masvingo: Blue Arrow/Greyhound, tel Harare (263) 4-729514. Tel Johannesburg (27) 11-3333671. *Express Motorways/Translux* Tel (263) 4-720393 or 725132. *Silver Bird* Tel Harare (263) 4-794777/8/9. Tel Johannesburg (27) 11- 3377215. *Zimibus* (minibus) Tel Harare (263) 4-720426. Tel Johannesburg (27) 11-8830380.

By rail There are no rail conncections to Masvingo or Great Zimbabwe.

GETTING AROUND

The choice is car hire, joining a package tour or using your own transport. Car hire is available from *Hertz*; contact Travelworld, tel (263) 39-62131. Day tour operators arrange hotel pick-ups. Call *United Touring Company* (UTC), tel (263) 39-62274 or 62131. Backpackers can catch the Morgenster Mission bus from the town centre. It goes to within 2km (1 mile) of Great Zimbabwe before turning south to the mission.

TOURS AND EXCURSIONS

Several Harare-based operators offer tours to Great Zimbabwe, sometimes combined with other scenic destinations: contact *Rainbow Hotels and Tours*, tel (263) 4-733781, and *United Touring Company (UTC)*, tel (263) 4-793701. For game-viewing pony trails, call *National Parks* on (263) 39-62913.

ACCOMMODATION

Pa-Nyanda Lodge Luxury safari lodge with game 11km (7 miles) south of Masvingo on the Beitbridge road. Tel (263) 39-63412, fax (263) 39-62000. P O Box 199, Masvingo.

Lodge of the Ancient City On a *koppie* overlooking woodlands and the Great Enclosure. Tel *Touch the Wild* (263) 9-44566/7/9, fax (263) 9-44696. Private Bag 6, P O Hillside, Bulawayo.

Great Zimbabwe Hotel Ideally situated near the Ruins. Small, comfortable rooms, open air patio dining. Tel *Zimbabwe Sun Group* (263) 39-62274, fax (263) 39-64884. Private Bag 7082, Masvingo.

Kyle View Holiday Resort Camping and rustic furnished chalets, self-catering but with a restaurant between Great Zimbabwe and Lake Mutirikwi. Tel (263) 39-52298, Private Bag 9055, Masvingo.

Norma Jeane's Lake View Chalets Self-catering accommodation in lovely gardens. Best in the area. Boats for hire. Tel (263) 39-7206, fax (263) 39-64205. P O Box 196, Masvingo.

Glenlivet Hotel Eleven bedrooms. Magnificent mountain backdrop and stunning sunsets. Family run. Swimming pool. Tel (263) 39-7611, fax (263) 39-62846. P O Box 146, Masvingo.

Mutirikwi Lake Shore Lodges and marina, 8km (5 miles) from Great Zimbabwe on Mutirikwi shore. Tel (263) 39-7151. P O Box 518, Masvingo.

Golden Spiderweb Lovely thatched chalets 69km (43 miles) north of Masvingo on the Harare road.

National Parks and Great Zimbabwe

Chalets and camping at **Great Zimbabwe**. Contact **Great Zimbabwe Hotel** 800m (½ mile) from entrance gate. Tel (263) 39-62274, fax (263) 39-64884. Private Bag 7082, Masvingo. **Mutirikwi (Kyle) Recreation Park** Rustic lodges on north bank overlooking lake, plus there is camping and caravaning. Tel *National Parks* Central Reservations, (263) 4-706077. P O Box CY826, Causeway, Harare. Camping also available on the southern shore fairly close to Great Zimbabwe at **Kyle View Holiday Resort** and **Mutirikwi Lakeshore Lodges**.

Masvingo town

Flamboyant Hotel (Protea Hotels). Good travellers' hotel 2km (1.2 miles) south of Masvingo. Tel (263) 39-62005, fax (263) 39-64126. P O Box 225, Masvingo.

Chevron Hotel Hotel actually in Masvingo near the Information Bureau. Tel (263) 39-62054. P O Box 245, Masvingo.

Budget and backpack

Backpackers Rest Mountain bike hire and swimming pool. Tel (263) 39-63960/63282. 13 Hellet Street, Masvingo.

Budget Accommodation 18 Kirton Street, near Information Centre. Tel Paw Paw, Harare (263) 4-724337.

Clovelly Lodge (pick-ups from town centre). Tel (263) 39-62346/64751.

WHERE TO EAT

Masvingo and Great Zimbabwe do not boast any great restaurants, but there is a good choice of simple, tasty food available.

Great Zimbabwe Ruins Curio shop with Cokes, chocs and chips and tree-shaded tables.

Great Zimbabwe Hotel Patio dining. Snack menu, weekend barbecues and à la carte on offer. Only 800m (½ a mile) from Great Zimbabwe entrance. Tel (263) 39-62274.

Wimpy 5km (3 miles) south of the town at Shell Garage and Great Zimbabwe turn off. Open late.

Igloo Takeaways Ice-cream bar in Josiah Tongogara Road, Masvingo.

The **Flamboyant** (tel (263) 39-62005), **Chevron** (tel (263) 39-62054) and **Kyle View** (tel (263) 39-52298) hotels all have restaurants, often with good, inexpensive meals; Kyle View also has patio barbecues on Sundays from 11h30. But if you are prepared to make the 40km (25 mile) journey, the best food in lovely surroundings is at the **Glenlivet Hotel**, tel (263) 39-7611.

Tea Cosy Meikles Store in Robert Mugabe Street. Light snacks and pastries.

CHURCH SERVICES

There are 17 Christian churches in Masvingo. These include Anglican, tel (263) 39-62536, DRC, tel (263) 39-62263 and Catholic, tel (263) 39-62956. Contact the Islamic mosque on tel (263) 39-62250.

HEALTH HAZARDS

There are hippos, crocodiles and bilharzia in the lake. There is not much malaria, more so in the nearby Lowveld, but visitors should take the usual prophylactics. Always be wary of the sun, especially when out horse-riding or on the lake.

USEFUL ADDRESSES AND TELEPHONE NUMBERS

AA Tel (263) 39-62563. Magic (Pvt) Ltd. Shop 5, Robert Mugabe Street, Masvingo.

Historical information Try *Belmont Press*, 36 Hofmeyr Street. Tel (263) 39-62633.

Master Angler (for fishing enquires). Tel Harare (263) 4-885560, fax (263) 4-883214. P O Box BW550, Borrowdale, Harare.

Medical Air Rescue Service (MARS) Tel (Harare) (263) 4-792304/791378, fax (263) 4-721233.

National Museums and Monuments of Zimbabwe (enquiries). Tel (263) 39-62080, fax (263) 39-63310. P O Box 1060, Masvingo.

Photographic Equipment and Film Gold Print. New Richards Building, Robert Mugabe Way, Masvingo. Tel (263) 39-63642.

Prehistory Society Tel (263) 4-302385. P O Box 867, Harare.

Publicity Association Information Bureau near the Railway Crossing and curio sellers. Open weekdays only, occasionally during holiday seasons on Saturdays. Tel (263) 39-62643. P O Box 340, Masvingo.

Wildlife Society Masvingo Branch. P O Box 655, Masvingo. Tel (Harare) (263) 4-700451.

THE LOWVELD AND GONAREZHOU

A Lowveld man or woman, they say, never refuses a drink – of anything – so hot and dry is this rugged, wild territory stretching from the Shashe River border with Botswana in southern Zimbabwe to the Chimanimani foothills far to the east.

The heart of the Lowveld, however, lies in the arid baobab and sand river country between Beitbridge and Hot Springs. Great chunks of the Lowveld are game sanctuaries, both private conservancies (including Save, Africa's largest) and national parks, of which Gonarezhou, the place of the elephant, is the best known.

Gonarezhou is the country's second largest game park situated in Zimbabwe's southeast corner. It is 150km (93 miles) long and borders on Mozambique's Banhine Parque and South Africa's Kruger National Park, the three forming a natural migratory triangle for the elephant and animals of the wild.

Some 25 years ago, 14 000 out of a total of over 50 000 animals were shot and killed in Gonarezhou, supposedly to contain tsetse fly and protect cattle ranching. However, the effect of this policy was devastating: 8 000 bushbuck and the same number of kudu, 13 000 warthog, 3 000 elephant and 1 100 buffalo were killed. Bush and forest clearance were other expedients.

It will take many years for nature to heal all these wounds and those caused by ruthless poachers, recent internecine warfare in neighbouring Mozambique and relentless 50 °C (122 °F) drought. As of January 1994, Gonarezhou was once again fully functional and open to everyone after having been closed to the public for many years.

For the purposes of administration, Gonarezhou is divided into the northern Runde region (Chipinda Pools) and Mwenezi River (Mabalauta Camp) in the south.

OPPOSITE: *Gonarezhou is famed for its baobabs; here one of these giant trees is magically etched against the evening sky.*

THE LOWVELD

BEITBRIDGE AND TULI

A new mile-wide bridge spans the Limpopo at Beitbridge, adding to the one first built in 1929. Spanking new immigration and customs halls in both Zimbabwe and South Africa have also been constructed, with such extras as air-conditioned duty-free shops. This does not necessarily mean that transit between the two countries is any faster, or that the queues of both people and long-distance trucks any shorter. In fact, were it not for the casual friendliness of both, the whole process could be rather tedious.

Messina, just 13km (8 miles) south of Beitbridge is a little mining town, while Beitbridge, 490m (1 608ft) above sea level on the Zimbabwe border, is an emporium of petrol stations. Both are as blindingly hot as only the Limpopo River Valley can be and both have hinterlands of baobabs, hot springs, cattle ranches and mile after mile of wooded hills and arid mopane plains, plus Kipling's fever trees, set about everywhere.

The real treasures are the kudu, giraffe and other game that wander across the road, usually at night, on the Zimbabwe side, and the untold riches underground. This is Zimbabwe's newly discovered diamond country, probably part of the same reef stretching across both sides of the Limpopo. It was also dinosaur kingdom 200 million years ago. Fossils of a *Massospondylus* have been found on nearby Sentinel Wilderness and much palaeontological work is afoot. Or under foot, with brush and magnifying glance.

Some 100km (62 miles) west is the lovely semi-circle of the Tuli Safari Area on the Shashe River. Fort Tuli, built by Cecil Rhodes' Pioneer Column when they invaded the country in 1890, was the first of several forts to ward off imminent Ndebele attacks.

Tuli is aptly named after the local word *utulili*, meaning dust. Only a flag now marks the fort where Mother Patrick and the Dominican Sisters started the country's first hospital in 1891. Frederick Courteney Selous built the road to Tuli for the Pioneer Column.

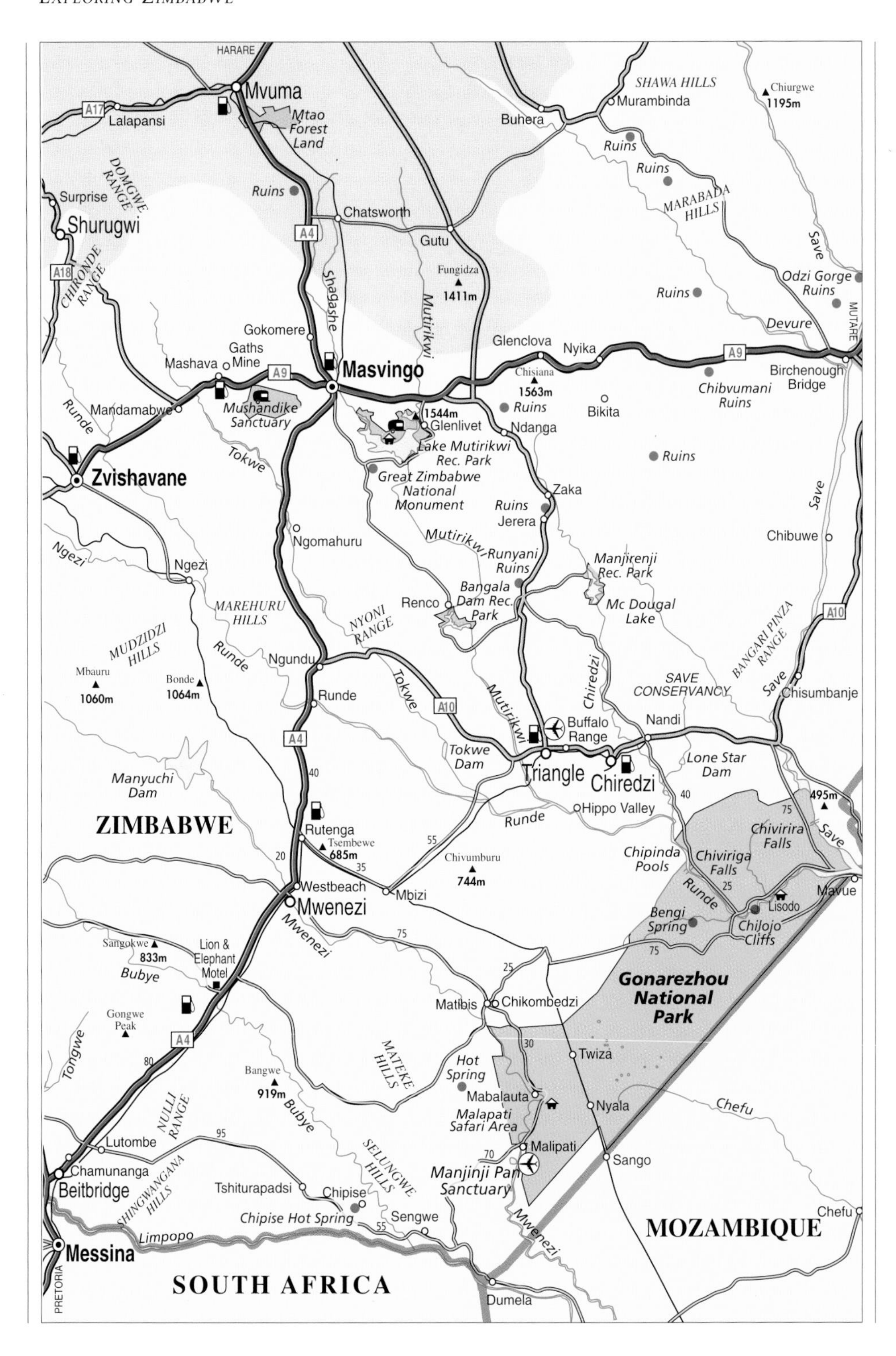

HARARE
Mvuma
A17
Lalapansi
Mtao Forest Land
DOMGWE RANGE
Surprise
Shurugwi
Ruins
Chatsworth
A4
Gutu
Buhera
SHAWA HILLS
Murambinda
Chiurgwe 1195m
Ruins
Ruins
MARABADA HILLS
Save
Odzi Gorge Ruins
Ruins
Devure
MUTARE
A18
CHIRONDE RANGE
Shagashe
Fungidza 1411m
Mutirikwi
Gokomere
Gaths Mine
Mashava
A9
Masvingo
Glenclova
Nyika
A9
Chisiana 1563m
Birchenough Bridge
Chibvumani Ruins
Runde
Mandamabwe
Mushandike Sanctuary
1544m
Glenlivet
Ruins
Ndanga
Bikita
Zvishavane
Tokwe
Lake Mutirikwi Rec. Park
Great Zimbabwe National Monument
Ruins
Zaka
Ruins
Jerera
Save
Ngomahuru
Mutirikwi
Runyani Ruins
Chibuwe
Ngezi
Ngezi
Manjirenji Rec. Park
Bangala Dam Rec. Park
Renco
Mc Dougal Lake
A10
MAREHURU HILLS
NYONI RANGE
BANGARI PINZA RANGE
MUDZIDZI HILLS
Runde
Ngundu
Mbauru 1060m
Bonde 1064m
Runde
Tokwe
A10
Mutirikwi
Chiredzi
SAVE CONSERVANCY
Save
Chisumbanje
Buffalo Range
Nandi
A4
Tokwe Dam
Triangle
Chiredzi
Lone Star Dam
Manyuchi Dam
40
40
495m
Hippo Valley
75
ZIMBABWE
Rutenga
Runde
Chivirira Falls
Tsembewe 685m
55
Save
Chivumburu 744m
Chipinda Pools
Chiviriga Falls
20
35
Westbeach
Mbizi
Runde
25
Mavue
Mwenezi
Lisodo
Mwenezi
Bengi Spring
Chilojo Cliffs
75
75
Sangokwe 833m
Lion & Elephant Motel
25
Bubye
Gonarezhou National Park
Matibis
Chikombedzi
Gongwe Peak
A4
Tongwe
MATEKE HILLS
30
Twiza
80
Bangwe 919m
Hot Spring
NULLI RANGE
Bubye
Mabalauta
Nyala
Chefu
Malapati Safari Area
95
Lutombe
SELUNGWE HILLS
Malipati
70
Chamunanga
Sango
SHINGWANGANA HILLS
Beitbridge
Tshiturapadsi
Chipise
Manjinji Pan Sanctuary
Chipise Hot Spring
Sengwe
Chefu
Limpopo
55
Mwenezi
MOZAMBIQUE
Messina
PRETORIA
SOUTH AFRICA
Dumela

The area was his hunting headquarters in Victorian days, and Tuli is still a beautifully wild land, rich in trees and game. Tuli also has the distinction of being the site of the first rugby game in Zimbabwe, played by the Pioneer Column in 1890, on the wide and dry sandy bed of the Shashe.

Just across the border in Botswana's Tuli-Mashatu is the largest herd of elephant on private land in the world. The old hunter-adventurer road is fascinating. It crosses Botswana and then the Limpopo into South Africa by cableway at Pont Drift, but there is no immigration post. Tuli today is a ghost village, but for those who like out-of-the-way places and for those with a sense of history, this hot, flat wilderness is fascinating.

CHIREDZI

Hunters Lager is made in Chiredzi, the cane-growing capital of the Lowveld, some 300km (190 miles) east of Beitbridge. And it is thirsty country indeed.

Chiredzi is also entry point for the Gonarezhou National Park. The town's rather convoluted name means a place where a fish can be caught on a line. It sits near a spaghetti junction of rivers, the Chiredzi, Save, Runde and Mutirikwi, all making their way down to Gonarezhou National Park. None of these rivers are very reliable, however, when it comes to providing water for either fish or sugar cane, except, perhaps, in torrential floods early in the year.

Chiredzi was started in the early 1960s to serve the needs of the fast-growing sugar cane project in Hippo Valley, irrigated by water from Lake Mutirikwi near Great Zimbabwe. Thomas Murray MacDougall grew the country's first cane in 1931. His home, now a small museum, is on nearby Triangle Estate, 15km (9.5 miles) west where the country's large petrol-from-cane ethanol plant is sited.

When the time for cutting the cane falls due, great fires are lit to sweep through the cane to make it easier to cut and handle. The giant Hippo Valley mill can process 440 tonnes of cane an hour. The Chiredzi-Triangle Lowveld area juxtaposes huge open fields of cane with swathes of indigenous forest. Cattle ranching was profitable here not so long ago but nowadays wild game animals are being re-introduced onto vast conservancies such as Save, Chiredzi and Lone Star, where the game-viewing and variety of wilderness scenery is unsurpassed.

Rural portrait: a young family at Hot Springs.

Bustling Chiredzi village has mainly 1960s buildings and a good range of banks, shops and facilities, plus a Wildlife Society Interpretive Centre. Like nearby Triangle, it has a rail linkup with the national network, and an airport (Buffalo Range). It also has crocodile and ostrich farms, Immigration Control and in Triangle, the most experienced wildlife translocation experts in the country.

LONE STAR

Bush coffee from baobab pips, honey from the baobab's white flowers, smoked monkey-orange and grilled *mbewa* mice, bones and all, are unusual, tasty Lowveld treats which you might just be able to persuade the rangers on Lone Star Wilderness Sanctuary to prepare for you.

The Lowveld is Zimbabwe's Texas, but here the longhorns are replaced by elephant, lion, rhino, buffalo and practically the whole spectrum of Africa's game on ranches such as Lone Star (40 486ha; 100 000 acres) not far from Chipinda Pools at Gonarezhou. Lone Star, between the Runde and Chiredzi rivers, is large enough to sustain practically every Lowveld habitat: mopane and munundo woodland and long grass plains highlighted by the occasional huge baobab; water courses of ghostly fever trees; sweet fruit marulas; and forests of hardwoods, thornveld, mountain acacias and cathedral mopane.

A 7km-long (4.5 mile) lake hemmed in by mountains like a Norwegian fjord forms one of the largest private dams in the country, and in a range of sunburnt hills called Malilangwe – the place of the sleeping leopard – there are possibly more of these elusive spotted hunters than in the Matobos. About 230 species of bird are also found here.

Lone Star has nearly all of Zimbabwe's species of eagles (longcrested excepted) and many of the owls. Bream, bass and barbel can be caught in the dam, provided the fish eagles don't get to them first. Lone Star's luxurious Induna Lodges are tucked away in a bowl of high cliffs, moulded into the rock.

BELOW: *Induna Lodge and lake in a bowl of Lone Star hills offers visitors the chance to see exquisite San paintings (left) among the overhangs.*

INTERESTING PLACES EN ROUTE

• Small roads cross from Mozambique at Dumela into the southern Lowveld but there are no customs or border posts. However, there is one at the Chicualacuala rail crossing into Gonarezhou on the Maputo line.
• If travelling from Harare, stop at the Great Zimbabwe Ruins near Masvingo, the ancient city after which the country is named.
• An alternate, less used route to Gonarezhou is to take the Birchenough Bridge road east from Great Zimbabwe which forks south to Zaka. There are ruins nearby and more 25km (15 miles) south of Zaka near Runyani/ Chivamba; from here, drive east for 20km (12.5 miles) to Manjirenji Lake and Recreational Park. Formerly Lake McDougall, the lake provides the rancher and cane-grower with boating and fishing in scenic isolation.
• Coming from Mutare, take the scenic gravel route to Chimanimani via Cashel. Turn to Chipinge via Skyline Junction Road, then down into the Lowveld again via Tanganda Halt. Cross the Save near Gonarezhou at Rupangwana (Quinton Bridge).
• At 3 200km^2 or 344 000ha (850 000 acres), the Save Valley Conservancy area is probably the largest privately owned conservation area in Africa. Consisting of 20 former cattle ranches (the fences between them have been removed) the area is now a major game area and wilderness resort.

GONAREZHOU NATIONAL PARK

GREY GHOSTS OF MABALAUTA

'When the spectre of drought haunts the land, the Lowveld ... is a desiccated region of gaunt leafless trees and shrivelled grass, dry water-courses and in the spring and early summer, blazing dehydrating heat', wrote Allan Wright in his *Grey Ghosts at Buffalo Bend*. Then comes the miracle of rebirth with the rains. Allan Wright, District Commissioner for the Lowveld for many years, was largely responsible for the creation of Gonarezhou National Park in 1975, incorporating his Buffalo Bend Reserve and flanking the Manjinji Pan 'island of water' Bird Sanctuary, both on the Mwenezi River.

TOP: *Gonarezhou, the second largest game park, has camp sites along the Runde River (above).*

Mabalauta is the headquarters of this National Park and site of the Swimuwini chalets at the sandy horseshoe loop and high cliff of the Mwenezi River at Buffalo Bend. Mabalauta is derived from the Shangaan *Palaurwa*, which means 'to sand down' a hunting bow from a *Ficus capreifolia* branch. The view downriver from Buffalo Bend stretches in a languorous sweep to distant heat-shimmered plains. The Mwenezi runs through southern Gonarezhou in a series of remote bird and game-viewing pools, then into Mozambique to join the Limpopo River.

The whole Gonarezhou area, particularly the south, has a history of invasion. Tonga-Hlengwe, and particularly Ndau-speaking folk, plus, of course, a few trans-Limpopo Venda, were some of the earlier inhabitants when General Soshangane and his Gaza impis stormed in during Shaka Zulu's time. It has been a melting pot ever since, the greatest sufferers unfortunately being the grey

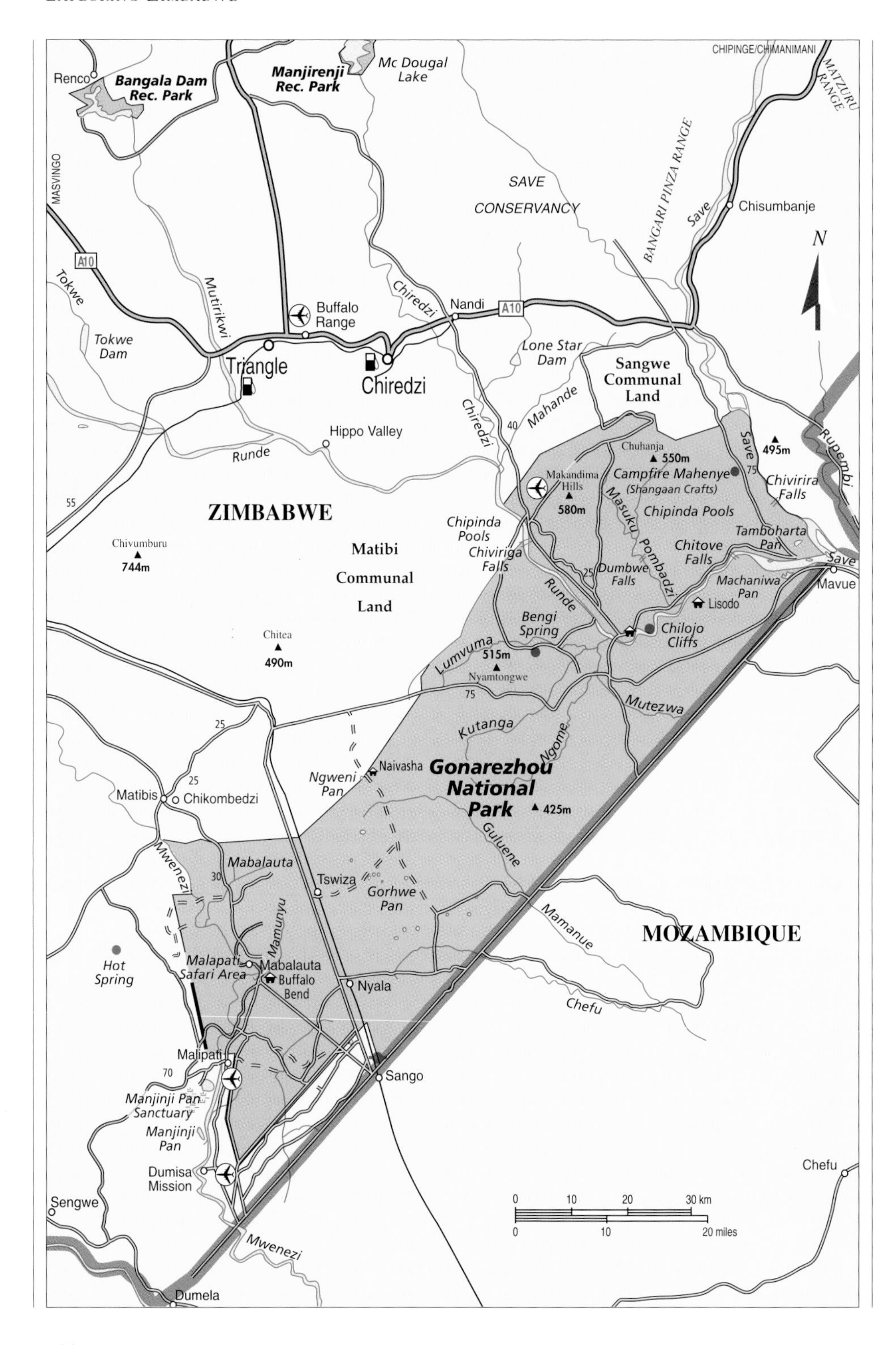

Renco
Bangala Dam Rec. Park
Manjirenji Rec. Park
Mc Dougal Lake
CHIPINGE/CHIMANIMANI
MATZURU RANGE
BANGARI PINZA RANGE
MASVINGO
SAVE CONSERVANCY
Save
Chisumbanje
N
A10
Tokwe
Mutirikwi
Chiredzi
Buffalo Range
Nandi
A10
Tokwe Dam
Triangle
Chiredzi
Lone Star Dam
Sangwe Communal Land
Chiredzi
40
Mahande
Hippo Valley
Runde
Chuhanja
550m
Save
495m
Rupembi
Campfire Mahenye
(Shangaan Crafts)
75
Chivirira Falls
Makandima Hills
580m
55
ZIMBABWE
Masuku
Chipinda Pools
Chipinda Pools
Tamboharta Pan
Chivumburu
744m
Matibi Communal Land
Chiviriga Falls
Pombadzi
Chitove Falls
Save
25
Dumbwe Falls
Mavue
Runde
Machaniwa Pan
Lisodo
Bengi Spring
Chilojo Cliffs
Chitea
490m
Lumvuma
515m
Nyamtongwe
75
Mutezwa
25
Kutanga
Ngome
25
Naivasha
Ngweni Pan
Gonarezhou National Park
425m
Matibis
Chikombedzi
Guluene
Mwenezi
Mabalauta
30
Tswiza
Gorhwe Pan
Mamanue
MOZAMBIQUE
Mamunyu
Hot Spring
Malapati Safari Area
Mabalauta
Buffalo Bend
Nyala
Chefu
Malipati
70
Sango
Manjinji Pan Sanctuary
Manjinji Pan
Chefu
Dumisa Mission
0
10
20
30 km
0
10
20 miles
Sengwe
Mwenezi
Dumela

ABOVE: *Baobab bark, elephant snack.*
BOTTOM: *The adorable rhino: bush tank.*

ghosts, the elephant. Remote and hot, a region of tsetse fly and malaria, the area's huge tusked mega-herbivores nevertheless attracted every crook and rascal with a gun.

A valley of lovely 15m-high (50ft) ironwood trees (*simbiri* in Shangaan and Zimbabwe's only stands of these *Androstachys johnsonii* giants), borders Mozambique. Ironwood smells like wild honey when it is cut or burnt. In the past it was used for railway sleepers in Mozambique and because it is so hard, white ants (or termites) have practically no effect on it.

At Ironwood Viewpoint on the Mwenezi, on a clear day one can see the aptly-named Crooks Corner and across to Mozambique. Pans radiate out north from the Mwenezi River which attract game after the rains. Beyond the railway line are others that can be reached on gravel roads by four-wheel-drive or high-clearance vehicles. They include the Manyanda Pan (place of honey-eating hunters) with its viewing platforms, Mafuku and Lipadwa, off Soshangane Drive.

White-striped nyala antelope are found in southern Gonarezhou, plus lion, a few rare suni, buffalo, sable and too many elephant for the parks' carrying capacity, one of the reasons why, using techniques pioneered in Gonarezhou, their translocation to other parks in Africa was undertaken. In the largest operation of its kind, 200 elephant were translocated from Gonarezhou National Park to Madikwe Reserve in South Africa, a distance of 1 000km (621 miles). Each elephant was herded by helicopter to a waiting truck where it was darted with a morphine-based tranquillizer, the legs tied, and then the giant beast was rolled gently onto rubber mats from where winches hauled it into a capture container. Here the elephant was revived with an antidote and now, back on its feet, it was coaxed into a linking 30-tonne-truck for the journey south.

Much care was employed throughout and to minimize separation trauma, the translocation truck contained the whole family. Water and food were administered in plentiful pre-departure supply. Hopefully, poached-out herds as far north as Kenya will benefit from this revolutionary technique.

The Sabi Star, or impala lily, blooms May to September in Gonarezhou. In the Yemen, where it was first identified, this succulent was known as the many-flowered plant. Part of its Latin name, *Adenium obesum*, hints at

its overweight baobab-like trunk, most of which is underground. Covered in white, pink-edged, star-shaped flowers, it favours rocky areas and is the leading lady of the Lowveld floral line-up. Sausage trees flourish along the Mwenezi River.

Be patient when looking for game in Gonarezhou. The distances are vast and you will seldom come across another vehicle. But the birding and the vistas along the river are awesome. Conservationists are hoping that one day the extensive wilderness areas of Zimbabwe's Gonarezhou National Park, South Africa's Kruger National Park and Mozambique's Banhine Parque may be linked in a massive, natural migratory triangle for the elephant that have been poached and culled for so long.

BELOW: *Mopane in the rains of summer and the Sabi Star (bottom) blossoms in winter's dry.*

Rivers of Gonarezhou

Near the wine-farming area of Marondera on the Highveld east of Harare, the Save, Zimbabwe's largest, most silt-threatened internal river, slowly begins its long journey to the Indian Ocean. In the sweltering Lowveld valley of hot springs and baobabs that flank the Chimanimani highlands, it is joined by the Odzi River from Nyanga where it is wide, sandy and suffers from terrible soil erosion.

The women dig deep in the riverbed for water as the Save, in parts, consists of 30m (100ft) of silt. On its banks of high trees are the Vapostore honey farmers. Dressed like apostles in knotted girdles, woollen caps and shepherd's crooks, these long-bearded men are the most hard-working and successful wild honey farmers in the country. The deep brown honey of a dozen flower tastes (even tobacco!) is gathered at night from log hives high up trees, when the bees are sluggish and slow to sting human harvesters.

Passing under the spidery span of Birchenough Bridge, with its perfect steel half-moon, the Save flows ever south past the Save Conservancy, the world's largest private game reserve on its western plains. It turns east at Quinton Bridge, heads past the ruins of an old Portuguese mission station and into Gonarezhou National Park, forming its northern border. Coursing over the wild purple basalt of the Chivivira Falls (*Chibilila* in Shangaan), it reaches and fuses with the Runde River and they flow together through a narrow green gap into Mozambique.

This easternmost spearhead of Gonarezhou is a swampy wetland lush with ebony, clambering blue-bark cordia, sycamore fig, marula fruit and huge wild mango, or mutondo trees, spreading their canopies along the rivers, while parts are forests of bushy, almost impenetrable ilala palms. In the sands that separate the shallow waters, the spoor of lion, hyaena and the great pancake plates of elephant footprints can sometimes be seen.

The Runde (river of great floods) forms part of the Lowveld irrigation complex that enables the growing of Zimbabwe's petrol-blend sugar. Joined by the Chiredzi, its

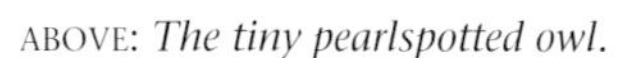

ABOVE: *The tiny pearlspotted owl.*
TOP RIGHT: *Fording the Save in the dry season near Mahenye Lodge.*
RIGHT: *Birchenough Bridge, a cat's cradle of steel.*

muddy and seasonal meanderings through forest banks, pans, baobabs and high cliffs provide the scenic focus for many of Gonarezhou's northern wildlife viewpoints, particularly where it joins the Save.

The Runde, which rises on Gweru town's golfcourse, was a real problem to Cecil Rhodes' 1890 invading column as the wagons almost capsized on the rocky riverbed. Today a long bridge sweeps across their early path while further to the east, the rail bridge which crosses the river, linking Chiredzi with the railway line to the coast, is the longest in the country at 418m (1 371ft).

Where the Runde joins the Save, having meandered its way through northern Gonarezhou, the altitude, at 90m (295ft), is the lowest in the country; if you are a walker or birder, this is Gonarezhou at its best. Here are the exquisite Tamboharta and Machiniwa marshy pans and riverine forests of huge trees as varied and majestic as Kew Gardens.

Tamboharta Pan in the wooded promontory leading into the confluence of the Save and Runde rivers is a water wonderland of spurwing geese, ducks, jacanas and herons, marsh grass, and nymph and lotus-lily blossom. Elephants often wade across the pan, pausing and grazing. On the far side of the Runde is Machiniwa Pan, surrounded by tall forests and situated under the Marumbini Hills where, in days of yore, there was a recruiting post for South Africa's gold mines.

The pinky-purple flowers of stud thorn that local people use for shampoo, wild yellow hibiscus, Mexican poppy and false foxglove, all grow in the sand.

The range of birds found here is tremendous, including Pel's fishing owl, Egyptian geese, hamerkop, yellowbilled storks and bateleur eagles. The Runde is up to 3km (2 miles) wide at the confluence. On the island in the middle is Mahenye Safari Lodge, hidden amongst a forest of Natal mahogany and wild mango trees. You can usually drive across the riverbed with the exception of a couple of days a year.

Hundreds of trees grow in the forests along the Runde River, and by its many pools in northern Gonarezhou. The toad tree (*Tabernaemontana elegans*) has dried shrivelled fruit, gaping, pale brown and pockmarked with warts, rather like a toad's head, and the latex of the tree can be used to curdle milk.

Plenty of lion occur in the vicinity, and you occasionally hear them roaring while you sit around the campfire at night. In the tangled Ngwathumeni Forest nearby, learn to identify an evening brown butterfly, a sycamore fig, wild mango, an assassin bug – and when to stay still if a lion is in the thicket ahead. It is always best to walk with a trained and armed guide. In the old days, the local Shangaan would hold an annual fish drive near Mahenye. Fishing requires special permission from National Parks. Some 108 species of reptiles and amphibians are found in the park including the marbled tree snake, Zanzibar puddle frog, soft-shelled terrapin and Warren's girdled lizard.

CHILOJO CLIFFS

These dramatic cliffs rise sheer from the quiet pools of the Runde in layers of ochre, pink, copper, white and yellow, and form part of a 32km-long (20 mile) sandstone massif. As you make your way along the dusty roads and mopane scrub of Gonarezhou, the Chilojo Cliffs are visible from a great distance. They form the most startling feature along the Runde River, especially when the sunset catches the quickly changing fire in the stone. They were called Clarendon Cliffs in colonial days, and the original Shangaan name *vulojo* means 'ripples on an elephant's palate'. Baobabs, aloes and a variety of trees seem to claw their way up to the base of these high, stark cliffs whose grandeur and vistas of endless wilderness sum up the spirit of Gonarezhou. In a day's drive you may well not see another living person.

The cliffs date back to what geologists call the 'chalk-deposit period' when much of Gonarezhou apparently faced a vast inland ocean. The sandstone has been eroded to

LEFT: *The flowing Runde River is often dry; elephants make use of this crossing (below) against the backdrop of the impressive Chilojo Cliffs.*

Chipinda Pools, the headquarters of Gonarezhou, is home to yellowbilled storks (above) and herds of brawny buffalo (left).

form gullies where the animals come to drink. It is an area of varied but not abundant wildlife and patience is needed, waiting beneath the canopy of nyalaberry and ebony trees at Fishan's Camp, to spot white-striped nyala, Lichtenstein's hartebeest, the more unusual suni antelope and even elephant.

Drive round the back of the cliffs and onto the plateau where the views across the flat, dusty woodlands and occasional mesa-like mountain are superb. The Chilojo plateau, with several big pans on top, stretches 15km (9.5 miles) east to the Mozambique border.

CHIPINDA POOLS

Chipinda Pools is northern Gonarezhou's headquarters. Here by the river and in the lea of Chwonja Hills, or the roaring lions as they are known in Shangaan, are lovely camp sites with open dining rondavels. National Parks have a base and small ecological display nearby. Unlike much of Gonarezhou, Chipinda's camp site is open year-round and is the entry point for the northern Runde-Save river portion of the park. It lies 33km (20 miles) east of the main Chiredzi-Birchenough Bridge road; the turn-off is 15km (9.5 miles) from Chiredzi, the Lowveld capital.

Attractive camp sites are situated further into the park at Chinguli and at another eight spots along the river, most with panoramic views across the Runde. Pokwe, Fishans, Lisodo and particularly Chilojo camp in front of the cliffs' fiery pink ramparts, are all remote and beautiful; the one facing 343m (1 125ft) Kundani Mountain is also worth the longish 4 x 4 drive.

Although drought has killed off some of Chipinda's huge, tagged trees, there are still plenty of bastard marula, ebony, African mangosteen, mahogany, white syringa and leadwood to shade the pools where hippo and crocodile bask. Chipinda means 'to flow through' and this the Runde does, just before the Chiviriga Falls, while some 15 rivulets flow into the wide Runde.

ADVISORY: THE LOWVELD AND GONAREZHOU

CLIMATE

Gonarezhou in the Lowveld is hot and semi-arid. Some 70% of its sparse rain falls in the November to February summer months. A mild June and July winter leads to temperatures in excess of 40 °C (104 °F) in the summer. Much of the park is only 150m (492ft) above sea level.

BEST TIMES TO VISIT

The dry season months, May to October, are the best, but from September it is very hot. During the sparse rains, the National Parks' camps at Chipinda Pools and Mabalauta are also open, but as travel on game-viewing roads is restricted, prior advice should be sought from National Parks.

MAIN ATTRACTIONS

The Tamboharta and Machiniwa pans near the Save-Runde confluence are pristine, bird-rich, waterlily wildernesses with the occasional elephant wading across the green vastness. The views looking up to the pink sandstone Chilojo Cliffs and the spectacular view of the twisting Runde and wooded plains from the top are a must. If it is big game you are looking for, head for Lone Star Reserve or Senuko on Save Conservancy.

TRAVEL

By air United Air usually operates several flights weekly from Harare, via Masvingo, to Buffalo Range Airport in Triangle-Chiredzi; call Air Zimbabwe for reservations. Tel (263) 4-575021. All three Safari Lodges (Lone Star, Save and Chiredzi) have airstrips.

By road Northern Gonarezhou is approached by road via Chiredzi, while the south is reached via Rutenga off the Beitbridge-Harare highway. The gravel road between the two is for four-wheel-drive vehicles only. Mahenye by road is 55km (35 miles) east of Chiredzi to the Quinton Bridge on the Save, then 44km (27 miles) south. Lone Star Reserve's turn off on the Chiredzi road is at the 135km-peg (84 mile) and then 17km (10.5 miles) to Induna. Save Conservancy and Senuko turn off is at Nandi then 49km (30 miles) north, partly on tar. All the main roads to Gonarezhou and to Chiredzi-Triangle from both the Beitbridge-Masvingo road and the Chipinge-Beitbridge road are full tar, as is the Chiredzi-Zaka-Chivu-Harare route.

GETTING AROUND

Although you can reach Chipinda Pools in a normal car, Gonarezhou requires a high clearance vehicle or four-wheel-drive.

TOURS AND EXCURSIONS

National Parks operate three-to-six-day **walking trails** in Gonarezhou. Tel (263) 4 706077.

Photographic safaris (vehicle or walking) are available at all the luxury lodges.

Biza Saddle Safaris near Gonarezhou offer horseback safaris lasting several days through a game ranch of 101 150ha (250 000 acres). Maximum six clients at one time. Shamamonga Bush Camp. Lots of game, buffalo, leopard, zebra, rhino. Tel (263) 4-495742, fax (263) 4-498265. P O Box GD305, Greendale, Harare.

ACCOMMODATION

Safari Lodges

Mahenye Wilderness Lodge, Save-Runde confluence, Gonarezhou. Raised riverbed luxury lodges made of red and white teak and panga panga wood. Decorated with river reed matting woven with ilala palm. Beneath huge trees on an island in the middle of the Save River. *Zimbabwe Sun Reservations*, tel (263) 4 736644 fax: (263) 4-736646. P O Box CY1211, Causeway, Harare.

Lone Star Reserve, Induna Lodge, Gonarezhou. The reserve is sculpted into a well-treed boulder valley facing a lake on a game reserve that has all the big five. Tel *Wilderness Safaris* (263) 13-4527/3371, fax (263) 13-4224. P O Box 288, Victoria Falls.

Senuko Lodge, Save Wildlife Conservancy, Gonarezhou. Thatch (and canvas blinds) chalets à la Shangaan with *en suite* facilities in rocky woodlands on Africa's largest private wilderness sanctuary, stretching nearly all the way from Birchenough Bridge to Chiredzi. *Zimbabwe Sun Reservations*. Tel (263) 4-736644, fax (263) 4-736646. P O Box CY1211, Causeway, Harare, or (Lowveld) tel (263) 31-2698, fax (263) 31-2617. P O Box 396, Chiredzi.

Turgwe River Camp, Humani Ranch, southeast Lowveld. Four tented thatched chalets for personalized game walks. Tel *Bushveld Safaris* (263) 4-796432, fax (263) 4-796432. 46 Stirling Heights, Josiah Tongogara/5th Street, Harare.

Sentinel Limpopo Safaris, Beitbridge area. Dinosaurs, palaeontology, horse trails, balancing sentinel rocks and leopard on the banks of the Limpopo River. Chalets under large trees. Tel/fax (263) 86-351. P O Box 36, Beitbridge.

Lion and Elephant Motel, Biri (Bubi) River. Comfortable chalets on the banks of the dry river. Old-fashioned breakfasts. Tall hunting tales and good biltong. 70km (45 miles) from Beitbridge. Tel (263) 14-336/2602, fax (263) 14 358. P O Box 148, Beitbridge.

Threeways Safaris Biri (Bubi) River. 65km (40 miles) north of Beitbridge. turn-off near service station for 5km (3 miles). Hemingway country. River bank, rustic, hunters chalets, paraffin lamps and home-cooking by the river. Tel (263) 14-or dial 0 and ask for Rutenga followed by 01320/01312. P O Box 49, Beitbridge.

Note: Coming from Harare the Great Zimbabwe Ruins makes a good stopover (Great Zimbabwe Hotel or the Lodge of the Ancient City, *see* pg. 94)), and from Nyanga, Hot Springs Resort south of Mutare or the Chimanimani Arms in the mountains (*see* pg. 131).

Other accommodation

Tambuti Lodge Hotel, Chiredzi, 8km (5 miles) from Chipinda Pools turn-off. On the banks of the Chiredzi River. Tel (263) 31-2575, fax (263) 31-3187. P O Box 22, Chiredzi.

Planters Inn, Chiredzi town. Comfortable, air-conditioned and convenient for businessmen. Close to three golf courses. Tel (263) 31-2281, fax (263) 31-2345. P O Box 94, Chiredzi.

National Parks accommodation, Gonarezhou. Rustic chalets at Mabalauta (Buffalo Bend). Gonarezhou and camp sites at Chipinda Pools. Contact Central Reservations, tel (263) 4-706077. P O Box CY826, Causeway, Harare.

The Beitbridge Inn, Beitbridge. Tel (263) 86-214, or **Peter's Motel**, tel (263) 86-309, are both air-conditioned. A new hotel is currently under construction.

WHERE TO EAT

There are no hotels, restaurants or shops in Gonarezhou. Visitors staying at the National Parks chalets or camp sites should come fully equipped. All the lodges have restaurants as do the hotels in or near Chiredzi. Buy your provisions in Chiredzi.

HEALTH HAZARDS

Malaria, bilharzia, dehydration, sunstroke and sun skin cancer. Take the necessary precautions. Wild animals are always dangerous.

USEFUL ADDRESSES AND TELEPHONE NUMBERS (CHIREDZI)

AA, Chiredzi Auto Electrical, Lion Drive, Chiredzi. Tel (263) 31-2897.

Air Charter and Travel Agent Lowveld Travel and Cane Air. Tel (263) 31-2295, fax (263) 31-2562. Mutual House, Chiredzi.

Airport, Buffalo Range. Tel (263) 31-2819.

Air Zimbabwe, Buffalo Range. Tel (263) 31-2363.

Car Hire Try Lowveld Travel. Tel (263) 31-2295, Mutual House, Chiredzi, or Chiredzi Car Hire, tel (263) 31-2462/2693.

Chiredzi Pharmacy, 77 Knobthorn Road. Tel (263) 31-2471.

Hospital, Chiredzi. Tel (263) 31-2388.

Immigration Control Tel (263) 31-2683. P O Box 90, Chiredzi.

Medical Air Rescue Service (MARS) Tel (263) 4-791378 (within Zimbabwe ring 14-791378/792304), fax (263) 4-721233.

National Parks, Central Reservations. Tel (263) 4-706077, fax (263) 4-724914. P O Box CY826, Causeway, Harare.

National Parks, Chipinda Pools. Tel (263) 31-2980. Private Bag 7003, Chiredzi.

National Parks, Mabalauta. Tel (263) 31-2980.

Post Office Tel (263) 31-2361.

Railways Tel (263) 31-2277.

Wildlife Society (Head Office, Harare). Tel (263) 4-700451. P O Box HG996, Highlands, Harare.

EASTERN HIGHLANDS

Seen from Mozambique, the 300km-long (190 mile) barrier of mountains that delineates the high plateau of Zimbabwe seems like the distant Valhalla of the mountain king: huge, green valleys shadowed by passing clouds, and chunky peaks alternately covered in mist and sunlight. Rising to 1 800m (5 906ft) and sometimes another 700m (2 300ft) higher, these trout lake, fruit orchard, coffee plantation and pine tree uplands are the holiday hideaways of Zimbabweans and visitors alike. Mutare, with its central avenue of palms, is the capital of this area and is situated astride the rail route from Harare to the coast, but there are half a dozen other holiday villages: Nyanga, Troutbeck, Cashel, Chimanimani, Chipinge and Juliasdale are spread along the downs and the high valleys, nearly all graced by English village churches with heavenly mountain vistas.

The Eastern Highlands begin 100km (62 miles) north of Nyanga village and cover three areas: Nyanga National Park, the Bvumba promontory near Mutare and the rugged Chimanimani Mountains in the far south. Nyanga is the largest and best known of the holiday areas. Sited in the northernmost part of the Eastern Highlands, it is a region of forests, wild flowers, waterfalls, rivers, open moorlands and Inyangani, the country's highest mountain at 2 593m (8 508ft). It was once covered with woodlands and stone-terraced farmlands, testimony to the times 300 years ago when Iron Age agriculturalists worked these slopes. Ziwa Ruins and Museum and Nyahokwe Mountain are only two of dozens of superbly maintained stone-wall ruin sites in Nyanga.

Mount Inyangani, the Mutarazi Falls and the forested 10km (6 mile) Pungwe Gorge are highlights of the area, accessed by good gravel roads and affording splendid viewpoints, while around the Udu, Nyangwe (Mare) and Nyanga (Rhodes) dams in the Nyanga National Park, pony trails give visitors the chance to appreciate the beautiful scenery. Trout fishing in the lakes and rivers is a popular pastime, and although there are game animals (wildebeest, kudu, waterbuck, leopard and baboon), Nyanga, and in fact all of the Eastern Highlands, is more attuned to walking, climbing and birding. You will seldom see a snake but the gaboon viper has been seen in Pungwe Gorge forest and berg adders from time to time in the mountains, particularly Chimanimani. Bring along a celestial map for the clear night sky of the mountains is perfect for studying the stars.

The less energetic can explore the many cosy hotels to enjoy tea and scones in front of log fires. Hired cottages in many of the lovely valleys or on the wooded slopes are the best way to holiday in the mountains; there are also half a dozen golf course hotels, including the 18-hole championship course at Leopard Rock. The Highlands also offer white-water rafting on the Pungwe River and a choice of two casinos.

OPPOSITE: *Grace and filigree lace beauty at Bridal Veil Falls, Chimanimani.*

NYANGA

Nyanga North

Extraordinarily wild, beautiful and mountainous, Nyanga North is one of the least-known areas of Zimbabwe. It is best approached either via the Nyamapanda-Mozambique border road or via Murewa and Mutoko. Murewa is a country town with a good hotel near the turn-off and a busy bus market. A little north of Murewa, gravel roads (a four-wheel-drive vehicle is not necessary) cut through small villages, heading almost due east for the Nyanga mountains.

On this route you will pass the old Nyangombe refugee camp, now closed but for many years the home of tens of thousands of Mozambican refugees. Keep asking the way and soon the mountains come into view. The villages you pass are remote, colourful and friendly; signs welcome you proudly to the local school, and the village centre will only boast a maize mill, table football, butchery

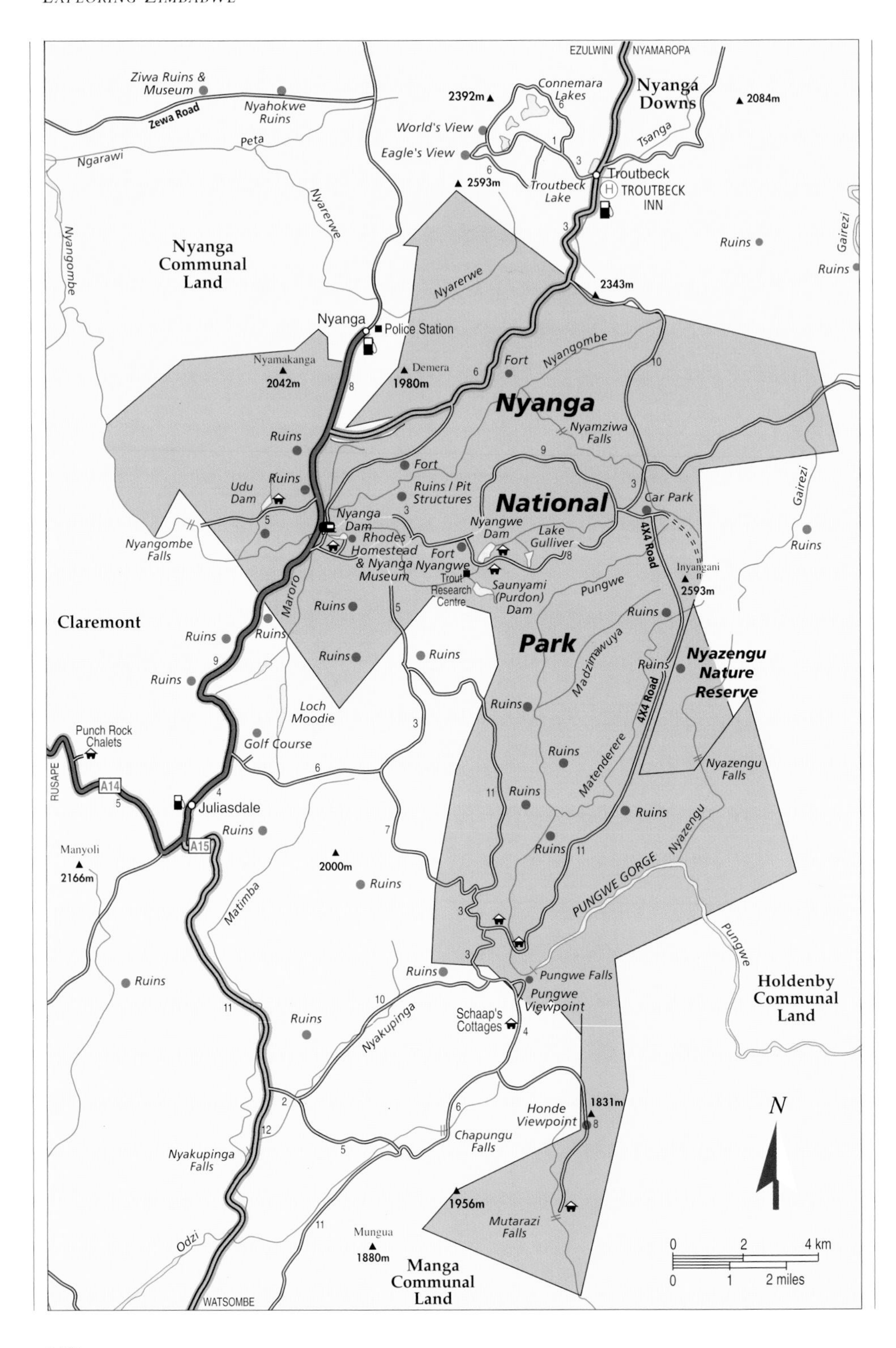
EZULWINI
NYAMAROPA
Ziwa Ruins & Museum
Zewa Road
Nyahokwe Ruins
Connemara Lakes
2392m
Nyanga Downs
2084m
World's View
Eagle's View
Tsanga
Troutbeck
TROUTBECK INN
Troutbeck Lake
2593m
Ngarawi
Peta
Nyarerwe
Nyangombe
Nyanga Communal Land
Gairezi
Ruins
Ruins
2343m
Nyanga
Police Station
Nyamakanga
2042m
Demera
1980m
Fort
Nyangombe
Nyanga
Nyamziwa Falls
Ruins
Fort
Ruins / Pit Structures
Udu Dam
Ruins
National
Car Park
Nyanga Dam
Rhodes Homestead & Nyanga Museum
Nyangwe Dam
Lake Gulliver
4X4 Road
Nyangombe Falls
Fort Nyangwe
Trout Research Centre
Saunyami (Purdon) Dam
Pungwe
Inyangani
2593m
Maroro
Ruins
Claremont
Ruins
Ruins
Park
Ruins
Ruins
Ruins
Nyazengu Nature Reserve
Ruins
Madzimawuya
Ruins
Loch Moodie
Punch Rock Chalets
Golf Course
Ruins
Matenderere
RUSAPE
A14
Nyazengu Falls
Juliasdale
Ruins
Ruins
Ruins
Manyoli
2166m
A15
2000m
Ruins
Ruins
Nyazengu
Matimba
PUNGWE GORGE
Pungwe
Ruins
Ruins
Pungwe Falls
Pungwe Viewpoint
Holdenby Communal Land
Ruins
Nyakupinga
Schaap's Cottages
Honde Viewpoint
1831m
N
Chapungu Falls
Nyakupinga Falls
1956m
Mutarazi Falls
Odzi
Mungua
1880m
Manga Communal Land
WATSOMBE
0
2
4 km
0
1
2 miles

and paraffin-lit store. You will be asked for lifts (and offered payment) and like most country folk, everyone is courteous.

Another route is to continue on the tar road until you get to Mutoko, 142km (88 miles) from Harare. Fuel up here. The Mutemwa Leprosy Village is here, made famous by Englishman, poet, musician, ex-Gurkha officer and mystic, John Bradburne, who stayed and cared for the patients during Zimbabwe's *chimurenga* (liberation war) and was eventually killed here. Beneath the 1 503m-high (4 931ft) Mutemwa Mountain (it means to be cut off), a group of husband and wife missionaries now look after Aids orphans, while round the other side of the mountain are some lovely old ruins, 6km (4 miles) on tar beyond Mutoko on the right, and a site museum. Also to be visited are rock art sites a little further on at Ruchera Cave.

Passing by the Luanze historic Portuguese ruins, drive onto Nyamapanda, the main entry point into Malawi and middle Mozambique, and a hive of action. Alternatively, take the All Souls Mission Road which runs uphill and down dale, passing through beautiful woodland country near the Mission. Its Italian-style church tower and frescoes is where Dr Luisa Guidotti worked during the Rhodesian war. Like her friend John Bradburne, she was also killed in a hail of bullets.

The road from here leads into Mudzi Communal Farming Area, dusty and poor, where young men play draughts with bottle tops. In the Chikwizo area, against a wooded hill, the road goes past the ruins of a small Gothic cathedral built long ago by Chikwizo's eccentric French parish priest, Peré Pichon, then begins to swing south to cross the long Ruenya River bridge. Nearby are 20-year-old signs warning of land mines – don't take any chances! You'll be able to buy basic foodstuffs anywhere along this route.

The area on the right, the woodlands of the 1 033m-high (3 389ft) Mount Chiwha quite near Avila Mission, is a wilderness area and plans are afoot to introduce trails here. The 40km-road (25 mile) to Elim and Ruangwe is flatter. Ruangwe, a district centre on a tar road with supermarket and petrol station, is in the lea of the hills and marks the northernmost part of the Nyanga range. A twisty, bumpy road leads through the northernmost mountain gap, past the Ruangwe police station and crosses a dozen small rivers that all flow into Ruenya River.

TOP: *Nyanga's magnificent mountains.*
ABOVE: *Rural life in Nyanga.*

This pass, with its rugged range of red striated mountains is particularly picturesque and announces the start of Nyanga proper. The gravel road from the pass to Nyanga village passes through the crowded Nyanga lowland communal lands, a highlight being the turn off to Ziwa Ruins (*see* p 121) and

TOP: *Cumberland Valley near Nyanga.*
ABOVE: *Early morning horse trail, Troutbeck.*

Museum, and Nyahokwe Mountain. The more comfortable route is the fully tarred road on the other side at Ruangwe. It is 60km (37.5 miles) back along this eastern side of the Nyanga range, flanking the Gairezi River and the Mozambique border, with a scenic detour that actually traces the border for part of the way. Initially you pass rocky, barefaced hills, then brooding, open valleys leading up to cloud-covered mountains. The vegetation is lush and tropical with thick stands of bananas, pawpaws and ilala palms, and along the river, liana-covered trees.

The area is decorated with huts and at Nyamaropa Irrigation Scheme near Regina Coeli (Queen of Heaven) Mission, cotton fields. Road signs are largely signs to schools. Soon you begin climbing, leaving the 20m-wide (65ft) border river and the Mozambique mountains behind, up the steep escarpment to the Nyanga Downs and Troutbeck.

Troutbeck

Troutbeck sits atop a great shoulder of mountain above Nyanga village. It is a tiny settlement with a bakery, craft shop, petrol station and the luxurious lakeside Troutbeck Inn. A good metal road winds up the mountain, past dwarf acacia trees huddled like witches in the wind and trailing lichen-grey old man's beard from their claw branches. Troutbeck Inn is a long, narrow hotel with a permanent log fire, a black tin roof, manicured lawns, trout-fishing lake, golf course and forested slopes.

Behind it, further up the mountain past streams and waterfalls, are the Connemara Lakes, a series of dams at 2 300m (7 546ft) surrounded by pine forests and holiday homes. A circular drive leads to the second of Zimbabwe's World's Views, a picnic site (with ablution facilities) run by the privately run National Trust. For the adventurous, a path twists upwards to a ruins complex. Everywhere the views are precipitous, falling 1 000m (3 281ft) sheer to the patchwork of smallholdings in the valley below.

Troutbeck has possibly the most attractive of Nyanga's English country-style churches, St Catherine's in the Downs, not far from the tumbling falls of the Tsanga River which rises on the World's View massif. The gravel road past the church twists down to a sawmill, then, with the Nyanga range on your right, reaches the pretty Gairezi River with its 10m-deep (33ft) boulder-hugging pools and wild strelitzias clinging to the cliffs. In early September watch out for the osprey raptor, one of the few birds that inhabits all the world's continents. This road, once across the river, will eventually take you round to the foot of Inyangani and the Aberfoyle tea estates.

Ezulwini

'Ezulwini' means heaven. And it is truly a haven and heaven of clouds, wild flowers, lakes, bracken slopes, waterfalls, daffodils and mountain ridges stretching 50km (30 miles) towards Mozambique. Sited 11km (7 miles) east of Troutbeck Village on the edge of the Nyanga massif, it provides an open vista of

TOP: *World's View near Troutbeck offers grand views of the Connemara Lakes.*
ABOVE: *A cabbage tree at Nyangombe Falls.*

rolling grass and mountain ranges floating in valleys of mist and blue haze to the Indian Ocean. Here at an average altitude of 2 000m (6 562ft) and as high as 2 400m (8 000ft), the gentle sighing of the wind is constant, broken only by the hum of bees and the chorus of nectar-sipping sunbirds.

Fig trees and tree ferns grow beside the Nyanhambe stream as it trickles through hidden loops over waterfalls until deep in the valley below, it becomes the Gairezi River. No matter what the season, there are always tiny flowers at your feet as you walk, 'lonely as a cloud', in these brisk uplands. Ezulwini's fruit farm produces apples and blueberries and at nearby Nyamoro farm, buy home-made butter, watch the cows being milked and treat yourself to a delicious cream tea in the garden while looking over fields of golden daffodils.

NYANGA NATIONAL PARK

Mount Inyangani

Climbing this mountain is a must. In fact, it isn't really a climb at all but a stiff hour's walk up a path from the car park at the foot of the mountain, then a 45-minute level walk to the peak. The local mountain club has marked out the trail with yellow signs because if the mist comes down (in which case sit tight and wait it out), it can be difficult to see the path past the lichen-covered rocks and marshy sedge.

The mountain is Zimbabwe's highest at 2 593,1m (8 508ft) but the plateau from which you start the ascent is about 2 000m (6 562ft). On your way up near the mountain stream is a misty dell of proteas and wild flowers. The views from the top down to the steep Honde Valley and across to Gorongosa mountain are spectacular. Behind you, on the western flank, is the Pungwe River valley.

On the eastern slopes of Mount Inyangani, along the deeper stream banks and on fire-proof rocky outcrops, you will find beautiful mlanje cedar (*Widdringtonia whytei*) trees, together with waxberry, yellowwood, Cape chestnut, forest fever tree, wild holly and many orchids growing on trees.

If you go down towards the Gairezi River in the east with its sequence of waterfalls descending through fold after fold of hills, you will need a compass and some knowledge of the mountains. Interesting ruin sites occur in the Inyangani area and the mountain is the birthplace of a dozen rivers, the largest of which is the Pungwe.

It is about a 20 minute drive from the main road to get to Inyangani car park, usually via Nyangwe Dam, longer from Pungwe Drift or Troutbeck. Visible from every direction, Inyangani can be seen 100km (62 miles) away at Eagle's Nest, Headlands, from everywhere in the Honde Valley and from Mutoko on the northern approach route.

Nyazengu Nature Reserve

Nestled into the lea of Mount Inyangani and surrounded by the Nyanga National Park, the privately owned Nyazengu reserve (1 250ha; 3 089 acres) offers walkers and bird-watchers a day's delightfully remote excursion. Hidden 5km (3 miles) from the Inyangani car park down a gravel road that reads 'No Entry' (the road is fine for reasonable clearance cars as far as Stonechat Cottage, which can be hired, and the trout pool where the trails begin), the reserve offers six trails, the longest being 12km (7.5 miles).

Tiny wild flowers thrive below the mist-roiled cliffs above you as the trail weaves in and out of montane forest, past Pig's Patch's green forested gloom, down to the Nyazengu River and the 90m (300ft) sheer waterfall into the Pungwe Gorge, then through golden grasslands, past ancient iron workings to the final steep descent alongside cascades, pools, tree ferns and rain forest. With a little luck you may spot Livingstone's louries in flight above the Nyazengu Falls. It is a stiff uphill

Honde Valley view: lonely hills and far horizons.

ABOVE: *A fruit and sculpture stall near the Claremont orchards, Nyanga.*
RIGHT: *The lovely Pungwe Falls.*

walk from the river to the four-wheel-drive road that links Pungwe Drift and Inyangani car park. Alternate trails include the Matendere Cascades, the Nyazengu rock pool falls and for an interesting diversion, the trip up Inyangani via Tucker's Gap, halfway along the open shoulder where the walks begin.

A small pride of lion roams the Nyanga National Park. They have even been seen by hikers on the gravel road that leads from Troutbeck to Mount Inyangani. The recently re-introduced wildebeest are aware of these predators but the only official mention of them is in the local trout fishing book and the Nyazengu trail leaflet. The latter advises: 'do not run, do not turn your back, face the animal, stay together and walk slowly backwards until you have moved out of the threat circle of the animal'. An encounter, hopefully, reserved for the few.

The Pungwe and a pride of waterfalls

The Pungwe is the largest of the 17 rivers flowing off the Inyangani massif. It rises on the western slope of Inyangani as the first tiny stream that you cross heading towards Nyazengu Nature Reserve. It is joined by the Madzimawuya, Matenderere and Tamburatedza rivers before leaping off the escarpment.

Many of these and other rivers have their own waterfalls and deep, cold pools which are reasonably difficult to access and are usually totally deserted. The Tamburatedza Falls flows into the deep, clear Pungwe pools, with more pools and falls further down towards the National Parks chalets at Pungwe Drift, a low-level bridge over which the water streams as you drive across.

This is not far from where the Pungwe races off the escarpment in a series of zig-zag falls down into the 10km-long (6 mile) forested ravine of the Pungwe Gorge that links it to the Honde Valley. The pools just before the lip are favourites with visitors, while the view site on the road above offers a stunning panorama of Inyangani, river, waterfalls, Pungwe Gorge and Honde Valley. The Pungwe Gorge is a delight for tree-lovers, and is home to the gorgeously patterned yellow, brown, purple and cream gaboon viper from whose deadly bite few recover.

The Nyanga Mountains are rich in waterfalls. The Nyangombe below Udu Camp and the Nyamziwa, also in Nyanga National Park, are well-known. Less visited are those further up the Nyamziwa towards Inyangani and in the western river valley below Claremont orchards. In fact, there are waterfalls and pools on nearly all of Nyanga's rivers. However, right of way hiking trails may not yet have been formalized on some private estates, so first contact a local farmer, plantation manager or the Nyanga Tourist Association before proceeding.

HONDE VALLEY

The Honde Valley was the hottest spot in the liberation war in what was then Rhodesia. The remains of the old earthenwork 'keep' can still be seen at Ruda growth point (a government-developed town) near the airstrip. The Honde is a wide, 40km-long (25 mile) and intensively cultivated valley separating the Nyanga massif and the range of Mozambique hills into which both the Honde and the Pungwe rivers disappear on their 300km-journey (190 miles) to Beira.

GONE FISHING – NYANGA TROUT

Nyanga is trout-fishing country with plenty of scenic and well-stocked rivers and lakes. The Gairezi River (four-wheel-drive country), reached via the northern shoulder of Inyangani, are the best 'reaches', but there is also good fishing in the Inyangombe, Madzimawuya (Pungwe tributary), Maroro, Matenderere, Tamburatedza, Pungwe, Mare and Nyamziwa rivers.

Nyanga has several hatcheries and a variety of dams stocked with trout: Nyangwe (formerly Mare), Udu, Purdon, Nyanga (formerly Rhodes) and the 'quality' Gulliver where, like Purdon, no boats are allowed. All the waters fall under National Parks and there are size, number and time restrictions.

Usually no fishing is allowed in Purdon and Gulliver dams during August and September and none allowed in rivers from June to September. Only artificial flies may be used and licences must be obtained on arrival at Nyanga National Park.

Trout were first introduced into Zimbabwe in 1905 in the Mare River. Rainbow trout are the norm, less common are brown trout. The record rainbow caught in 1956 in the Odzi River weighed 3.827kg (8lb 7oz). Rainbow can be as large as 4.5kg (10 pounds), usually taken on wet flies such as Walker's Killer, Kemp's Favourite, Connemara Black and Pheasant.

Trout are usually caught on fly rods – made of split cane in the old days and today of glass or carbon fibre of about 2.6m (9ft) in length – line and fly. In Nyanga, a no. 7 double paper floating line is recommended by the experts. A 9cm (3.5in) diameter reel will suffice and most will learn how to cast if they are shown. Come with your own equipment as there is none for hire in the National Parks. Flies can usually be purchased at Kashmir Trading in Nyanga village. The best book to read is *The Flycatcher's Nyanga* by Peter StJ, Turnbull-Kemp published by the National Trout Anglers' Society. P O Box UA 204, Union Avenue, Harare.

Solitude, silence and beautiful mountains are for many the lures of Nyanga's trout fishing rivers.

The valley, with its visitor-friendly tea estates hidden away in the north up against the eastern buttress of Mount Inyangani, can be approached on a tarred road off the main Juliasdale to Mutare highway. It winds rapidly down the escarpment past a huge granite cliff almost the height of the mountain wall. The road zigzags torturously down through cultivated lands; the drop is steep, 1 500m (4 921ft) in 20km (12.5 miles), affording views of the valley with its schools, buildings and banana-lush homesteads. In the distance, huge granite needles rise from the surrounding hills like volcanic plugs. There are vistas of mangoes, sugar cane, pawpaws and bananas and two lovely river crossings: the Pungwe with its montane forest valley leading up to the escarpment, and the rapids near the Eastern Highlands Tea Estate (where pepper is for sale) over the Nyamingura River.

The view past the rippling waters and lush riverine vegetation looks straight up to Inyangani's sun-dappled mistlands, nearly 2 000m (6 562ft) above. The road climbs into the emerald green of the tea-growing estates and coils around the steeply sloping hills and the darker taller coffee bushes, interspersed with gum and flamboyant trees. Pickers with their large wicker back-baskets harvest the tea bushes. This is a high rainfall area and clouds continually drift past the massif.

Mutarazi Falls

The approach to Mutarazi Falls lies just off the Pungwe scenic road past a lovely thatched cottage with spectacular views of Inyangani and the Far and Wide Adventure Camp. Mutarazi was once a separate park but is now incorporated into the Nyanga National Park. The 7km (4.5 miles) road winds through a heavily wooded escarpment.

From the camp site, with its montane trees and deceptively gentle river pools, a track lined with bracken and wild flowers leads innocently to a tree and promontory view site of the Falls, where you clutch onto rock and tree for dear life above the huge, beautiful abyss which seems to be suspended over the whole Honde Valley.

The Nyanga region is a paradise for hikers.

The slender spume of the Mutarazi Falls (the second highest in Africa) lies to your right as it gently floats off the escarpment and mists its way down 762m (2 500ft) to the rain forest below, lush and dark green against the wet, black precipice. The Falls can clearly be seen from the Honde Valley below, as are the nearby Mutarira Falls. Both flow into the Honde Valley. The best view of the valley, if you have a head for heights, is the nearby Honde View. Follow the road signs on the Mutarazi scenic road to a cleared area which leads to several boulders literally perched on the cliff edge 1 500m (4 921ft) above the valley. Basic camping and picnic facilities are available at Mutarazi.

Nyafaru and Aberfoyle

Until recently there was only a rough track to Aberfoyle but now a good, twisty gravel road, 22km (14 miles) from Troutbeck, leads off the Nyanga Downs for a further 65km (40 miles) of sheer, remote mountain pleasure to Nyafaru and Aberfoyle. Allow two hours' driving time; the only traffic you are likely to see is the daily bus, the occasional mountain pack donkey and small boys clearing cattle from the road. You will pass patches of fleshy-leaved *mzanje* trees (the tiny orange fruit is sweet and a rural market staple) and many cabbage trees. Centres of population are usually near schools. Nyafaru, perched on its mountain eyrie, is a primary school and agricultural co-operative with a non-operative windmill generator.

Aberfoyle Club (honey and carved wooden toilet seats for sale) welcomes visitors to its golf course, tennis courts, swimming pool and chalet accommodation. The impressive Chipote Falls are within walking distance and pink tipachina flowers grow in profusion. The Inyangani backs onto Aberfoyle, facing the estates, while as you drive north, the Mozambique mountains soar 1 888m (6 194ft) upwards.

In this ideal walking country, occasional long-drop loos have been discreetly placed at hill crests along the road. If you run out of water don't hesitate to ask at a hut; the people are generous and usually speak English. The plastic sacks you see villagers carrying on their heads are filled with locally milled maize meal. There are dozens of stone-walled ruin sites and many a hillside where, if you know how to look at the grassed-over slopes, the terracing of ancient farmers can be seen. Forty-three kilometres (27 miles) from the metal road turn off is a wide 'Lorna Doone' valley between imposing hills. There is an unnamed bridge here, while beyond the V-gap in the hills – climb the ridge 50m (165ft) to the right – is a lovely waterfall and deep, delightful pools. This twisty mountain road offers 360° views of mountains and valleys, precariously perched huts, pineapple gardens, waterfalls and dark green gorges.

Nyanga's ancient stone ruins

Chipped stone tools of the early Stone Age in Nyanga testify to the fact that man was living here 50 000, possibly even 350 000 years ago. Although there are few rock paintings done by these hunter-gatherers, the ones at Diana's Vow on the road between Rusape and Juliasdale are possibly the finest of their kind of the 30 000 throughout Zimbabwe. At Harleigh Farm nearby, visit the handsome stone wall ruins of the late 17th-century *zimbabwe* type. Farming and herding communities moved into Nyanga at the beginning of the third century AD, built permanent village complexes and established skilled pottery.

TOP: *The Honde Valley is a fertile valley rich in tropical fruit and emerald-green tea plantations (bottom).*
CENTRE: *Workers with wicker back-baskets harvest the abundant tea bushes.*

A later influx of Iron Age communities erected sunken stone-lined pit structures in which they kept livestock, and as the population increased and the need arose to clear more land for agricultural purposes, terraced farming slopes were extended over an increasingly wide area. Stone-wall terracing created suitable level space for cultivation and was a way to dump unwanted stones. Positioned along the contours of slopes and valleys, they stabilized the difficult terrain and prevented soil erosion.

On the perimeter platform raised around the sunken stone pit were sited huts and granaries. Entrance into the pit was through a tunnel and every pit in this high rainfall area had a drain hole. These homesteads were separated from each other by agricultural fields. A good deal of energy was needed for this type of cultivation and for the construction of the stone *mushas* (kraals) and stock pens. Livestock farming was an important aspect of the economy in the 16th and 17th centuries. Sorghum and millet were the staple crops while imported glass beads found in archeological excavations at Ziwa testify to trading contacts with the Swahili and Portuguese of the East African coast.

Treasure Trove

In the Nyanga uplands, the stone-lined pit structures built 400 years ago by Sena-speaking Tonga people, migrants from the Zambezi Valley, can be seen at many sites, one just past the Warden's office at Nyanga (Rhodes) Dam. Even more dramatic are the lichen-grey circular 'forts' dotted on top of *koppies* near Nyangwe (Mare) Dam and Chawomera off the Troutbeck road. With their grand vistas, they make lovely picnic spots.

West of Nyanga village is a treasure-trove of dry-walled stone circles and enclosures, while up Nyhakowe Mountain is a boma almost of Great Zimbabwean proportions, guarded by a member of the National Museums and Monuments. The guide will lead you through the ancient stone mountainside village, its ore smelting 'factory', furnace and 'dare' convention centre looking up to a

Impressive ruins at Nyahokwe mountain.

grand panorama of mountains. Nyahokwe was probably the home of a substantial ruling group or chief. Lovely ruins near the great pyramid of Ziwa mountain, which stands boldly 400m (1 312ft) above the plain 11km (7 miles) west of Nyahokwe, can also be visited. The Ruins, roundel after roundel of drystone walls and enclosures, is a major part of the Nyanga ruins, a proliferation spread over 8 000km^2 (3 089 miles^2) of mountains, lowlands and even Mozambique.

Nyanga's high rainfall was adequate to support the crops of the Sena community resident in the mountains. They were hemmed in on all sides by rival and more powerful political groups, such as the Barwe and the Manyika. Thus, with little room for expansion, they were forced to maximize the natural resources by intensive terrace farming.

The small site museum at Ziwa has picnic sites shaded by thatched umbrellas. You will often see 'Van Niekerk Ruins' on maps. These and the Ziwa Ruins are one and the same. Major P.H. Van Niekerk was one of several Boer families Cecil Rhodes encouraged to settle in Nyanga at the beginning of this century. Van Niekerk helped the archaeologist Dr Randall MacIver to study the Ruins in 1905.

Nyanga's many ruins can often be spotted by the tell-tale presence of brightly coloured aloes and clumps of trees. Many of these are fruit trees (wild fig, marula, mzanje, huhash and num-num among some 30 others) and testify to the ancients' fondness for a taste of honey in an otherwise tough life.

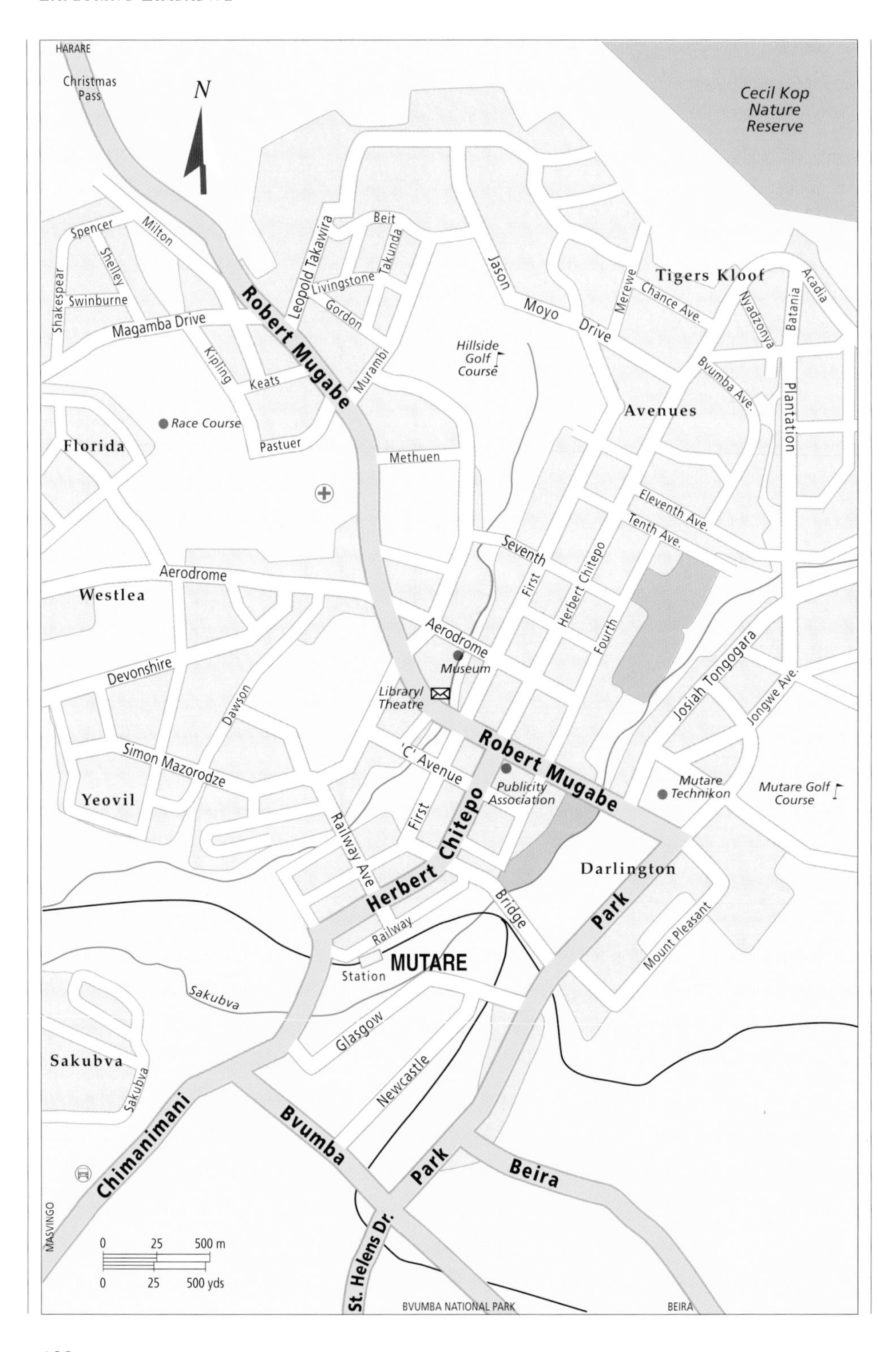
HARARE
Christmas Pass
N
Cecil Kop Nature Reserve
Spencer
Milton
Shelley
Shakespear
Swinburne
Magamba Drive
Kipling
Keats
Leopold Takawira
Beit
Takunda
Livingstone
Gordon
Murambi
Robert Mugabe
Jason
Moyo
Drive
Merewe
Tigers Kloof
Chance Ave.
Nyadzonya
Batania
Acadia
Hillside Golf Course
Bvumba Ave.
Plantation
Avenues
Race Course
Florida
Pastuer
Methuen
Eleventh Ave.
Tenth Ave.
Seventh
First
Herbert Chitepo
Fourth
Aerodrome
Westlea
Aerodrome
Museum
Devonshire
Library/ Theatre
Dawson
Josiah Tongogara
Jongwe Ave.
Simon Mazorodze
Robert Mugabe
'C' Avenue
Publicity Association
Mutare Technikon
Mutare Golf Course
Yeovil
Railway Ave
First
Herbert Chitepo
Darlington
Bridge
Park
Railway
Mount Pleasant
MUTARE
Station
Sakubva
Glasgow
Sakubva
Sakubva
Newcastle
Chimanimani
Bvumba
Park
Beira
St. Helens Dr.
MASVINGO
0 25 500 m
0 25 500 yds
BVUMBA NATIONAL PARK
BEIRA

Mutare, gateway to the Eastern Highlands, is set in splendid surroundings.

BVUMBA

MUTARE

The sunsets atop Mutare Heights overlooking mountains, valleys and red-streaked skies are pyrotechnic. A torturous road leads to the top and as evening falls, the lights of the town in the valley below sparkle as cars wind their way off the Zimbabwe plateau road from Harare down Christmas Pass.

Tall palms grace Herbert Chitepo Street, Mutare's main thoroughfare. Zimbabwe's fifth largest town with a population estimated at 200 000, Mutare is surrounded by mountains, fruit farms and some of the most sought-after scenery in Zimbabwe. It retains an unhurried, one-street-town atmosphere even though it is the main rail and road link to Beira and the Mozambique coast.

The name Mutare means a piece of metal, after the gold discovered 100 years ago in nearby Penhalonga through which the Mutare River flows. This historic mining town, 17km (10.5 miles) distant on the least used road to Nyanga, has a lovely garden at its southern exit, where the Pioneer Sisters Memorial commemorates three stalwart English nursing sisters who, 100 years ago, walked 241km (150 miles) from Beira to nurse the prospectors. A church built entirely of corrugated iron still stands in Penhalonga.

Motor assembly plants, petroleum refining, timber processing and food canning are four of Mutare's industries. At Sakubva market you can buy crafts and *ishwa* (grilled flying ants) in season. Also worth a visit is the chunky Catholic cathedral, down the road from the Information Bureau and market.

Murahwa's hill has Iron Age ruins while only 3.5km (2 miles) from the city centre, Cecil Kop Nature Reserve, the 1 500ha (3 705 acre) poachers' haunt that became a wildlife sanctuary, sits on the hills overlooking both town and Mozambique. Run by the Wildlife Society, it has bush trails, water holes, view platforms and game that includes giraffe, elephant, sable, crocodiles and white rhino. Around 200 butterfly species are found in the park, as are silvery-cheeked hornbills.

The exhibits at Mutare's museum are particularly well laid out while 1897 Utopia House Museum, former home of Victorian poet and philanthropists Kingsley and Rosalie Fairbridge, is an antiquarian's bonus. Jenny's Cottage, the *koppies* and the trails on Mapor Estates along the Odzi River are also worth a visit. La Rochelle in the Imbeza Valley, the Norman towered home of the Courtauld family, features flower and orchid gardens and a braille wilderness trail, one of only two in southern Africa, the other being at Kirstenbosch National Botanical Gardens in Cape Town. There is also a private game park and winery at Odzi, ancient Fort Gomo Kadzamu 16.5km (10 miles) beyond Penhalonga, Odzani Falls, the huge new Osborne Dam and the Methodist Africa University.

Often treated as a convenient entry to the surrounding mountains, Mutare's attractions are varied enough to warrant a longer visit.

BVUMBA BOTANICAL GARDENS

About 500 species of butterfly occur in Zimbabwe and ten times that number of moths, and many of these are found in the Eastern Highlands, especially the Bvumba. The turn-off to the Bvumba lies 1.6km (1 mile) south of Mutare on the Chipinge road. It is a 30km (18.6 mile) promontory of mountains, mist, forest, proteas and coffee farms high over

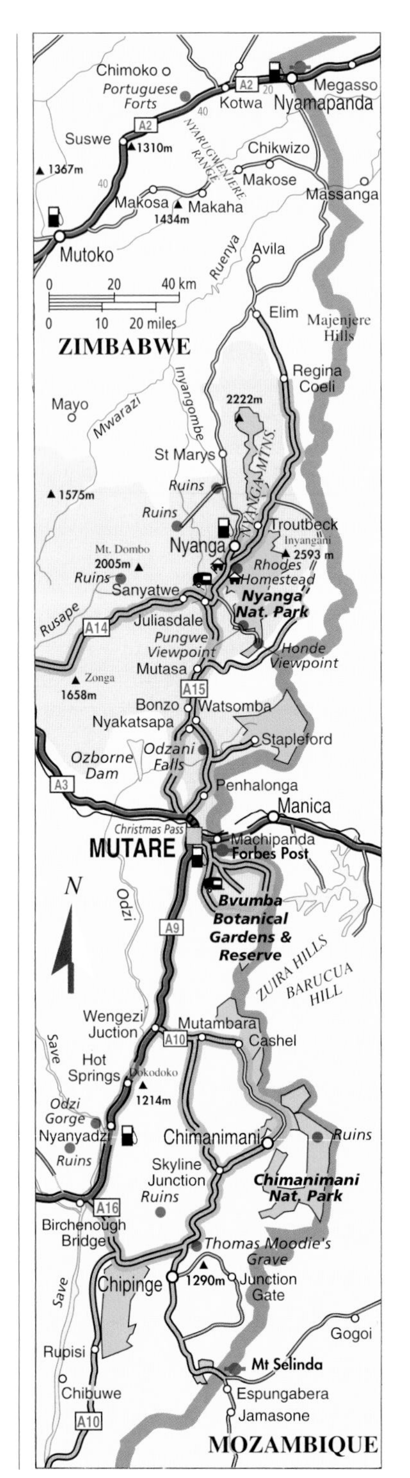

Chimoko
Portuguese Forts
Kotwa
Nyamapanda
Megasso
Suswe
1310m
1367m
Nyarugwenjere Range
Chikwizo
Makose
Makosa
Makaha
1434m
Massanga
Mutoko
Ruenya
Avila
0 20 40 km
0 10 20 miles
Elim
Majenjere Hills
ZIMBABWE
Regina Coeli
Mayo
Mwarazi
Inyangombe
2222m
St Marys
Nyanga Mtns.
Ruins
1575m
Ruins
Troutbeck
Inyangani
2593 m
Mt. Dombo
2005m
Nyanga
Ruins
Rhodes Homestead
Sanyatwe
Nyanga Nat. Park
Rusape
A14
Juliasdale
Pungwe Viewpoint
Honde Viewpoint
Mutasa
Zonga
1658m
A15
Bonzo
Watsomba
Nyakatsapa
Stapleford
Ozborne Dam
Odzani Falls
A3
Penhalonga
Manica
Christmas Pass
MUTARE
Machipanda
Forbes Post
N
Odzi
Bvumba Botanical Gardens & Reserve
A9
Zuira Hills
Barucua Hill
Wengezi Juction
Mutambara
A10
Cashel
Save
Hot Springs
Dokodoko
1214m
Odzi Gorge
Nyanyadzi
Ruins
Chimanimani
Ruins
Skyline Junction
Ruins
Chimanimani Nat. Park
A16
Birchenough Bridge
Thomas Moodie's Grave
Chipinge
1290m
Junction Gate
Save
Gogoi
Rupisi
Mt Selinda
Chibuwe
Espungabera
Jamasone
A10
MOZAMBIQUE

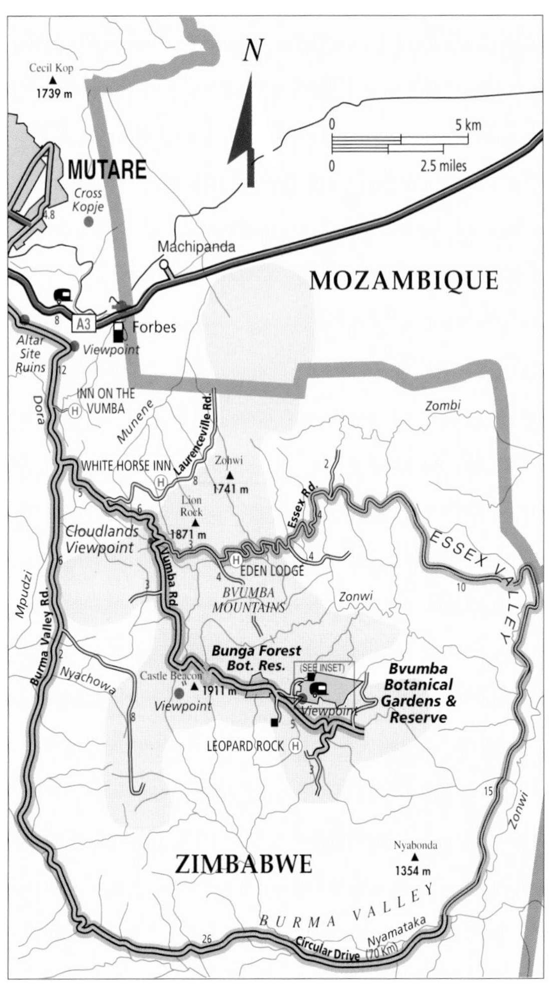

N
Cecil Kop
1739 m
0 5 km
0 2.5 miles
MUTARE
Cross Kopje
Machipanda
MOZAMBIQUE
A3
Forbes
Altar Site Ruins
Viewpoint
Inn on the Vumba
Dora
Munene
Laurenceville Rd.
Zombi
White Horse Inn
Zohwi
1741 m
Lion Rock
1871 m
Essex Rd.
Cloudlands Viewpoint
Vumba Rd
Eden Lodge
Essex Valley
Mpudzi
Burma Valley Rd.
Bvumba Mountains
Zonwi
Bunga Forest Bot. Res.
(See inset)
Bvumba Botanical Gardens & Reserve
Nyachowa
Castle Beacon
1911 m
Viewpoint
Viewpoint
Leopard Rock
Zonwi
Nyabonda
1354 m
ZIMBABWE
Burma Valley
Circular Drive (70 Km)
Nyamataka

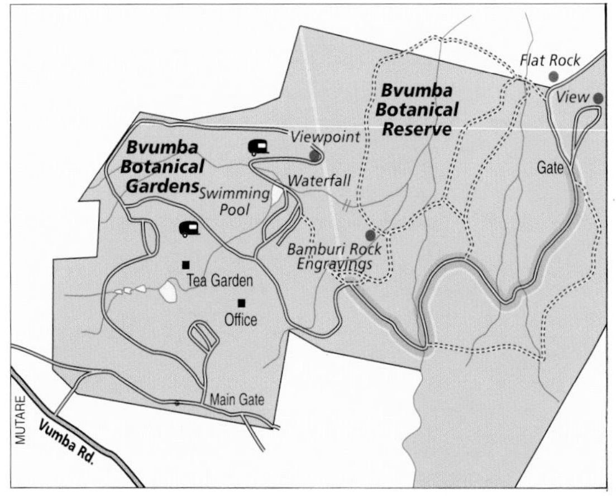

Flat Rock
Bvumba Botanical Reserve
View
Viewpoint
Bvumba Botanical Gardens
Gate
Waterfall
Swimming Pool
Bamburi Rock Engravings
Tea Garden
Office
Main Gate
Mutare
Vumba Rd.

Mozambique, with a 70km (43 mile) circular drive around its Burma Valley base. The Bvumba has breathtaking views, particularly across to what is known as the Himalaya Mountains as seen from Mavusa coffee farm below the golf course at Leopard Rock Hotel.

The Bvumba Botanical Gardens is a visual feast: banks of azaleas, tree ferns, orchids, aloes, fuchsias, hydrangeas, annuals and lily ponds set amidst 30ha (74 acres) of montane forest groves, pathways, streams, wooden bridges and lakes. A bird-watcher's paradise of outstanding variety, species found here include the wood owl, bronze sunbird and augur buzzard. Both camp site and tea garden fully exploit the magnificent views which stretch across the mountains to Mozambique 1 000m (3 281ft) below.

Bunga Forest straddles the main road just before the Gardens. Paths lead through the moss-tangled lianas, ferns and fairytale forest to the escarpment edge. It was given to the nation by Sir Lionel Cripps and forms a canopy over the main Bvumba road near a shaded picnic bower and historical plaques. At the foot of the path that leads up to the crest of Leopard Rock, or more correctly Chinyakwaremba, local folk sell delightful hand-sewn tray cloths decorated with colourful village motifs. Atop this 'hill of tired legs' the view is panoramic.

There are many lovely walks in the Bvumba with its gentle climate, down Cascades Road into Essex Valley, at Seldomseen Ornithological Centre, near 1 911m (6 270ft) Castle beacon, along White Horse Inn Road, around the National Parks Bvumba Gardens and down to Hivu Nursery on the main road where at journey's end, there are passion fruit drinks, good coffee, and baskets woven from local forest vines.

The Burma Valley drive is lovely. Most of it is on tar past long plantations of bananas, then mangoes, macadamia nuts, burley tobacco and coffee. Fifty percent of Zimbabwe's bananas are produced here, as well as the best cheese in the country, 'Vumba', at Crake Valley Farm.

BELOW: *La Rochelle near Mutare and the Bvumba Botanical Gardens (top right), famed for their orchids (bottom right) and other flowers.*

Golfers enjoy the course at the luxurious Leopard Rock Hotel (top); gum trees (above) and reed frogs (left) flourish in the mist and champagne air of the Bvumba mountains.

EN ROUTE TO CHIMANIMANI

Hot springs and mountain roads

The Odzi River rises north of Mutare while the Save begins near Marondera. The two flow the length of the mountains south of the Bvumba, then merge and flank the Chimanimani lowlands where the honey is sweet and the baobabs huge. The journey from Mutare to the mountains leads to Wengezi Junction. Here the scenic road runs via Cashel to Chimanimani village. A more direct route passes tomato farming villages and gum tree plantations to Skyline Junction where a spring flows out of the mountain.

Perhaps the most interesting route, if not as spectacular, is the main Lowveld river road to Hot Springs. This resort near Nyanyadzi overlooks the Maranke hills between the Odzi and Save rivers. It is a refreshing oasis of pools, ilala palms, bougainvillaea and hundreds of birds. The road then runs past baobab-fringed foothills to Birchenough Bridge, a 60-year-old 330m-wide (1 083ft) steel arch bridge over the wide Save where cattle drink in the pools and village women do their washing. On the eastern bank is a long line of 'tuckshop' stores selling baobab fibre carpets, drums and baskets.

The road divides three ways here: one crosses the bridge to Masvingo, one heads south to Gonarezhou and the Lowveld, while the other leads past an army camp to wind upwards through deeply wooded mountains, once rich in buffalo, to the rolling saddles of coffee downs outside Chipinge village. The local club is the social centre of this one-street town with its mists, dripping bamboos and flamboyant trees. Thomas Moodie, a Scots Afrikaner from the Free State, trekked here in 1893 as part of CJ Rhodes' effort to forestall any Portuguese territorial ambitions. Moodie is buried in a stone oxen and wagon square beneath acacia and jacarandas at the start of the Skyline Junction road. Chipinge is home to Zimbabwe's best known tea, Tanganda, after a river of the same name.

Beyond Chipinge is Chirinda Forest, a botanical reserve of huge hardwoods including the possibly dying 1 000-year-old red mahogany, 66m (210ft) high and 16m (52ft) round in the Valley of the Giants. A boma of mango trees acts as a buffer zone around the forest and an Interpretive Centre has been built to preserve the area's unique ecology, butterflies and insect life. A rare blue ground orchid (*Callianthus natalensis*) can be found along the mountainous trails in the forest.

Six kilometres (3.7 miles) up the Skyline route from Chipinge Junction to Chimanimani is the little known Ponte Italia bridge. A twist of the road, hidden by tall grass, marks the spot. A plaque commemorates where, in September 1944, Italian POW'S constructed a culvert over a tributary of the Rusitu River.

The road now winds past huge mountain-gripping stands of pine, wattle and blue gums, then down past the sawmill's sawdust furnace glowing through the night to Chimanimani village. There is a picturesque if somewhat steep side trip off the Skyline Road down into the Nyahode Valley and up again halfway along the Chimanimani road.

CHIMANIMANI

The Chimanimani area encompasses a village and a mountainous National Park. The village consists of an old-fashioned Raj-like hotel, tiny church, petrol station, a few stores and a tennis club. Near the hotel is a well-tended arboretum, information bureau that

INTERESTING PLACES EN ROUTE

- The usual Harare to Mutare route goes via the wine-producing town of Marondera (74km; 45 miles), with Imire Private Game Park and Sable Safari Lodge. Turn south 68km (42 miles) from Harare and 3km (2 miles) before Marondera, and follow the signs for 38km. Tel (263) 4-731856, fax (263) 122-354. Private Bag 3750, Marondera.
- Malwatte Farmhouse Restaurant and Craft Gallery at the 82km-peg (51 miles) on the Harare-to Mutare Road. Tel (263) 79-3239. Open 365 days, 08h00-17h00. Pony trekking, crafts and accommodation are available.
- Pink Elephant's rock paintings is just beyond Headlands. Look out for the cattle auction yards and hotel sign to your right, 130km (80 miles) from Harare. Turn left onto Baddeley, a mainly gravel road for about 15km (9.5 miles). The famous Diana's Vow Painting lies 5km (3 miles) south. The Pink Elephant's road, reasonably maintained and scenically splendid, flanks the western shoulder of the Nyanga mountains. It passes through pretty wooded hills, especially in the Mt Dombo area. It comes out onto the tar road halfway between Rusape and Juliasdale, then again at Cumberland Valley Road and Nyanga village. It is only intermittently signposted. Keep heading north, and east if you want to reach the tar road. An army training ground and firing range is in the vicinity.
- Juliasdale has petrol, hotels (Pine Tree Inn recommended), stores, a pretty church (Good Samaritan) and Visitor Information Centre.
- If you are travelling from Beira, stop at Chicamba Real Dam, 45km (28 miles) from the Zimbabwe border where there is good bass and bream fishing. Gorongosa National Park further east needs to be restocked with game; Gorongosa mountain lies outside the park.

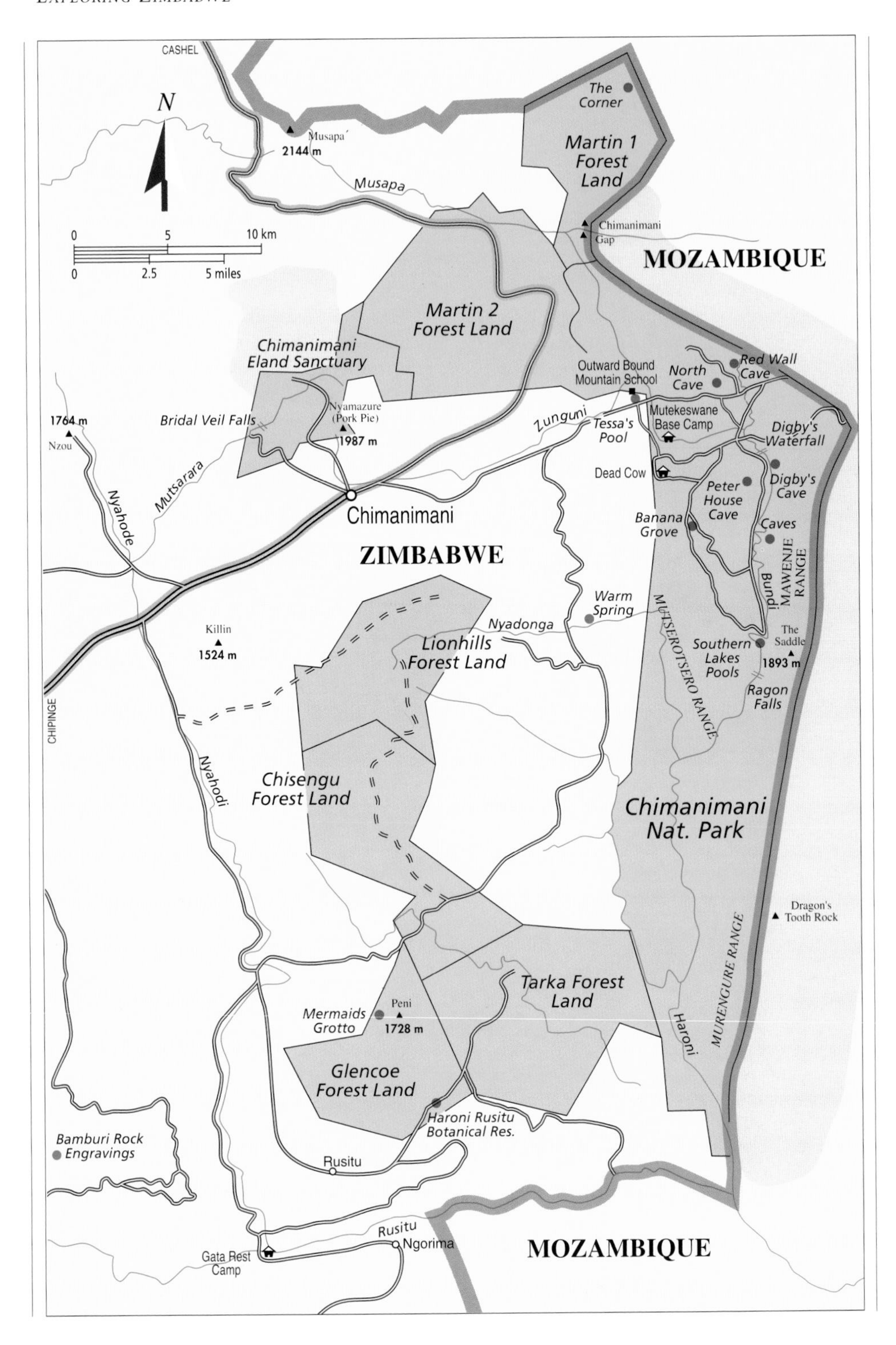
CASHEL
N
0
5
10 km
0
2.5
5 miles
Musapa
2144 m
Musapa
The Corner
Martin 1 Forest Land
Chimanimani Gap
MOZAMBIQUE
Martin 2 Forest Land
Chimanimani Eland Sanctuary
Outward Bound Mountain School
North Cave
Red Wall Cave
1764 m
Nzou
Bridal Veil Falls
Nyamazure (Pork Pie)
1987 m
Zunguni
Tessa's Pool
Mutekeswane Base Camp
Digby's Waterfall
Dead Cow
Digby's Cave
Peter House Cave
Mutsarara
Nyahode
Chimanimani
Banana Grove
Caves
ZIMBABWE
MAWENJE RANGE
Bundi
Warm Spring
MUTSEROTSERO RANGE
Killin
1524 m
Nyadonga
Lionhills Forest Land
Southern Lakes Pools
The Saddle
1893 m
Ragon Falls
CHIPINGE
Nyahodi
Chisengu Forest Land
Chimanimani Nat. Park
Dragon's Tooth Rock
MURENGURE RANGE
Tarka Forest Land
Mermaids Grotto
Peni
1728 m
Haroni
Glencoe Forest Land
Haroni Rusitu Botanical Res.
Bamburi Rock Engravings
Rusitu
Rusitu
Ngorima
Gata Rest Camp
MOZAMBIQUE

sells good honey, an Eland Sanctuary up Nyamzure (Pork Pie) hill. Bridal Veil Falls, 6km (3.7 miles) from the hotel, is a parkland of tall indigenous trees leading to a sylvan pool and delicately tiered series of falls. Sited near the source of the Nyahode River, the waterfall's tracery of spray is perfectly framed by mosses, orchids, ferns, lianas and strelizia trees on the cliffs.

In the Haroni Rusitu lowland forest at the southern foot of the Chimanimani, the rare trees (panga panga, Haroni fig and forest newtonia, for example) are home to such birds as the chestnutfronted helmetshrike, found only in this reserve in Zimbabwe, the rare redwinged warbler, the multi-coloured Angola pitta and the long-tailed green coucal. There is also an interpretive centre here.

To go trout fishing in the Chimanimani Mountains in the Bundi River you will have to carry your rods, food and camping equipment to the plateau from the Mutekeswane Base Camp. This, the best route up, is a two-hour climb via Bailey's Folly to the mountain hut. Chimanimani is a hiker's paradise of undisturbed mountain splendour.

Geologists believe it came into existence millions of years ago when its white quartzite massif cracked into folds against Zimbabwe's central plateau. Two-thirds of the range lies in Mozambique, the border unmarked, and the park is no more than 7km (4.5 miles) wide. Walking in the Chimanimani is not a Sunday stroll but an adventure for ardent hikers, so come equipped with strong shoes, a hat, food, a compass and water, although the water along the way is drinkable. Caves provide shelter and hikers should keep an eye out for berg adders and sudden storms. Avoid straying into Mozambique which will soon be declaring its side of the mountains a national park. Good walks from the mountain hut include the 40 minute hike to Skeleton Pass, the all-day Banana Grove trail to the Southern Lakes, and a three-hour climb up Mount Binga (2 437m; 7 996ft).

The Bundi plateau with its cracked strata formations, waterfalls and winds is wild. The River can come down in flood leaving you holed up in a cave atop this remote buttress where storms, ravines and sudden precipices are the norm. Serious hikers should avoid hiking during the school holidays as the mountains become a little crowded.

The ruggedly beautiful Chimanimani range.

ADVISORY: EASTERN HIGHLANDS

CLIMATE

In the Highlands the air is much cooler than anywhere else in Zimbabwe, often very cold in June and July, and the mountain and forest surrounds encourage the year-round burning of log fires in the hotels. Rain falls from November through March, when many of the wild flowers bloom. In spring (August), the new leaves on the msasa trees set the mountain slopes afire with a quilt of colours.

BEST TIMES TO VISIT

The coolest months, May to September, have the most sunshine and least rain, ideal weather for hiking, climbing and horse riding. The November to March summer rainy season is also very pleasant.

MAIN ATTRACTIONS

World's View Nyanga, Nyahokwe Mountain Ruins, and the drive from Troutbeck to Aberfoyle (gravel road most of the way) are three of Nyanga's many attractions. The country's highest mountain hike, Inyangani, or the one around Nyazengu Nature Sanctuary, are excellent.

Mutare town is worth a morning's visit and is the entry point for the lovely forested Bvumba mountains. The Bvumba Botanical Gardens are stunning. There are birds at Hot Springs, Birchenough Bridge is impressive and the drive from the Save Valley up to Chipinge through coffee farms and then to Chimanimani is worthwhile. Return along the scenic route via Cashel. Climbers will head for Chimanimani mountains, birders for Haroni-Rusitu.

There are six golf clubs in the Eastern Highlands.

TRAVEL

By air There are light-aircraft strips at Mutare, Nyanga and Chipinge.

By road A daily Harare/Mutare coach service operated by *Express Motorways*. Tel (Harare) (263) 4-720392, fax (263) 4-731677. Tel (Mutare) (263) 20-64868. Luxury *Blue Arrow* coaches, Fridays and Sundays. Tel (263) 4-729514, fax (263) 4-729572. *DSB Coachlines* operate a twice weekly luxury minibus to Juliasdale and Nyanga. Tel (263) 4-733741, ext 312. The roads to all three areas are mostly tarred (gravel roads that do occur are accessible to passenger cars). Car hire is available in Mutare: *Europcar*. Tel (Harare) (263) 4-752560, fax (263) 4-752083; tel (Mutare) (263) 20-62304, fax (263) 20-62367. *Hertz*. Tel (263) 20-64784.

By rail Daily trains run between Harare and Mutare. Tel (Harare) (263) 4-73393306, fax (263) 4-73393470. Tel (Mutare) (263) 20-62801/62825.

GETTING AROUND

A car is essential, although backpackers with patience will have no difficulty getting lifts. UTC (United Touring Company) arrange all-inclusive excursions to Bvumba and Nyanga from Mutare, tel (263) 20-64784 or (Harare) (263) 4-793701, fax c/o (263) 20 62128. P O Box 270, Mutare. Manica Chambers, 92 Herbert Chitepo Road, Mutare.

TOURS AND EXCURSIONS

Trout fishing Practically everywhere. Permits purchased at National Parks offices in the mountains: *Nyanga National Park and hatchery*, tel (263) 298-274 or 384. P O Box 2050, Nyanga. *Chimanimani*, tel (263) 26-2555. Private Bag 2063, Chimanimani. For futher information, contact *Master Angler*, tel (263) 4-885660, fax (263) 4-883214 P O Box BW550, Borrowdale, Harare.

Horse riding Again *National Parks*, Juliasdale Camp 'n Cabin, Nyanga. Also *Troutbeck Inn* and *Leopard Rock Hotel*.

Birding Everywhere, but *Haroni Rusitu Chimanimani Reserves* are well thought of. Also the *Chirinda Forest* area.

Ancient Ruins *Ziwa Site Museum* and *Nyahokwe. Nyanga Historical Museum*. Rhodes Nyanga Hotel.

White-water rafting and kayaking Pungwe River, Nyanga. Tel *Far and Wide* (263) 29-26329. P O Box 14, Juliasdale.

Mutare Museum, Victory Ave, Mutare. Tel (263) 20-63630.

UTC Tours from Mutare. Burma Valley cheese, banana and coffee farms. Tel (263) 20-64784, fax c/o (263) 20-62128.

Cecil Kop Nature Reserve, Mutare.

Mountain bike hire See *Far and Wide*, Juliasdale Village. Tel (263) 29-26329. (They also offer a number of other excursions.)

ACCOMMODATION

There are some 20 hotels and 30 other establishments in the Highlands. The cottages are self-catering, picturesque, remote and restful.

Cottages

NYANGA

Ezulwini A far-off place with heavenly views. Tel (263) 298-61121. P O Box 12, Troutbeck.

Stonechat Cottage Splendid Rob Roy isolation right beneath Inyangani. Tel (263) 4-303518. 128 Upper East Road, Avondale Harare.

Mountain Haven High up near World's View. Connemara Lakeshore. Tel (263) 4-721696 Private Bag 232A, Harare.

Silver Rocks Chalets Juliasdale fruit farming area. Tel (263) 29-394. P O Box 27, Juliasdale.

Granny's Folly 20 minutes' walk from the Gairezi River, breathtaking views across to Mozambique. Tel. (263) 22-2696. P O Box 31, Wedza.
BVUMBA
Badgers' Bend One cottage and two flatlets near Leopard Rock on a coffee farm. Tel (263) 20-210310/81354. P O Box 545, Mutare.
Cloud Seven Close to White Horse Inn. Swimming pool. Tel (263) 20-219617. P O Box 1111, Mutare.
Twin Streams Bird-watcher's paradise in montane forest. Tel (263) 20-215125. P O Box 812, Mutare.
CHIMANIMANI
Frog 'n Fern Cosy; includes lovely farm breakfast. Tel (263) 26-2294. P O Box 75, Chimanimani.
CHIPINGE
Buffelsdrift Remote farm in lovely forested mountains. 39km (25 miles) from Birchenough Bridge on the Chipinge road. P O Box 69, Chipinge.

Large hotels

Manica Hotel Mutare city. Tel (263) 20-64431, fax (263) 20-64466.
Troutbeck Inn Troutbeck, Nyanga. Trout lake, golf course, horse-riding. Tel (263) 298-305, fax (263) 298-474.
Leopard Rock, Bvumba. Top golf course. Casino. Tel (263) 4-733071, fax (263) 4-791484.
Chimanimani Hotel, Chimanimani Village. Old Raj-style rustic touch. Tel (263) 26-2511/13.
Rhodes Nyanga. Cecil Rhodes' old farmstead, recently refurbished. Rainbow Hotels and Tourism Group, tel (263) 298-377, fax (263) 298-477.

Safari lodges and luxury

Pine Tree Inn, Juliasdale, Nyanga. English cottage hotel. Best cream teas in the mountains. Tel (263) 29-25916, fax (263) 29-388.
The Castle Unique battlement guarding the keep to Leopard Rock. Book months ahead for exclusive maximum six group. Superb cuisine. Tel (263) 20-210320. Private Bag V7401, Mutare.
Mawenje Mountain Lodge Chimanimani. Brand new. Tel (263) 26-25441, fax (263) 26-2886.
Hot Springs Resort An oasis in the Lowveld 40km (25 miles) north of Birchenough Bridge flanking the mountains. Tel (263) 26-2361, fax (263) 26-2328.
Kiledo Lodge Chipinge mountains (self-catering). *En suite* facilities. Four thatched lodges. Tel *Sunlink* (263) 4-729025, fax (263) 4-728744, or direct, tel (263) 27-2944. P O Box 11, Chipinge.

Small hotels

Valley Lodge, Mutare. Tel (263) 20-62868.
Eden Lodge, Bvumba. Tel (263) 20-62000.
The Village Inn, Nyanga. Tel (263) 298-336
White Horse Inn, Bvumba. Tel (263) 20-60325.
Inn on the Vumba, Bvumba. Tel (263) 20-60722.

Budget, backpack and different

Aberfoyle Country Club, Honde Valley. Tel/fax (263) 4-729457, or direct, tel (263) 28-385.
Border Home, Mutare town. Tel (263) 20-63346.
Camp and Cabin, Juliasdale. Tel (263) 29-202 (recommended).
Mapor Farm, south of Odzi. Tel (263) 204-3072 (or ask for Odzi 0-3013).

National Parks

National Parks have lodges in Nyanga and camp sites in Nyanga, Bvumba and Chimanimani. Tel (263) 4-706077. P O Box CY826, Causeway, Harare.

WHERE TO EAT

All the larger hotels have restaurants. Best to ring first. You can nearly always get a meal at any of the areas' country clubs. The better restaurants include:
White Horse Inn, Bvumba. Tel (263) 20-60325.
Pine Tree Inn, Juliasdale. Tel (263) 29-25916.
Hot Springs, Nyanyadzi. Tel (263) 26-2361/2368.

HEALTH HAZARDS

Puffadders on sun-warmed mountain tracks, berg adders on rock climbs, mist up Inyangani, and pepper ticks in the grass that itch like crazy.

ANNUAL EVENTS

At the end of August and early September the msasa trees come out in their spring finery, a dozen shades of flaming brown, yellow and red, carpeting sections of the mountains.

USEFUL ADDRESSES AND TELEPHONE NUMBERS

AA Tel (263) 20-64422, fax (263) 20-64478. Fanum House, 10 Robert Mugabe Ave, Mutare.
Chimanimani Tourist Association Village Green. Tel (263) 26-2294. P O Box 75, Chimanimani.
Kashmir Trading Co, Nyanga Village (everything including troutflies). Tel (263) 298-229. Provisions can be purchased in Juliasdale, Nyanga, Troutbeck (and bakery), Chipinge and Chimanimani, and Mutare. Fuel is available in all the villages.
Manicaland Publicity Association Tel (263) 20-64711. P O Box 69, Mutare, cnr Robert Mugabe/ Herbert Chitepo Streets, Market Square.
Medical Air Rescue Service (MARS) Tel (263) 20-66466.
National Parks Central Reservations Tel (263) 4-706077. P O Box CY 826,Causeway, Harare. (Nyanga (263) 298-274384.)
Nyanga Tourist Association, Library, Village Green, P O Box 110, Nyanga.
Nyanga Tourist Association, Juliasdale, c/o Camp & Cabin. Tel (263) 29-202.

HARARE

Harare's high-rise buildings seem to compete with one another in glass and steel modernity in this neat city with its sensible grid pattern streets, bright sunlight and long avenues of flowering trees, but it is only when you walk First Street Mall or mingle with the queues at bustling Mbare Musika market and bus terminus that you realise Harare is pure Africa: colourful, noisy and friendly.

Named after the area's ruling 19th-century Shona chiefdom Neharawa, and founded as Salisbury with the arrival of Cecil Rhodes' gold-seeking Pioneer Column in 1890, Zimbabwe's capital lies at 1 500m (4 921ft) on the high central plateau. A city of 2.5 million people, it is spread across a 70km (45 mile) patchwork of high-density workers' suburbs, which includes the huge Chitungwisa satellite town on the periphery, and leafy residential areas with English names such as Borrowdale, Belvedere and Belgravia. Harare is a city of wide, clean streets, manicured trees and lovingly tended Botanic Gardens where the city orchestra plays at lunchtime. It is nearly always sunny by day but on winter nights in June and July, it can be freezing.

Although an industrial city, its heavy engineering, motor assembly, chemical, textile and food processing plants are neatly tucked away, the whole surrounded by farmlands of wheat, cattle and green swathes of tobacco, the country's top export. Harare boasts five-star hotels, 14 golf courses, a race course, great music, over 70 restaurants and is the world's most exciting stone sculpture centre.

As the nation's capital, it hosts Parliament, High Court, University and Museum, plus sophisticated road, air and telecommunications that make it the obvious entry point for the wilderness areas of Hwange game reserve, Victoria Falls, the Zambezi River and Eastern Highlands. But you can also safari in Harare by visiting Lake Chivero Game Reserve, Larvon Bird Gardens or the Mukuvisi Woodlands, while a necklace of privately run wildlife reserves within an hour's drive of the city offer practically all of Africa's big game. Imire, not far from the vineyards of Marondera on the Mutare road, even does rhino protection patrols on elephant back.

OPPOSITE: *Harare, possibly the world's most exciting stone sculpture centre, shimmers in the evening light (right).*

The People

Zimbabwe struggles to find a national dress other than the simple 'Zambia' (a wrap-around skirt) of village women, but Harare's streets provide a colourful display of proud urbanites who enjoy dressing up, the young in cool Harlem fashion, the men in sober business suits and the women in elegant West African styles.

Most of the country's small population of whites live in Harare. Everyone speaks English, is friendly and supermarket assistants carry your purchases to the car. The downside is that there are often long queues at the banks, civil servants can be frustratingly slow and jaywalkers abound. Rich and poor all seem to have domestic help and most watch either football or cricket. You will also find people of Euro-Africa, Chinese and Indian descent, and there is a substantial diplomatic and donor community. Harare hosts the country's unsustainably large civil service.

Zimbabwe has been independent for over 15 years and its population is literate, confident and sophisticated, with every profession from medical surgeon to film producer well

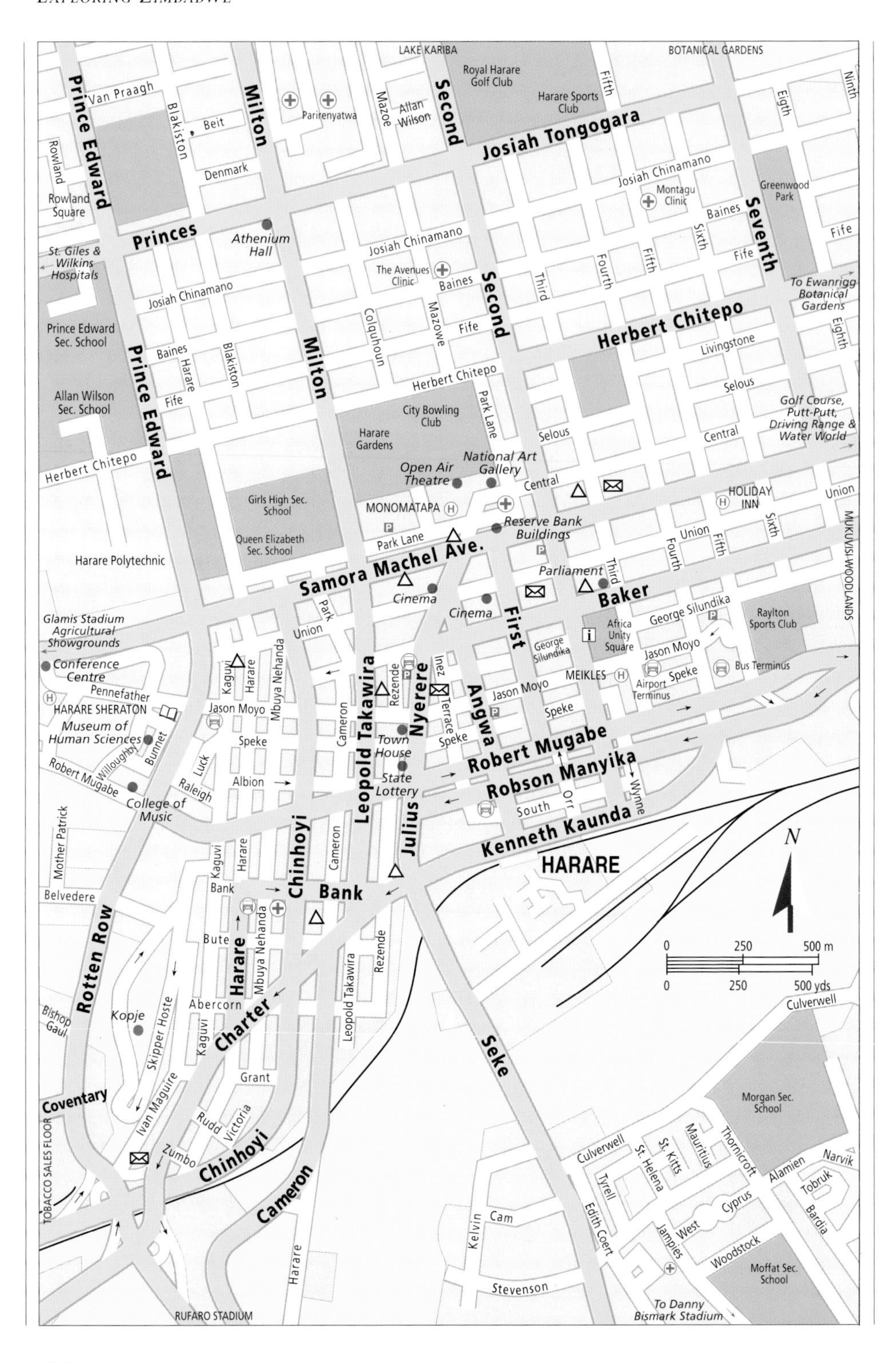
LAKE KARIBA
BOTANICAL GARDENS
Royal Harare Golf Club
Harare Sports Club
Prince Edward
Van Praagh
Blakiston
Beit
Milton
Parirenyatwa
Mazoe
Allan Wilson
Second
Fifth
Ninth
Eigth
Josiah Tongogara
Rowland
Rowland Square
Denmark
Josiah Chinamano
Montagu Clinic
Greenwood Park
Baines
Seventh
Princes
Athenium Hall
St. Giles & Wilkins Hospitals
Josiah Chinamano
The Avenues Clinic
Baines
Second
Third
Fourth
Fifth
Sixth
Fife
To Ewanrigg Botanical Gardens
Prince Edward Sec. School
Colquhoun
Mazowe
Fife
Herbert Chitepo
Livingstone
Eighth
Baines
Harare
Blakiston
Milton
Herbert Chitepo
Allan Wilson Sec. School
Fife
City Bowling Club
Park Lane
Selous
Golf Course, Putt-Putt, Driving Range & Water World
Harare Gardens
Selous
Central
Herbert Chitepo
National Art Gallery
Open Air Theatre
Central
Girls High Sec. School
MONOMATAPA
HOLIDAY INN
Union
Reserve Bank Buildings
Queen Elizabeth Sec. School
Park Lane
Union
Sixth
Fifth
Fourth
MUKUVISI WOODLANDS
Harare Polytechnic
Samora Machel Ave.
Parliament
Third
Cinema
Baker
Cinema
First
Raylton Sports Club
Glamis Stadium Agricultural Showgrounds
Park
Union
Africa Unity Square
George Silundika
George Silundika
Conference Centre
Mbuya Nehanda
Harare
Kaguvi
Leopold Takawira
Rezende
Nyerere
Inez
Terrace
Angwa
Jason Moyo
MEIKLES
Jason Moyo
Airport Terminus
Speke
Bus Terminus
Pennefather
HARARE SHERATON
Jason Moyo
Cameron
Speke
Museum of Human Sciences
Willoughby
Bunnet
Speke
Town House
Speke
Robert Mugabe
Luck
Robert Mugabe
Albion
Raleigh
State Lottery
Robson Manyika
Wynne
College of Music
Julius
Orr
South
Mother Patrick
Kenneth Kaunda
HARARE
N
Harare
Cameron
Kaguvi
Bank
Chinhoyi
Bank
Belvedere
Rotten Row
Bute
Harare
Mbuya Nehanda
Rezende
0
250
500 m
0
250
500 yds
Abercorn
Charter
Leopold Takawira
Culverwell
Bishop Gaul
Kopje
Skipper Hoste
Kaguvi
Seke
Grant
Morgan Sec. School
Coventary
Ivan Maguire
Rudd
Victoria
TOBACCO SALES FLOOR
Zumbo
Chinhoyi
Culverwell
St. Helena
St. Kitts
Mauritius
Thornicroft
Alamien
Narvik
Tyrell
Tobruk
Cameron
Kelvin
Cam
Edith Coert
West
Cyprus
Bardia
Jampies
Woodstock
Harare
Moffat Sec. School
Stevenson
RUFARO STADIUM
To Danny Bismark Stadium

subscribed. Only in the high-density areas will you find poorer folk among the plethora of small entrepreneurs and commuters.

Salesmen and women regularly travel to South Africa on shopping trips, while others, from tailors and tuck shop owners to bicycle menders and backyard mechanics, are always ready to undercut established firms. Fast foods are the city dwellers' normal fare with Coca-Cola an addiction that at times even supplants mother's milk. Crime is relatively low but does exist.

DOWNTOWN HARARE

Harare is a neatly laid out city, its wide streets lined with flowering jacarandas, flamboyants and cassias. It is perfectly safe to walk through even at night, although Harare is not a night city; shops close around 17h00 and nightlife in the city centre, with the exception of restaurants and cinemas, is limited. The suburbs, especially music-rich Highfields, usually offer more entertainment.

To get an idea of the city, drive west to east along Samora Machel Avenue, then turn right into Second Street and park. Walk down bustling **First Street Mall** with its craft shops, trees, benches and boutiques. A morning's stroll will reveal the old iron-balustraded **Victorian houses** of Robert Mugabe Avenue, the 1895 **Market Hall**, the old **Guild Hall** in Baker Avenue West, and the beautifully restored 1901 **Cecil House** at the corner of Second Street and Central Avenue. The **Anglican Cathedral** facing the gardens of **Africa Unity Square** (formerly Cecil Square) took 50 years to complete, while the nearby **Lonrho Building** was built in 1910. The **Town House**, built in 1950, boasts a lovely floral clock that includes the national Zimbabwe Bird.

Some lovely old **colonial houses** line the avenues between Herbert Chitepo and Josiah Tongogara, and the restored mansion housing the **Canadian Embassy** in Leopold Takawira Street is very handsome. The **Harare Gardens**, with its Italian restaurant, occasional open-air theatre and annual book

TOP: *Basket weavers at a Peoples Craft Market.*
ABOVE: *Monomotapa Crowne Plaza, a landmark.*

fair near the **Monomotapa Crowne Plaza Hotel**, and the **National Art Gallery**, are also highlights. Harare is only a hundred years old but the skyline is decorated with a profusion of futuristic glass and concrete spires. If it's historical interest you're after, head for the **Museum of Human Sciences** (formerly Queen Victoria) near the Sheraton Hotel or the **National Archives** on the Borrowdale Road, which holds 40 000 books and 30 000 photos of Zimbabwe's past. The 7km^2 (2.7 miles^2) of **Botanical Gardens** with nearly every one of Zimbabwe's 750 species of tree and plant are also worth a visit.

Shopping

The shops, after years of draconion import restrictions, now stock a reasonable range of imported goods at optimistic prices. Stone sculptures, leatherwork, crafts and cotton clothes are worth buying. **The National Handicraft Centre** on the southern edge

Mbare Musika, the nation's largest market.

of town is excellent, while downtown craft outlets include **Zimba** in the Samora Machel Parkade, **Rado Arts** in First Street and **African Adventures** on Julius Nyerere Corner. African prints can be bought at **The Trading Company**, local novels at **Grassroots Books** and for general purposes, try **Barbours,** the upmarket department store.

Electronic goods are expensive, as is film. Footwear is good value, food is reasonably cheap and fruit in season excellent. South African wines are surprisingly cheap and Scotch costs much less than in Scotland.

Suburban buys include colourful prints at **Danhiko**, home-made paraffin lamps, wire toys, briefcases made from oil cans, Weya paintings at **Cold Comfort Farm** and dozens of roadside crafts. **Borrowdale Village**, 10km (6 miles) from town is a popular shopping complex with over 120 outlets.

Entertainment

The liveliest music in Harare is out of town. Keep an eye on the weekend *Herald* for music by Thomas Mapfumo, Oliver Mtukudzi, Barura Express and anything from Zaire. Zimbabwe is not yet geared for single women in nightclubs so go in a group to such haunts as Club Hide-Out 99, Mushandira Pamwe, Sanganayi Inn, Skyline, Club Saratoga and Machipisa, mainly in the high-density suburbs where the nightlife swings.

Two television stations and several radio networks compete in Afro-pop. Local theatre is largely amateur with the exception of the superb Tumbuka contemporary dance company. Fifteen cinemas provide entertainment, while special interest clubs range from mountaineering to sky-diving.

Zimbabwe is sport-mad with soccer heading the list, followed by cricket, rugby, golf, squash and aerobics, with fourteen golf courses dotted around the city. Horse racing (and betting) is popular. Swimming pools and tennis courts are found at all major hotels. Harare boasts over 70 restaurants; prices are low and the service superlative. Local white wines are very drinkable, the reds, headache-prone.

MBARE MUSIKA

The nation's largest and noisiest market is the colourful, people-packed Mbare Musika near Rufaro Football Stadium, a pickpocket mecca and bus terminus 10 minutes from town on the southern outskirts of the city. Vendors try to attract your attention to their lavish displays of baskets, cone-shaped snuff balls, masks, soapstone carvings, spears, beadwork and gourds covered with intricately coloured telephone wire.

Shake-shake Shona music blares from buses and hair salons as you cross the road to the huge vegetable market where at least one of the Emergency Taxis (E.T.'s) is a 40 year-old Morris Minor. The strips of tractor tyre inner tube on sale are for tying parcels onto bicycles. Past the pyramids of tomatoes and pumpkins, the sellers of *n'anga* herbal medicines sit sagely among the stalls dressed in leopard skin hats, their mysterious bottles promising potency and instant cures. Buy a street snack of grilled *chibage* (corn on the cob), watch women make plastic bags sealed over a paraffin flame, and peruse the tools from Korea, the dusty cassettes and a host of other consumer delights.

Near the fast food stores, and where the soft drinks caps are bedded into the tarmac and the table football is furious, live-wire conductors entice you onto rickety buses piled high with fencing wire, chickens, bicycles, bedsteads and boxes. Hawkers dart in and around the buses offering, on cardboard

ABOVE: *The Boterekwe troupe of dancers perform at Chapungu Kraal at weekends (bottom right).* TOP RIGHT: *Heroes' Acre, a tribute to liberation.*

trays, a single cigarette, boiled eggs, bananas, boiled sweets and earrings. Near the bus lines and advertisements for beer are the sellers of combs, headscarfs and bargain-priced canvas carryalls, known as comrade bags, lined with fertilizer plastic.

Vibrant and friendly, Mbare may well be the highlight of your Harare visit.

HEROES' ACRE

Covering much more than an acre, Heroes' Acre is a great ceremonial burial ground to the 25 000 Zimbabweans who died in the civil war that led to the nation's independence in 1980. Sited on 57ha (140 acres) of msasa woodland, the monument features a bronze statue of the Unknown Solider; two men and a women, young guerilla fighters, look out heroically across the valley to distant Harare, frozen in vigilance on their pedestal of polished black Mutoko granite.

North Korean artists helped design the Z$18M project with its soaring 40m-high (130ft) needle column topped with an eternal flame, clearly visible at night from the Harare-Bulawayo highway. Two handsome bass relief murals depict the 16 year-old liberation struggle. A war museum is planned. Amai Sally Mugabe, wife of Zimbabwe's first President, is buried here, as is General Josiah Tongogara who led the largest guerilla army in the struggle. Buses bring parties of school children to be shown around by soldiers.

A permit to visit the site must be obtained at the Ministry of Information, Public Relations Office (Floor 5, Linquenda House, Baker Avenue), in Harare. To reach Heroes' Acre from here, travel 7km (4.5 miles) along Samora Machel Avenue.

CHAPUNGU SCULPTURE PARK

Tengenenge sculpture community, 150km (95 miles) north of Harare, is the largest of Zimbabwe's sculpture parks but Chapungu Kraal and Sculpture Park, with 12 resident artists, is the most accessible.

MUSIC AND SCULPTURE

Traditional *mbira* thumb-piano music was played at religious ceremonies to evoke the ancestral spirits. In modern times, Stella Chiweshe and Ephat Mujuru have done much to preserve the music and many popular musicians have found inspiration in its tinkling, haunting chant. Popular African music can be traced back to the 1930s with the adaptation of the Western zither by musicians such as Nhau Nzvenga and 1m-tall (40in) Ngoroma 'Chiremba'. Then it was the turn of the guitar, accordian, saxophone and for poorer folk in mine compounds, the *Tsava Tsava* weekend illicit brew dances. August Musarurwa's *Skokiaan* was top of the pops on the American hit parade in 1954, later to become known worldwide when Louis Armstrong adapted it as *Happy Africa*. The late 1950s produced hits such as *Pata Pata* from Dorothy Masuka, Zimbabwe's first international female star.

Then came the liberation war and Thomas Mapfumo's combined popular and political *mbira* music. He was followed by Oliver Mtukudzi, Susan Mapfumo, Storm and the Green Arrows. With independence new bands emerged: Bhundu Boys, Harare Mambos, Devera Ngwena and others. In Harare you can go to an all-night *pungwe* of traditional music. *Pungwes* were political conscientization gatherings held during the liberation war. The Federal Hotel, Solo's Nightclub, Club Saratoga, Hotel Nyamutamba in Chitungwiza dormitory town, Machipisa and Mushandira Pamwe in Highfields come alive at weekends with a mix of *mbira*, Zairean rhumba, *mbira* blues and marimbas that reflect the wry humour of township life, the war, and the trials of rural people in an urban setting.

Stone sculpture was first fostered in the 1960s with the opening of the National Gallery, the emergence of sculptor Joram Mariga and the nurturing of Gallery Director Frank McEwen who formed the Workshop School. Tom Blomefield converted his labour force on his farm Tengenenge north of Harare to carving. Between 1962-1972, 7 000 works were sold. Great names emerged: Bernard Takawira, John Takawira, Nicholas Mukomberanwa, Thomas Mukarobgwa. Since 1980 independence, a second generation of sculptors has emerged depicting traditional folklore subjects, while artists such as Muzondo and Tapfumo Gutsa have incorporated political messages and the use of wood and metal.

In Harare, Chapungu is particularly worth a visit (*see* p. 137). Also go to Stone Dynamics, Matombo, Vhukutiwa Gardens in Milton Park and the National Gallery. Look out for works by Bernard Matemera, Albert Mamvura, Joseph Ndandarika and Sylvester Mubayi.

Traditional marimba players entertain guests at the Victoria Falls Hotel.

Over 200 stone sculptures are displayed on the lovely lawns of Chapungu Kraal, about 8km (5 miles) to the east of Harare where some of Zimbabwe's best-known sculptors can be seen at work. Chapungu means bateleur eagle in Shona and this crimson-faced bird with its ruffled haughty head of mythological importance (the spirit messenger of the high savanna) is the first sculpture you see at the car park entrance which leads past the lake into Chapungu. Beneath filigreed msasa trees, the 7ha-park (17 acre) of lake, lawns, rockeries and reconstructed 19th-century Shona village, displays works that range from mystical 3m-high (10ft) creations to small, take-home carvings.

Traditional dancing by the innovative Boterekwa troupe can be seen at Chapungu at weekends where there is a thatched restaurant which serves light meals. Guided tours are offered, a permanent exhibitions curator is on site and *mbira* thumb-piano music can always be heard in the background as you marvel at the giant works.

LARVON BIRD GARDENS

Over 180 species of birds (eagles, vultures, flamingoes, sacred ibis and water fowl, to name a few) can be viewed at the spacious Larvon Bird Gardens, 18km (11 miles) from Harare along the Bulawayo road (turn left at Lake Service Station).

Set in open farmland, a miniature bridge shaded by palms and weeping willows leads over the lake past the ostriches to the aviaries. Signs direct you past quiet benches along grassy walkways to the soaring raptor aviary with its bateleur and fish eagles.

In the tropical walk-through aviary, with its miniature forests and pools, are butterflies and a myriad darting birds. The individual units in the Gardens are spacious and well-treed, providing each species with its normal habitat. A large parrot enclosure boasts representatives of these colourful birds from all over the world.

The restaurant at the lake, where there is a craft shop, is shaded by huge thorn trees. Larvon Bird Gardens are open from 10h00 daily.

Elegant wattled cranes are some of the many feathered wonders at Larvon Bird Gardens.

EWANRIGG BOTANICAL GARDEN

A great sweep of grassed valley fringed by msasa woodland frames the terraces of aloes (57 varieties in all), and the many other flowers in the Ewanrigg Botanical Garden, 40km (25 miles) east of Harare. The June-July winter months are the best months to see the spectacular displays of prickly leafed plants

INTERESTING PLACES EN ROUTE

- Gweru, 164km (102 miles) from Bulawayo, houses the country's military museum on Lobengula Avenue. Boggie's clock tower in the centre of town was erected in 1937. Its hands read 10h50 for 10 years until repaired in 1991. 9km (5.5 miles) from town is the Antelope Game Park.
- Sebakwe Dam and Recreational Park, 39km (24 miles) east of KweKwe town, offer woodlands mountain scenery, game and fishing.
- Ngezi Dam and Recreational Park has prolific birdlife. Turn right at Battlefields after 38km (24 miles). It is then 72km (45 miles). National Parks chalets, fishing, game walks. Beware of crocodiles.
- Between Mutare and Harare (263km; 163 miles), the two favourite places to stop for a snack and to browse, are Halfway House near Headlands and Malwatte near Marondera. But there are much cosier farmhouse tea-gardens between Mutare and Rusape. Look out for Mad Maggie's caravan.

with their cone-shaped spears of flaming red and yellow aloes. They grow wild in many parts of the country, particularly at Great Zimbabwe and near the ruins complexes of the Eastern Highlands, but Ewanrigg has the country's greatest collection.

The open Gardens, run by the country's National Parks, were started as a private garden in the 1920s by farmer Harold Christian. Today, a languid stroll through beautiful parkland will take you past banked terraces of barberton daisies, fuchsias, bamboos, cacti, ancient cycads, a herb garden, a water garden and of course, aloes for Africa. Plants can be purchased and there are lovely picnic and barbecue sites beneath shady trees, rich in the darting of sunbirds.

LAKE CHIVERO RECREATIONAL PARK

The game reserve on the south bank of Harare's premier dam, Lake Chivero is this park's main attraction. The turn off is 37km (21 miles) west of the capital along the Bulawayo road. The park's gravel roads meander in and out of open plain and msasa woodland where zebra, giraffe, white rhino, sable, impala and wildebeest can be seen. There are picnic sites by the waters, San (Bushman) paintings, marked game trails and rustic bungalows, named after birds, on a rocky knoll overlooking the lake.

Lake Chivero Recreational Park (formerly Lake MacIlwaine) is Harare's weekend playground offering boating, sailing, waterskiing and bream fishing. Swimming is not recommended as there is both bilharzia and crocodiles. The dam wall, built in 1952, holds back the 16km-long (10 mile) lake. Together with its sister lake, Manyame, 40km (25 miles) away, they provide Harare with its water. There are 10 000 dams in Zimbabwe, many used for recreation and all vital in a country whose annual rainfall is concentrated over a three-month summer period.

Holiday facilities on the north bank of Chivero (it has its own access road) include a thatched hotel, restaurant, tea garden and many sailing and boating clubs. The Lion Park (it also has elephant) halfway back to Harare is worthwhile for a first sighting of lions in the wild, while the Snake Park and Cold Comfort Farm make interesting stops on the road back to Harare.

MUKUVISI WOODLANDS

From the view platform overlooking the pan where the elephants come to drink, and beyond across a grassy game plain to the distant msasa trees, you almost forget that you are only a few kilometres from Harare city centre. The hum of distant traffic reminds you that the 277ha-sanctuary (685 acres)

TOP LEFT: *Fisherwoman at dusk, Lake Chivero.*
BOTTOM LEFT: *At least fifty-seven varieties of aloes are found at Ewanrigg Aloe Gardens.*

bordered by the nigh vanished Mukuvisi River, was miraculously snatched in 1980 from the hands of developers and preserved as a magnificent green lung in the eastern suburbs of Harare.

Headquarters of half a dozen wildlife organizations, it also boasts a shop, restaurant and conference centre. A paved pathway leads down between trees to the 'Close Encounter Area' where lily ponds are home to small buck and a myriad waterfowl.

Guided trails into the thickly wooded wild area reveals a rich flora of trees, including munondo, msasa, waterberry and mzanje with its delicious orange fruit. The park has giraffe, zebra, impala, sable and tsessebe, among others, a checklist of butterflies and 230 bird species, including rareties such as African finfoot, Narina trogon and Ayres eagle. A trip to Mukuvisi is a genuine wilderness experience, particularly for city children and business visitors who cannot escape to Hwange or the Zambezi. Mukuvisi is run by the Zimbabwe Wildlife Society.

These young elephants are residents of the Mukuvisi Woodlands, just outside Harare.

DOMBOSHAWA

A huge granite footstool balances atop the ascent route to Domboshawa National Monument: twinned granite domes, one covered in green trees, the other bald, about 27km (17 miles) from Harare. Follow the arrows up

HARARE CIRCULAR DRIVE

A day's picnic outing of some 150km (95 miles) could start at Epworth balancing rocks, those featured on the country's $10 note. Its lies 12km (7.5 miles) from downtown Harare on the Chiremba Road. A 20-minute country drive from here past farmlands, rural stores and low-level bridges will bring you to the village of Ruwa on the main Mutare road with its colourful cotton rug factory, bakery and sculpture gallery.

Nine kilometres (5.5 miles) north along the road flanking Ruwa's shopping centre, are the Brassart and Country Bumpkin farm shops. Continue on this road for another 15km (9.5 miles), then turn right at the 21km-peg (13 mile) onto the Arcturus road, not far from the cement works.

Soon after this a winding gravel road will bring you to Chishawasha Mission with its 100-year-old German twin-towered brick church, the oldest in the country after Matabeleland's Inyati. Inside is probably the most magnificent brass chandelier in Zimbabwe. A word of advice: there are mission stations all over Zimbabwe; if you break down, ask for Brother Mechanic.

At the next tar road turn right, then left, onto the Umwinsidale Road. On this wooded, hilly road you will pass vineyards, paddocks, Patrick Mavros' silver sculpture studio, even a castle. The road leads west into the Crowhill, then Borrowdale roads, a distance of 17km (10.5 miles). Turn left after 4km (2.5 miles) and stop for tea and browse at Borrowdale Village's shopping complex, then head down Edinburgh Road and right into Teviotdale/ Alpes, leading past Wingate golf course.

Turn left at the next T-junction for some 30km (20 miles) via the verdant Christon Bank ostrich-farming area to the main Mazowe road in the west. Head right to Mazowe with its orange orchards, Manzou Game Park, old hotel and even older gold mines. If you like, return to Harare along the gravel road past the hotel.

TOBACCO ROAD

The huge Tobacco Sales Floor in Gleneagles Road on the outskirts of Harare is superb live entertainment. An average of 17 000 chunky 100kg-bales (220 pounds) of tobacco packed tightly in hessian are auctioned daily April through October. Half a dozen auctions take place at once as buyers from all over the world move rapidly up the 40-bale lines facing the auctioneer who chants the bids. Buyers 'pike' each other's competitive bids with a nod, a wink, a crooked finger, indicating their price to the accompaniment of the auctioneer's dizzying rhyming monologue. Trolleys, like small trains, fetch 20 bales at a time to be auctioned in the vast hall the size of several playing fields, heartblood of Zimbabwe's economy.

Tobacco, a Caribbean Indian word, was introduced into Zimbabwe by the Portuguese. This *nyoka*, or snake as it was called, was widespread in the central and eastern parts of the country by the time the first English settlers arrived. It was a Jesuit priest, Father Boos, who grew the first commercial crop at Chishawasha Mission near Harare and by 1904 Virginia flue-cured tobacco was being produced for the first time ever outside the USA.

It only takes five seconds for a bale to be sold at Harare's tobacco floors as the auctioneer 'rolls' the bidders. 170 million kilograms (375 million pounds) sold in a season. Ten per cent of Zimbabwe's 13 million population is dependent on the revenue from tobacco, the country being the world's largest exporter, followed by Brazil and the USA, although China is the largest grower. It accounts for over Z$2 billion annually. Tour groups and individuals are welcome at the Floors. Ring the Public Relations Officer on 263-4-668921.

The world's largest tobacco sales floor.

A country of granite outcrops and balancing rocks: school children ascend Domboshawa (top) and Epworth's splendid equilibrium (above).

the streaked rock for about 15 minutes to the first of three rock overhangs. Ancient San paintings of giraffe, zebra, elephant and kudu can still be seen here, testimony to a long-forgotten people whose spiritual life was focused in group trance-like dance.

Open year round and managed by the Zimbabwe's National Monuments and Museums, Domboshawa makes a pleasant morning's outing. It has an interpretive centre and a small crafts shop (with welcome cold drinks after the climb), while a private company is currently completing thatched rondavels, a performing arts venue and restaurant. In the meantime, thatched barbecue sites have been erected within the perimeter.

Other rock art sites are found some 11km (7 miles) further at Ngomakurira, the place of drumming spirits, and at least four others in this Masembura-Chinamora area, part of a total of 30 000 throughout Zimbabwe.

ADVISORY: HARARE

CLIMATE

December to February is the rainy season with an average of 15 days of rain each month. Otherwise Harare is sunny nearly year round with eight hours of sunshine daily; October is the hottest month just before the rains. Harare, 4 823ft (1 470m) above sea level, is nearly always cool at night and during mid-May to mid-August, log fires are the norm. Harare's climate is one of the world's most equable.

BEST TIMES TO VISIT

These are largely determined by the best times to visit the other major attractions as Harare is not really a tourist attraction in itself. From June to July there are warm days and cold, sometimes freezing, nights. These, through to September, are the optimum months for Harare and all of Zimbabwe, especially for game-viewing. August to September are ideal if you intend visiting the Eastern Highlands. The hot month, when everyone waits for rain, is October and is sometimes called suicide month.

December to February is the rainy season with sudden torrential downpours often in the afternoon and spectacular lightning storms. It is also the best tigerfishing time. From March to May, Harare has very comfortable sunny days, cool in the evenings.

MAIN ATTRACTIONS

Harare has a bonanza of stone sculpture galleries and sculpture parks. Mbare Musika vegetable and crafts market should not be missed with its bustling, colourful, local flavour. It is also the country's largest bus terminus. The Tobacco Sales Floors, the world's largest, is great fun. Heroes' Acre just out of town recalls the cost of the independence struggle. A touch of the African wild is provided by Mukuvisi Woodlands, Lake Chivero Game Reserve, the Lion Park, Larvon Bird Gardens and Ewanrigg Aloe Gardens. The Harare Gardens and the National Botanical Gardens are fresh green lungs in the city.

TRAVEL

Harare is 1 142km (710 miles) from Johannesburg, 570km (354 miles) from Beitbridge, 560km (348 miles) from Beira, 889km (552 miles) from Victoria Falls, 368km (229 miles) from Kariba, 310km (193 miles) from Great Zimbabwe, 268km (167 miles) from the Nyanga mountains, 480km (250 miles) from the Matobo Hills and 730km (545 miles) from Hwange National Park.

By Air Harare is served by a dozen airlines, linking it directly with London and other European capitals, plus Nairobi, Johannesburg, Cape Town and Australia. A *bus shuttle service* links Harare airport with the city. Internally, Victoria Falls, Hwange Game Reserve and Lake Kariba (but not Great Zimbabwe or the Eastern Highlands) have daily Air Zimbabwe flights from Harare. Tel (263) 4-575021) for these and other destinations. Airstrips and private charter aircraft occur throughout the country; tel *Executive Air*, (263) 4-302248, *United Air*, tel (263) 4-731713 or *Safari Transfers*, tel (263) 4-302422.

By Road An excellent network of good tarred roads links every town and holiday resort, as well as all of Zimbabwe's neighbours. Driving is on the left-hand side and the speed limit is 120kmph (75 miles p/h). Beware of game at night and animals in unfenced rural areas. Road markings are often not up to standard. Practically no area of Zimbabwe cannot be reached by two-wheel drive. Fuel stations are often open 24 hours in the city and on the main highways (otherwise 07h00-19h00) and are usually never more than 100km (62 miles) apart.

Luxury buses can be taken internally and from Johannesburg, Bulawayo, Victoria Falls and Mutare. *Silverbird*, tel (263) 4-794777, *Blue Arrow, Greyhound*, tel (263) 4-729514, and *Zimibus*, tel (263) 4-720426. The **city bus service** is mainly operated by *ZUPCO*, tel (263) 4-739107, but may involve waiting. The adventurous could try a commuter omnibus minibus, an Emergency Taxi or a rural bus, all at Mbare market terminus.

By Rail The *National Railways of Zimbabwe*, tel (263) 4-73393000, operates daily services to Mutare, Bulawayo and Victoria Falls, while South Africa's *Spoornet* has a popular weekly overnight run to Johannesburg, tel (263) 9-66528.

GETTING AROUND

Car hire firms include *Europcar*, *Avis* and *Hertz*. **Taxi ranks** are available outside the large hotels, or at the corner of Union and Angwa streets near the cinemas. For **bicycle hire**, contact *Bush Trackers*, tel (263) 4-303025. **Safari and tour operators** include *Shearwater* and *United Touring Co.* For **city tours**, try *Kalambeza Safaris*, tel (263) 4-793999.

ACCOMMODATION

It has been the practice in some Zimbabwe hotels to charge different rates for locals and visitors. This should soon be phased out, but visitors still have to pay bills in foreign exchange. Five- and four-star hotel ratings are a little exaggerated in Zimbabwe, but prices by international standards are good.

Safari and Harare Countryside

Carolina Wilderness, 39km (24 miles) on Beitbridge Road. Two luxury double storey A-frames overlooking lake. Tel/fax (263) 4-736772.

Cresta Pamuzinda Safari Lodge, 86km (53 miles) on Bulawayo Road. Airstrip. Game-viewing. Tel (263) 62-8-292 (Selous), fax: (263) 4-794655.

Dombawera Game Park and Lodge, 140km (87 miles) on Bindura, then Matepatepa roads. Horseback trails, prolific birdlife, self-catering. Tel (263) 4-751331, fax (263) 4-751333.
Hippo Pools, 150km (95 miles) along Shamva Road on banks of Mazowe River in Umfurudzi Safari Area. Walking trails. Tel & fax (263) 4-708843.
Imba Matongo Five thatched lodges, Glen Lorne suburb. Tel (263) 4-499013, fax (263) 4-499071.
Imire They guarantee the big five and offer elephant-back safaris. Tel (263) 4-731856, fax (263) 4-795301. Tel Lodge direct (263) 22-354.
Landela Lodge, 29km (18 miles) on Mutare Road. Farmhouse. Excellent cuisine. Tel/fax (263) 73-2332 or tel Landela Safari Group on (263) 4-734043, fax (263) 4-750785.
Larkhill Farm Cottages, 70km (45 miles) on Mutare Road. Self-catering. Tel (263) 179-24372.
Mbizi Game Park (Harare airport, then 9km; 5.5 miles). Old farmhouse and self-catering cottages. Giant aloes. Tel (263) 4-572886, fax (263) 4-700812.
Mhondoro Wilderness, 157.5km-peg (98 mile) on Kariba Road. *En suite* thatched chalets. All the big game including leopard and rhino. Tel (263) 4-792648, fax (263) 4-733009.
Murage Wilderness The place of animals. Family orientated. 140km (90 miles) from Harare on Bulawayo road. Tel (263) 68-2273, P O Box 146, Eiffel Flats, Zimbabwe.
Mwanga Lodge on Bally Vaughan Game Park (48km [30 miles] on Shamva Road. Buffalo, elephant. Tel (263) 4-708304, fax (263) 4-728744. Tel Lodge direct on (263) 74-22721.
Mwena Game Park, 75km-peg (45 miles) on the Bulawayo Road. Private game reserve. Nine chalets. Hyaena, jackal and lion. Tel (263) 67-8-270. Selous.
Thetford House, turn at 22.5km-peg (14 mile) on Mazowe Road. Gracious residence in Christon Bank farming area, Harare North. Tel/fax (263) 4-724728.
Zindele Game Park, 65km (40 miles) on Mazowe Road. Plus guest farm. Tel/fax (263) 4-721696.

Luxury Select (with star ratings)

Kasisi Gardens***** Luxury garden flats, 37 Oxford Road, Avondale. Tel (263) 4-335120, fax (263) 4-339483.
Meikles***** Old-style elegance. Established 1915. Facing the fountains of Africa Unity Square. Good cuisine. Tel (263) 4-795655, fax (263) 4-707754.
Monomotapa (Holiday Inn Crowne Plaza)***** Overlooking Harare Gardens near National Gallery. Tel Zimbabwe Sun Group (263) 4-704501, fax (263) 4-791920. Central Reservations: tel (263) 4-736644, fax (263) 4-736646.
Sheraton***** Relaxed, American-style hotel. Popular gazebo bar and pool. Tel (263) 4-729771, fax (263) 4-728450.
Best Western Jameson**** Small, refurbished. Samora Machel Avenue. Popular Tiffany's Restaurant. Tel (263) 4-794641, fax (263) 4-794655. Central Reservations, tel (263) 4-703131.
Holiday Inn**** Friendly, efficient service, conveniently situated. Tel (263) 4-795611, fax (263) 4-735695.

Medium Range

Bronte Hotel English country garden family hotel. Old-fashioned table d'hôte meals. Tel (263) 4-796631, fax (263) 4-721429.
Courteney Hotel Small hotel whose restaurant L'Escargot has a big reputation. Quiet surroundings. Tel (263) 4-706411.
Cresta Lodge Value for money, value for service businessman's hotel on the eastern fringe of the city. Tel (263) 4-726401, fax (263) 4-726405.
Cresta Oasis Good Value. Easy to reach in Baker Ave. Tel (263) 4-704217, fax (263) 4-790865.

Budget, Camp and Backpack

Hillside Backpackers' Lodge 71 Hillside Road, 3km (2 miles) from railway station, 10 minutes by bus from town. Old farmhouse with log fires and cold beers. Pick-ups available from airport. Tel (263) 4-721929.
Red Fox Hotel** Mock Tudor in leafy suburb. Greendale Ave off Samora Machel. Tel (263) 4-495466, fax (263) 4-723230.
Russell Hotel 116 Baines Ave. Good Value. Tel (263) 4-791894/790565.
Executive Hotel 126 Samora Machel Ave/4th Street. Tel (263) 4-792803, fax (263) 4-791240.
Mushandira Pamwe Hotel Highfield high-density suburb. African music nightly. Tel (263) 4-64356.
Coronation Park Camp Site, 6km (4 miles) Mutare Road. Tel (263) 4-486398.
Hunyani Hills Hotel Country hotel overlooking lovely Lake Chivero. 29km (18 miles) on Bulawayo Road, turn left. Tel (263) 62-2236.
Lake Chivero Camping Sites (National Parks) North Bank, 29km (18 miles) Bulawayo Road. Turn left at Shell Gararge. Tel (263) 4-706077/8.
Other popular backpacker pads are **Sable Lodge** (Lodge 95), 95A Selous Ave, tel (263) 4-726017; **Kopje Lodge**, 38 Fort Road, recently renovated, pizzas. Tel (263) 4-790637.

WHERE TO EAT

Adrienne's Second Street Shopping Centre, near Reps Theatre. Parisian style. Tel (263) 4-335602.
Alexanders 7 Livingstone Ave. Varied menu, good welcome. Old Victorian House. Tel (263) 4-700340.
Aphrodite Taverna Greek atmospher and food. Strathaven Shopping Centre. Tel (263) 4-335500.
Delhi Place Indian cuisine. Greystone Park Shopping Centre. Tel (263) 4-883178.

DV8 Groombridge Shopping Centre, The Chase. Gammon steaks on the patio. Tel (263) 4-745202.
Guido's (Italian). Montagu Shopping Centre. Pasta family meals plus coffee bar. Tel (263) 4-723349.
Good *hotel restaurants* are **Bagatelle** and **La Fontaine**, both in the Meikles Hotel (tel (263) 4-795655), **La Chandelle** in the Sheraton (tel (263) 4-729771) and **L'Escargot** in the Courteney Hotel (tel (263) 4-706411).
Italian Bakery Best cappuccino and croissants. Avondale Shopping Centre. Tel (263) 4-339732.
Le Français Monomotapa Hotel. Old established French restaurant. Tel (263) 4-704330.
Mandarin Cantonese Cuisine. Upstairs in Ivory House near Meikles Store, Robert Mugabe Ave. Tel (263) 4-726227.
Pearl Garden, Chinese and Thai cuisine. Lewisam Shopping Centre, Enterprise Road. Tel (263) 4-495199.
Ramambo Lodge Marimba band and safari game meat braais. Also crafts and sculptures. Cnr Samora Machel and Leopold Takawira. Tel (263) 4-792029.
Roots of Africa Traditional African fare served on cast iron plates and seated (if you like) on a mat. Cnr Livingstone/7th Street. Tel (263) 4-721494.
Sherrol's in the Park (Italian). Edwardian palms in Harare Gardens. Tel (263) 4-725535.
Sitar Newlands Shopping Centre. Inexpensive Indian cuisine. Tel (263) 4-729132.
Squabbles Newlands Shopping Centre. Good seafood, intimate dining. Tel (263) 4-732940.
Wombles Ballantyne Park Shopping Centre. Wildwest sized steaks. Popular. Tel (263) 4-882747.

HEALTH HAZARDS

There are crocodiles and bilharzia in Lake Chivero. Malaria prophlyactics should be taken if travelling beyond Harare, Bulawayo or the Eastern Highlands. The tap drinking water is perfectly safe. Aids is a major disease in Zimbabwe. Beware of sunburn.

ANNUAL EVENTS

The Harare Agricultural (and Industrial) Show and the Zimbabwe International Book Fair are both held annually in August.

USEFUL ADDRESSES AND TELEPHONE NUMBERS

AA Fanum House, Samora Machel Ave, Cnr Julius Nyerere. Tel (263) 4-752779, fax (263) 4-752522.
Airlines: *Air France* Tel (263) 4-703868; *Air Zimbabwe* Jason Moyo/Third Street, tel (263) 4-575021/737011; *British Airways* Tel (263) 4-794616; *Ethiopian Airways* Tel (263) 4-790705; *Kenya Airways* Tel (263) 4-792181; *Lufthansa* Tel (263) 4-793861; *Qantas* Tel (263) 4-751228; *SAA* Tel (263) 4-738922; *TAP* Tel (263) 4-706231.
Banks: *Barclays* Tel (263) 4-729811/758281; *Standard Chartered* Tel (263) 4-753212; *Zimbank* Tel (263) 4-735011/757471.
Car Hire: *Avis* Tel (263) 4-751542. *Europcar* Tel (263) 4-752559 or 752560, fax (263) 4-752083. *Fleet* Tel (263) 4-752208. *Hertz* Tel (263) 4-704915.
Embassies (*see* full list in telephone directory under Diplomatic Missions): *Australia* Tel (263) 4-794591. *France* Tel (263) 4-498096. *Germany* Tel (263) 4-731955. *Italy* Tel (263) 4-497279. *Japan* Tel (263) 4-757861. *Kenya* Tel (263) 4-790847. *South Africa* Tel (263) 4-707901. *United Kingdom* Tel (263) 4-793781. *United States of America* Tel (263) 4-794521.
Emergency (Ambulance, Police, Fire) Tel 99. But 999 shortly.
Golf Try Royal Harare, tel (263) 4-702920. Josiah Tongogara and Fifth Street.
Hospital (Casualty). Parirenyatwa General. Ministry of Health. Mazowe Street. Tel (263) 4-794411.
Medical Air Rescue Service (MARS) Tel (263) 4-791378/792304, fax (263) 4-721233.
National Parks Reservations Botanical Gardens. Borrowdale Road/Sandringham Drive. Tel (263) 4-706077, fax (263) 4-724914. P O Box CY 826, Causeway, Harare.
Pharmacies Try QV Group First Street. Tel (263) 4-700621, or Day & Night Union Avenue/Angwa Street Tel (263) 4-722678.
Photographs and Film Developing Try Photo Inn, First Street and Baker Avenue, tel (263) 4-758251, or Gold Print, George Silundika Avenue (between Angwa & First). Tel (263) 4-732623.
Post Office Julius Nyerere Street/Baker Avenue. Tel (263) 4-794491.
Private Hospital (Avenues Clinic). Baines Avenue/Mazowe Street. Tel (263) 4-732055.
Private doctors See front of Harare telephone directory: Medical Practitioners.
Publicity Bureau Africa Unity Square. Cnr Second Street and Jason Moyo. Tel (263) 4-705085/6/7. P O Box 1483, Harare.
Safari Operators: *Safari Par Excellence*, Travel Centre, Jason Moyo Ave, tel (263) 4-720527. *United Touring Co*, Travel Centre, Jason Moyo Avenue, tel (263) 4-793701. *Shearwater*, cnr First & Baker streets, tel (263) 4-757831. *Phileas Fogg Travel*, Newlands Shopping Centre, tel (263) 4-786491.
Secretarial Services Try *The 'Boss'* in Borrowdale Shopping Centre. Tel (263) 4-882032.
Taxis: *Al Taxis* Tel (263) 4-706996. *Rixi Taxis*, tel (263) 4-753080.
Telephone Directory Enquiries Dial 962; **International Booked Calls** Dial 966; **Local Trunk Calls** Dial 967; **STD** Dial 110 (then country, city and number).
Wildlife Society of Zimbabwe, Mukuvisi Woodlands. Tel (263) 4-700451.

THE ZAMBEZI RIVER AND MANA POOLS

The Zambezi, mysterious and majestic, starts its unseen journey in remote northwest Zambia, not far from where that other great African waterway, the Congo, has its source. One thousand kilometres (620 miles) downstream, the now mile-wide Zambezi hurtles over the Victoria Falls, then fills the massive Kariba and Cahora Bassa lakes, and only ends 2 700km (1 678 miles) later in the tangled, shark-infested delta at the Indian Ocean.

The Zambezi is wild, its rapids and islands, lush banks, forests and swirling reaches largely uninhabited and visited only by rafts of snorting hippos and sandbanks of crocodiles. But no part of this restless, ancient river has quite the ethereal 'dawn of creation' feel as the 300km (190 miles) stretch from the spidery Chirundu Bridge to Kanyemba on the Mozambique border, which incorporates the Mana Pools National Park. It was named after a series of long and game-rich pools along the alluvial flood plain left by the river's meanderings centuries ago. Mana Pools, a UNESCO World Heritage Site with banks of giant *Acacia albida* (apple-ring thorn), mahogany, fig, tamarind and sausage trees, flanks the wide Zambezi and faces the high, blue mountains of the Zambian Escarpment.

Here the profusion of game that gathers by the river in the dry season is legendary. It is a wilderness where there are no houses, few people, dirt airstrips and nearly 400 species of birds; it is pristine safari country for walking, canoeing, touring or just sitting on the riverbank; it is hot, rugged, infested with both tsetse and malaria, and immensely beautiful. As it has been since the dawn of time.

The rich Ingombe Ilede burial grounds near Chirundu are witness to 1 500 years of river trade, initially between the local Mbara and Arab adventurers and later with the Portuguese who travelled up the Zambezi, described by Vasco da Gama as 'the river of good omens', as far as Kariba. David Livingstone saw it as 'God's highway to the sea' that would eradicate the slave trade. His wife Mary is buried in an almost forgotten grave near the river's delta. Only 50 cars at a time are allowed into the park, few motorcraft on the river and the silence without forbidden ghetto blasters is tangible.

Evenings are a benediction as the sun plays on the waters and hills in a minuet of ever-changing colours. It is indeed an untouched Eden, and one that during the rains at Christmas, turns into a flooded water wonderland of pans and pools, of water lilies, wild flowers, lianas and lush green trees. Silent, pristine and exquisitely beautiful in the mists of morning and the dappled sunlight of noon, Mana Pools is the riverine Venice of the wild.

OPPOSITE: *To many, Mana Pools, Zimbabwe's unspoilt Eden, sums up the magic of Africa.*

EAST TO KANYEMBA

In the far north of Zimbabwe at the remote gravel crossroads linking Harare with the lower Zambezi Valley, is the Makoni Store with hand-painted Coke sign, about 75km (45 miles) from Kanyemba. Peasant farmers' wives in colourful cloth wraps sit patiently on the *stoep* (verandah) waiting for the day's solitary bus to arrive, while inside, the khaki thread and tins of bully beef are 30% more expensive than in Harare, the local policeman refreshes himself from a bucket marked 'drinking water' which comes with a mug and a sign warning of cholera.

The rattle route from here down to the Zambezi Escarpment through Dande Safari Area passes bushbuck, buffalo and rocky ridges of msasa trees. After the first November rains, lush greenery carpets the sides of the roads, while below the bridge, women dig in the sandy riverbed for the family's water. Near Kanyemba one senses the road is coming to an end as there are regular signs such as 'Welcome to D Zineza bus stop'.

Kanyemba is named after a 19th-century Portuguese-speaking warlord, José do Rasario Andrade, who traded in beads, guns, cloth and female slaves in return for gold packed in porcupine quills. In some remote areas of

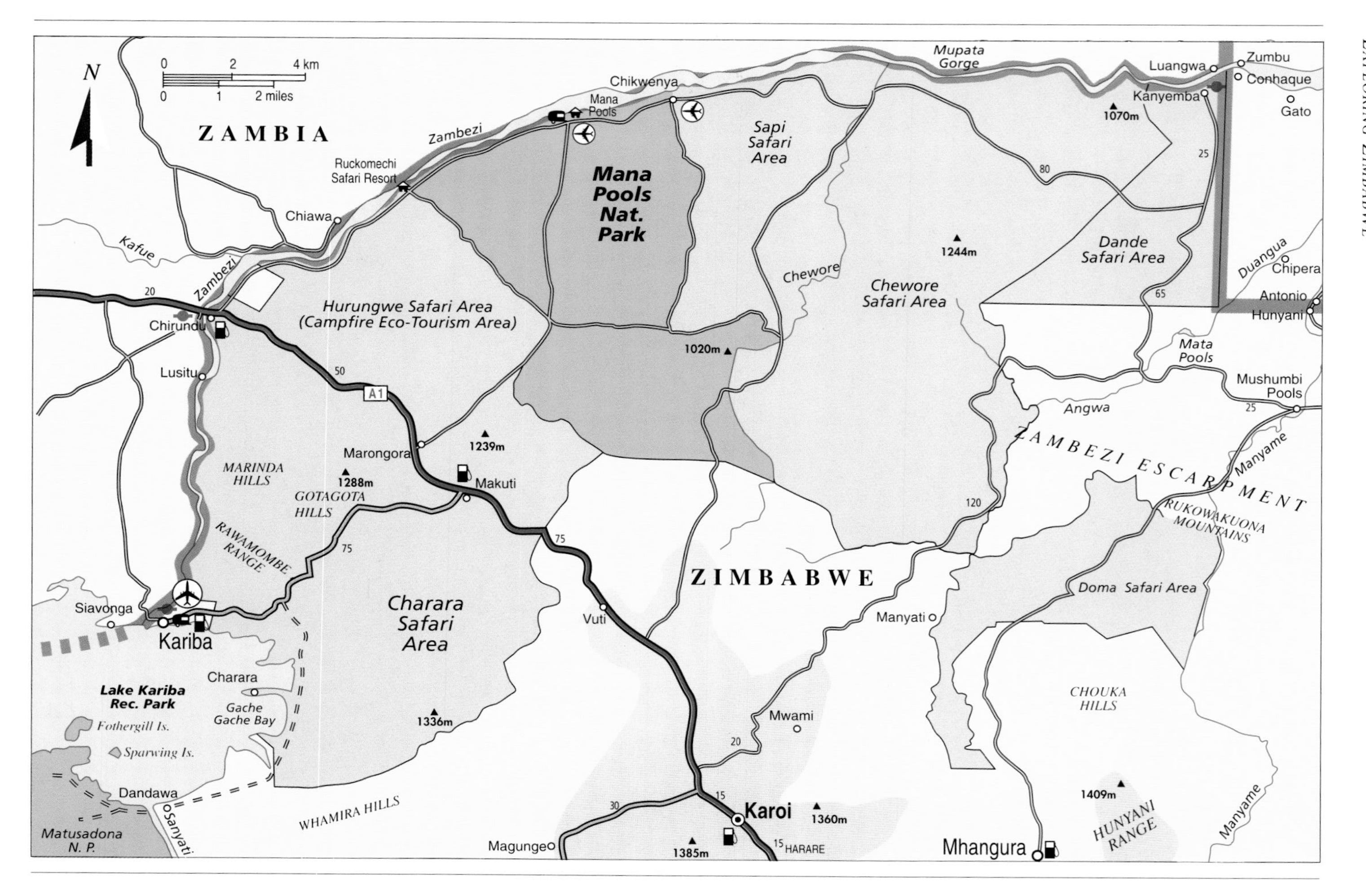

ZAMBIA
ZIMBABWE
ZAMBEZI ESCARPMENT
Mana Pools Nat. Park
Sapi Safari Area
Chewore Safari Area
Dande Safari Area
Doma Safari Area
Hurungwe Safari Area (Campfire Eco-Tourism Area)
Charara Safari Area
Lake Kariba Rec. Park
Matusadona N. P.
RUKOWAKUONA MOUNTAINS
CHOUKA HILLS
HUNYANI RANGE
MARINDA HILLS
GOTAGOTA HILLS
RAWAMOMBE RANGE
WHAMIRA HILLS
Karoi
Kariba
Makuti
Marongora
Vuti
Mhangura
Manyati
Mwami
Magungeo
Chirundu
Lusitu
Chiawa
Siavonga
Ruckomechi Safari Resort
Chikwenya
Mana Pools
Mupata Gorge
Kanyemba
Luangwa
Zumbu
Conhaque
Gato
Chipera
Antonio
Hunyani
Mushumbi Pools
Mata Pools
Angwa
Manyame
Chewore
Zambezi
Kafue
Duangua
Charara
Gache Gache Bay
Sanyati
Dandawa
Fothergill Is.
Sparwing Is.
1070m
1244m
1020m
1239m
1288m
1336m
1360m
1385m
1409m
HARARE
A1
0 2 4 km
0 1 2 miles
N

Zimbabwe you may still be offered such quills. He had an army estimated to number several thousand. Today Kanyemba, where the massive Luangwa River joins the Zambezi, where Zambia, Mozambique and Zimbabwe meet, and where for centuries traders have bargained and armies clashed, is a small administrative centre consisting of a few *musha* villages, a clinic, a police camp (it is advisable to check in here), Chief Capota's kraal and an abandoned District Commissioner's camp on the edge of the river beneath tamarind trees. Their brown peapod-like fruit are delicious.

Apart from the occasional Chikunda-speaking fisherman, today restricted to the riverside as, due to cross-river poaching, dugout canoes are discouraged, Kanyemba appears almost deserted.

Kanyemba looks out across the Zambezi to the misty Madzansua Mountains of Mozambique. Zumbo village in Mozambique and Feira in Zambia were all part of this ancient Portuguese trading post with a once-beautiful church. Some 3km (2 miles) west is the Mwanzamtanda River with its luxury Zambezi Camp overlooking the rugged Chewore Hills. Zambezi Hippo Trail Safaris collect clients from Kanyemba airstrip to take them 25km (15 miles) into Mozambique to their bird and fishing camp on Lake Cahora Bassa.

CHIKWENYA

A torch is a useful item at Chikwenya as you make your way from your thatched safari chalet to the dining area on the edge of the dry Sapi riverbank, for elephant, buffalo, lion and dozens of other animals don't care a

THE HEFTY HIPPOPOTAMUS

Twitching pink ears and big watching eyes characterize the hippopotamus whose greyish black skin, sensitive to the sun, was never hairy in spite of the folk tales. The hippo is usually seen in small family groups in the shallow waters of the Zambezi or along the Matusadona shores of Lake Kariba.

Hippo, in ancient Greek, means water-horse but is classified by the experts as a land mammal, and when you see one chomping away at night on the shore grass, it looks perfectly at home. But don't get in front of its access route to the river because it can outrun man or woman and is notorious for ignoring 'give way' signs. In fact, the 1 500kg (3 308 pound) hippo is responsible for more fatalities in the wild than either elephant, lion or buffalo, and yet is the favourite subject of Zimbabwe roadside woodcarvers. Canoeists are very wary of these giant, seemingly harmless beasts that emerge puffing, grunting and blowing from under the waters, as they can chomp through a canoe like a hotdog. Its huge-toothed yawning is in fact an aggressive display.

Hippo can sometimes be seen walking underwater. In the Zambezi they can walk submerged for up to six minutes. The hippo also has webbed toes to help it swim. It establishes pear-shaped territories bulging out into the river, likes to graze at sundown eating 130kg (287 pounds) per feed and will sometimes forage up to 30km (20 miles) in a night.

Some 3 000 hippo live at Mana Pools.

Hippos like to tuck themselves into the water away from too much sun. It is also in the water that they mate. Calves are hidden in reed beds and any nosy crocodiles would be wise to keep their distance. Other than the occasional baboon punch-up and the mournful wailing of hyaena, no animal is quite as noisy as the hippo. Its grumping and snorting can be heard all night, one roar followed by a tailing-off of several more.

hoot if you are there or not and will wander through the camp to feed on some favourite patch of grass or to drink at the river. Chikwenya, beneath huge apple-ring thorn and Natal mahogany trees on the eastern edge of Mana Pools National Park, was named after Chief Chikwenya and means a scratchy place, perhaps because one of the trees was a favourite elephant rub. It is usually accessed by small charter aircraft at the camp's strip nearby, a 45-minute flight from Kariba.

The Zambezi, as it forks left and right of Chikwenya Island, is at its widest (5km; 3 miles) here, and sometimes noisiest; hippos seem to love the waters of Chikwenya and will graze in great rasping tearaways in the evening on the shore. Chikwenya faces the blue mountains of the Zambian Escarpment rising 600m (1 969ft) above the multi-islanded backwaters of the Zambezi, playground of water birds such as Egyptian and spurwing geese, goliath herons and jacanas.

The Sapi riverbed, domed by gnarled trees, is ideal for walking trails, a speciality of Chikwenya, the first photographic safari camp to be opened in the Zambezi Valley. Pioneered by ex-naval officer Rob Fynn, it has, over the years, attracted the very best of Zimbabwe's conservationists and guides, including John Stevens, Geoff and Veronica Stutchbury and legendary Ura de Woronin, raconteur and writer who lived in the Valley for 50 years and who was killed by an elephant at Chikwenya, some say willingly because he felt his time had come.

INTERESTING PLACES EN ROUTE

- Mazowe Dam and citrus estates is 40km (25 miles) from Harare. Look out for oranges on sale and stop for tea at the old Mazowe Hotel. The Mazowe hills hide some old but still operating gold mines, while some of the original wild citrus stock was introduced by the Portuguese 400 years ago.
- Zombepata Cave Rock Paintings are located on a private farm, Chikonyora, 24km (15 miles) beyond Guruve. The paintings in the cave feature elephant and San abstract motifs. Contact the owners in advance.
- Mavuradonha Mountains. This is not the most direct route to Kanyemba but for those who like to digress, the Wildlife Society's rustic A-frame chalets Wilderness Camp with its mountains, pools and birds is worthwhile. It is 150km (95 miles) from Harare on the Mvurwi-Centenary road. The 40km-stretch (25 mile) from Muzarabani to Mahuye to link up with the Kanyemba road is rough.

Chikwenya was recently purchased by the Zimbabwe Sun Group who, although trained to urban luxury, have maintained the deliberate bush atmosphere of the thatched, semi-open chalets facing the Zambezi, each with a shower beneath the stars. Mosquito nets are used at Chikwenya and in the bush, not so much for mosquitoes but to keep at bay such delightful creatures as geckos that plop at your feet and the tiny, colourful frogs that love the shower walls. There is every type of big game, too, lion and leopard, packs of mottled hunting (wild) dogs, waterbuck with target circles on their rumps, warthogs, eland, sable and rare nyala antelope, and always crocodiles suntanning on the sands.

But don't always look for the big ones. Equally fascinating are the insects and spiders, ferocious little honey badgers, the dung beetles and termites, the butterflies and the continual pageant of birds in the *Albida* trees where the elephant, standing on rear legs, reach as high as 8m (26ft) to feed.

Lofty Acacia albida *canopy at Chikwenya.*

All the magnificent animals of the wild at Mana: elephant (above), leopard (right), waterbuck (bottom right).

MANA POOLS NATIONAL PARK

The pristine wilderness of Mana Pools, a World Heritage Site on the Zambezi, lies between the dry and sandy Sapi and Ruckomechi rivers. Although there is an airstrip, most visitors drive the 84km (52 miles) from the Chirundu road. Mana faces a series of sand and reed islands in the Zambezi where waterbirds browse and where hazy mountains seem to erupt from the river's edge.

It is an area of huge riverine forests and open, clay-flooded plains. The park reaches back 50km (30 miles) across a wide mopane woodland plain, home to practically all of Africa's animal species, to the hot, baobab-dotted hills of the escarpment leading up to Zimbabwe's cool and agriculturally bountiful central plateau. Massive tracts of safari hunting area surround Mana, guaranteeing its isolation, while the local Zambezi Society is ever vigilant to the threat of hydroelectric dam-building, oil, coal and uranium exploration, all mooted and to date effectively diverted.

The Zambezi Valley lies at an altitude of only 500m (1 649ft) and there is no permanent human population on the Zimbabwe side. Phalanxes of ilala palms, teased by 'dust devils' before the summer rains, give way to mahoganies, ebonies, winterthorns, figs and mangosteens in this 2 870km^2 (1 108 miles^2) park. Hot, dry and flush with the game of Africa, Mana supports buffalo, lion, leopard, nyala, eland, wild pig, sable, zebra and occasionally a flash of cheetah and endangered wild dog. One of the reasons why, in the dry season, the animals concentrate on the 3km-wide (2 mile) stretch of alluvial river terraces, which flank the entire Zambezi and become flood plains in the rains, is the presence of the huge *Acacia albida* trees which leaf in the dry season providing life-saving nourishment for the animals. At Ndungu camp site a large, sandy beach stretches out from the riverbank. Here twisted figs and lianas as thick as a man's thigh grow upwards in gargantuan cat's cradles. At Musangu Lodge you can rent a double-storey hideaway at the water's edge beneath *Acacias*, overlooking plains of river grass. Yellow waterpeas, water primroses and particularly the white and purple water hyacinth decorate the surfaces of backwaters and forgotten lagoons at Mana. At the water's edge, crowned plovers display angrily at any intruder. Here, too, great white egrets tread daintily through the shallows.

The river is rich in bream, vundu, nkupi, chessa and, above all, tigerfish. Many of the riverine camp sites in Mana National Park are named after fish and you will see knots of local women at Nyamepi, the main camp and Park Headquarters, returning with their day's catch wrapped in cloth on their heads.

The pools from which the park gets it name, particularly the 4km (2.5 mile) Long Pool and Chine Pool near Nyamepi, are

CANOEING SAFARIS

Canoeists on the tranquil Zambezi.

The most peaceful and rewarding a way to experience the awesome beauty of the Zambezi is on a canoeing safari.

The Sena of the Zambezi Delta and the water people of the Caprivi river systems, together with the Korekore, Kalolo and Tonga of the Zambezi, have all used the ancient trees that grow along Africa's rivers to make dugout canoes. Today it is the turn of two-man 5m-long (18ft) fibreglass canoes piloted by young guides with a taste for adventure. There is a macho cachet attached to canoeing: 'Men and women who have an affinity with the untamed', as advertized by Shearwater Adventures, one of the largest tour operators. But you don't have to be an expert or even superfit, while companies such as John Stevens' Bushlife Zimbabwe even lay on such back-up facilities as prepared camps, luxury tents and chilled wine. Kariba is the kick-off point for many three-to-nine day canoeing safaris. Canoes are often berthed at hotels and transported overland to Chirundu bridge as needed. The unique aspect to canoeing is that your presence on the water, provided you are quiet, does not upset the animals and birds and you can often cruise very close to grazing beasts. Hippo have to be circumnavigated as they don't like their territories invaded while, unless you go down to the river to bathe, crocodiles are seldom interested in you.

After an eventful day on the river, in which you possibly witnessed jittery impala doing gymnastic leaps or a buffalo being attacked by a crocodile, evening approaches in a canvas of pastel colours. Tents are pitched on a sandy island mid-river to reduce the risk from passing elephant and curious predators. Supper is prepared, a sleeping mat used to shield camp table and gas fire from the wind, a cut-off plastic bottle doing similar duty for the chef's candle. Out on the river even the plovers are still and all is quiet as the sun dies in a blaze of burnished gold across the waters.

The uniqueness of a night on a Zambezi riverbank is soon apparent: Kalahari Ferrari's, or rain spiders, skitter in manic glee at your feet, a python slithers away in your torchlight and buffalo wander past your tent to drink. In the distance a hyaena revs up its chilling whoopsong, baboons squabble, a lion grunts for its mate. By the time morning comes and you crawl out from under your mosquito net, you feel a bit like Indiana Jones.

surrounded by jigsaw puzzles of dried mud, death traps at times for buffalo when crocodiles come calling. End of year sees great cloud formations in a thousand colours and shapes building in the high skies of Mana. When the rain falls, an avalanche of water turns the alluvial riverbanks into flood plains of pools, pans and waterlogged reaches. The trees, flowers and insects luxuriate, but the animals migrate to higher, safer ground and man does not venture into the park at all, for the clinging black soil can swallow a tank. Mana's fairytale re-birth is witnessed only by the occasional silent canoeist cruising past.

To many, Mana sums up the magic of Africa: a huge wild river of hippo and crocodiles, laced with pools and islands, framed by rugged mountains and alive with game. Mana Pools and the 300km (190 mile) stretch of river it embraces from Chirundu to Kanyemba is an unrivalled wilderness. The park is open April through October, although safari lodges go through until end-November.

TOP: *Water hyacinth flowers adorn quiet corners of the Zambezi River where the buffalo (above) come down to bathe.*

RUCKOMECHI

Ruckomechi Camp on the Zambezi River comprises a 30km² (12 mile²) arc of flood plain, jesse bush, mopane veld and riverine forest. Reached by speedboat from Chirundu, Ruckomechi is regularly voted as having the best safari lodge in Zimbabwe. And with its setting beneath giant apple-ring thorn trees on the high banks of the Zambezi, it is hard to beat. The view is spectacular: great stretches of river and sandy islands, noisy with hippos, and beyond, the Zambian mountains.

At the lodge's open, thatched A-frame bar, the lapping of water below is soothing as you watch a mardi gras of birds go by: giant kingfishers, Egyptian geese, grey herons, carmine bee-eaters and always the trill of emeraldspotted wood doves. In the overhead winterthorn hundreds of weavers chatter, while beyond the open dining hut, the wind shimmers the grass near Henry's Chanel, a waterway of blue and white water-hyacinths. Henry was a hippo who fancied the spot as his exclusive territory and was prone to upset canoes who dared to venture in.

Ruckomechi Camp, famous for its open-air bath and loo-with-a-view, and for a cricket match played by mad Englishmen one Christmas day on a crocodile island in the river, means little cup, after the wild pumpkin gourd local folk use to dig for water in the dry riverbed. For a few weeks early in the year, the Ruckomechi River comes down in flood, an event that is seldom witnessed except perhaps by school children on a bush orientation course during the off-season summer months, when it is too wet, hot and hard of access for less hardy adult visitors.

The Zambezi at Ruckomechi is shallow but not recommended for swimming: crocodiles are notoriously catholic in their tastes. This prehistoric reptile, whose lineage goes back 140 million years, can reach 5m (16ft) in length and attacks in an explosive lunge, the length of its body, then sinks back again into the muddy waters of this primeval river.

Zebras (top left) and impalas (left) in separate symphonies of camouflage colours, while visitors take a stroll at Long Pools (above), all at Mana Pools.

CHIRUNDU

Chirundu village and border post, 363km (226 miles) northwest of Harare, is largely a memory of long-gone sugar estates and a line-up of long-distance trucks heading for Lusaka. Here you will also find the 415m-wide (1 362ft) steel bridge over the Zambezi, built in 1939 and named after Otto Beit, brother of the financier-philanthropist who gave his name to the Alfred Beit Bridge built in 1934 over the Limpopo. But the Zambezi, only 370m (1 214ft) wide at Chirundu, does have its own attractions, particularly for fishermen who usually stay in the tree-top Tiger Safaris chalet on the river, or at one of the Mongwe Fishing camps at Kakomomarara. Chirundu is also the point where many canoeing safaris begin, while those operated by Zambian companies but with Zimbabwean clientele, start further east at the Kafue River confluence. Ruckomechi can also be reached from Chirundu, either by speedboat or overland along an axle-cracker highway that fringes the river and where game is so prolific you halt every few minutes.

Wildlife

Mana and its surrounding safari hunting areas through which the game move, covers an area of 11 000km^2 (4 247 miles^2), two thirds the size of Hwange park. It has an enormously rich and varied animal population. It is famous for its riverside buffalo, its elephant that cross the shallow Zambezi in desultory file, its hippo 'cities' and its tigerish little honey badgers, symbol of the park. But it also has side-striped jackal, banded mongoose, warthog, lion, cheetah, beautifully dappled wild dogs, nyala, waterbuck with target circles on their rumps, Sharpe's grysbok antelope, spotted hyaena, leopard, kudu and impala, sometimes known as Mana chickens for the way they skitter and scatter about in perpetual panic. There are turtles and tortoises, as well as crocodiles and pythons, cobras and mambas, and in the waters, lungfish, tigerfish, chessa, vundu, nkupe and bream.

Mana was once the home of Zimbabwe's largest black rhino population. The demand for a rhino horn ingredient in traditional medicine in the Far East has resulted in ferocious poaching by gunmen in the pay of organized crime syndicates. This rhino mafia, whose tentacles stretch from Kenya to as far as Cape Town, has corrupted businessmen, politicians and even military units in many countries of southern and East Africa, and has subtly and relentlessly tried to besmirch the good name of leading game rangers and conservationists. Fortunately, sufficient radio-tagged rhino have been saved and now survive in maximum security zones throughout Zimbabwe where their movements are monitored day and night by anti-poaching patrols. Over 200 poachers have been killed and now the net is closing in on those who employ them. Soon the black rhino may return to flourish once again in the tangled jesse bush of Mana, their favoured home.

Bird-watching

Because of its varied habitats, nearly 400 species of birds are found along the river and back through the mopane forests to the rugged escarpment. They include bateleur eagles, huge saddlebilled storks, jacanas, guineafowls, woodpeckers, hornbills, bee-eaters and vultures. Sitting by the riverbank, you can hardly keep up with the fly-pasts.

Vegetation

You will see ilala palms, leadwoods and rain trees, tamarinds with their delicously tart fruit, figs and shaving-brush combretum. Down below the escarpment it is baobab country, trees that live up to 2 000 years, when their soft pithy trunks that store water are not eaten by elephant.

The distinctive terrain is carpeted with heavy grass, particularly in the mountains. Skeletal mopane trees, beautiful in their coats of summer green on the wide escarpment floor, and dry deciduous clumps of fussy jesse bush dominate the valley nearer the Zambezi River.

The rivers that rush down to the Zambezi in the rains support fringing canopies of tall riverine forests, while the alluvial plains of the Zambezi itself and the older islands are story-book forests of giant albida, mahogany and sausage trees.

SAUSAGE TREES

Parts of Mana, especially near Nyamepi Camp, look like a Christmas gathering of delicatessen owners. It seems that every second tree is decorated with giant salamis. The fruit can weigh up to 10kg (22 pounds), is long, grey with a rough skin and at times, half a metre (20in) in length and 18cm (7in) thick. It is best not to camp beneath a *Kigelia*, enticingly shady as the 18m-high (60ft) trees may be.

The *Kigelia* is part of the jacaranda tree grouping, the lovely purple-flowered tree of Brazil. The dark crimson flowers of the sausage tree are even more beautiful, up to 15cm (6in) across, with a velvety feel to them. Animals that can reach them, such as elephant and baboon are happy to ignore the flower's rather awful smell and munch on them. Some bats find them delightful.

In Zimbabwe an extract from the fruit is used to make a skin-cancer cream. It is rubbed on pre-cancerous skin lesions and even warts. The sausage tree has always had a variety of traditional medical applications: to increase mother's milk and to help infected grazes, while the fruit and bark, ground and boiled in water, is given to children with diarrohea. It is

Kigelia africana, *the sausage tree.*

even used, perhaps less effectively, to treat syphilis and rheumatism. Although it should not be eaten (the fruits are believed to be inedible), it is, the seeds roasted, the fruit baked and added to home-made beer to assist the fermentation process. The powder is also supposed to make babies nice and chubby when rubbed on their arms and tummies.

The round-topped sausage tree grows in many parts of Zimbabwe but particularly likes hot and potentially moist low-lying areas such as Mana Pools.

ADVISORY: THE ZAMBEZI AND MANA

CLIMATE

The Zambezi Valley can be hellishly hot and as humid as Rangoon, but this changes in winter with a breeze off the river and mists above the water. September is a good month: the migrant birds arrive and wildlife concentrates at the river. June and July are the most comfortable months to visit. At 400m (1 312ft), the Valley temperature never drops much below 20 °C (68 °F) and is often 40 °C (105 °F). The rainy Christmas season makes the flood plains impossible to cross, even for big trucks.

BEST TIMES TO VISIT

September (spring) is probably the best month. The coolest months are June and July. Mana Pools National Park is closed November to end-April, but canoeing safaris are usually available year-round except for mid-January to end-February.

MAIN ATTRACTIONS

A canoeing safari is the perfect way to explore the silent beauty of the river and its prolific game and birdlife. National Parks walking trails are good, the luxury safari camp's trails even better. In fact, three nights at either Ruckomechi or Chikwenya is likely to be the high spot of your African holiday. Bring binoculars for the many birds and a field guide to identify both them and animals.

TRAVEL

By air Small airstrips at Kanyemba in the east (and nearby in Mozambique and Zambia) and also at Chewore River, Chikwenya, Mana Pools National Park and one 8km (5 miles) from Chirundu. There is no strip at Makuti, the turn off to Kariba, or at the Marangora National Park's entry point to Mana Pools. Air Zimbabwe operates a daily flight to Kariba and from there to Hwange and Victoria Falls.

By road The adventurous route is north of Harare via Mvurwi and Guruve to Mahuye at the foot of the Zambezi escarpment. Up to this point it is tarred, a distance of 200km (125 miles), thereafter it is 170km (105 miles) on dirt to Kanyemba with a 4 x 4 vehicle recommended in the rainy season. The journey through the valley along 'Hunter's Road' halfway between the river and the escarpment is best in a 4 x 4 and essential on the lower route flanking the river. Either is a hard day's drive.

The usual route to Mana Pools is on the excellent national road from Harare via Chinhoyi and Karoi to Makuti, the last place to refuel and overnight, a distance of 300km (190 miles). From here proceed 16km (10 miles) on the Chirundu main road to the Marongora National Parks Office where entry permits can be obtained up to 15h30, provided park accommodation has been pre-booked. The access road to Mana Pools National Park lies a further 6km (4 miles) down the escarpment where visitors turn right onto gravel for a remote 43km-ride (27 mile) across rivers, and past baobab and mopane trees at the foot of the escarpment to the park's Nyasikana entrance gate. A four-wheel-drive vehicle is not essential. It is then another 42km north to Nyamepi Mana Pools Camp. There are no stores or fuel at Mana. Last chance for both is at Makuti or the Chirundu border post. Hitch-hiking is not allowed in the park, but backpackers with savvy do visit.

By land and water Safari companies usually transfer their guests into the park by small aircraft from Kariba or a combination of landcruiser to Chirundu and then speedboat. Chirundu lies 125km (80 miles) from the Zambian capital of Lusaka. Increasingly, Zimbabwe visitors are using Zambian canoe and safari camps and vice versa. Several companies operate in both countries. A four-wheel-drive is best at Mana as there are many steep river gullies.

TOURS AND EXCURSIONS

A variety of safari operators book the smaller, more exclusive National Parks 'special' camp sites and then package tented and canoeing safaris to the public, using these or other sites as their base. Facilities provided usually include either camping equipment or comfortable twin-bedded mosquito-proofed tents, bush showers, safari toilets, battery operated lights, camp chairs and tables, wholesome home cooking plus chilled beer, wine and drinks. Some are exceptionally luxurious.

Flip Nicholson Safaris Tel/fax (263) 4-738143. P O Box UA501, Harare.

Goliath Safaris Tel/fax (263) 4-708843. P O Box CH294, Chisipite, Harare.

John Stevens Safaris Thus described by author Wilbur Smith: 'A safari with John Stevens is one of the most memorable experiences of the African veld'. Tel Bushlife (263) 4-496113, fax (263) 4-498265. P O Box CH84, Chisipite, Harare.

Shearwater (largest operator of canoeing safaris with canoes based at Kariba Breezes Hotel) Tel (263) 4-757831, fax (263) 4-757836. P O Box 3961, Harare, or Kariba, tel (263) 61-2433, fax (263) 61-2459. P O Box 229, Kariba.

There are numerous other operators, including some excellent operators in Zambia.

ACCOMMODATION

Safari Lodges:

Cahora Bassa Camp (Kanyemba) Fishing and birding camp with thatched two-bedded chalets overlooking a grassy flood plain lies 25km (15 miles) inside Mozambique at the headwaters of Cahora Bassa, in effect the 7km-wide (4.5 miles) joint

Zambezi-Luangwa rivers. Untouched, unexplored, undeveloped. * 350 species of bird life. * Tigerfish, bream, vundu, bottlenose, chessa. Tel African Adventures (263) 4-751331, fax (263) 4-751333. P O Box A88, Avondale, Harare.

Zambezi Camp (Kanyemba) 14 tents under thatch. Recently opened 3km (2 miles) west of Kanyemba overlooking the Chirombwe mountain across the Zambezi in Zambia and the Chewore hills of the Zambezi Valley. * Exclusivity in a recently opened area. * Superb fishing and bird-watching. * Transfers by small aircraft to Kanyemba. * Access to Cahora Bassa Lake, Mozambique, and Luangwa River, Zambia. Tel (263) 73-2567, fax (263) 73-2612. P O Box 139, Ruwa, or c/o Run Wild, tel (263) 4-792333, fax (263) 4-792342.

Ruckomechi Run by Shearwater Adventures, it sits unfenced on the edge of the high Zambezi riverbank beneath giant albida trees looking across the river to the Zambian mountains. Open 1 April to 30 November. * Accommodation in 10 thatched bungalows, *en suite* facilities. * Game drives. * Canoe trips. * Walking trails with armed guide. * Fully equipped conference centre. Tel (263) 4-757831, fax (263) 4-757836. P O Box 3961, Harare.

Chikwenya Wilderness beauty and thatched Tonga-style chalets at the confluence of the Zambezi and Sapi rivers. The Zimbabwe Sun Group recently refurbished and took over the camp. Open 1 April to 30 November. * Specially adapted canoe boats for river game-watching. * Bush walks. * Hand-crafted pottery and rough timber tables in the open air, tree-shaded dining area. Tel (263) 61-2359, fax (263) 61-2240. Private Bag 2081, Kariba.

Chipembere Safaris Pfundundu Lodge Southern boundary Mana Pools. * Hiking trails * Campfire Project. Tel/fax (263) 61-2946. P O Box 9, Kariba.

Cloud's End Hotel (Makuti) *En route* to Mana or Chirundu, a convenient place to overnight. Row of comfortable hilltop chalets among trees and bougainvillea with spectacular views down the escarpment to Kariba. 'Out of Africa', hard-drinking Hemingway bar with trophies and tall tales. Tel (263) 63-526. P O Box 3334, Harare.

Tiger Safaris Chalet (Chirundu) One 4-bedroomed, self-catering but fully equipped chalet very high over the Zambezi and literally on the edge of the water. Rather like a tree-house. * One party only. * Boats for hire (obligatory part of chalet hire). * Magnificent views of river and bridge. * Photographic river safaris available. Tel (263) 637-633. P O Box 1, Chirundu.

Kayila Lodge (Zambian Bank) Thatched A-shaped *en suite* units, each with its own veranda on the Zambian edge of the Lower Zambezi floodplain opposite Mana Pools National Park. * Huge, soaring thatched bar and dining area. * Luxurious facilities. * Day and night game drives. * Hikes into the escarpment that hovers high over the camp. Tel Safari Par Excellence (263) 4-720527, fax (263) 4-722872. P O Box 5920, Harare.

Mongwe Fishing Camps (National Parks) Camping only. 19km (12 miles) downstream from Chirundu by car on the Kalisho Springs Road, or by private motorboat. Ablution facilities and water. No supplies. Apply to National Parks. Tel (263) 4-706077. P O Box CY826, Causeway, Harare.

National Parks Board Two-bedroom lodges (8 beds) and 4-bed lodges at various points along the Zambezi, together with half a dozen rustic camping sites (named after fish) with open shelters and ablution facilities. Nyamepi, the Parks Headquarters, has many fairly rough camp sites beneath trees in a magnificent riverine setting. The staff are always helpful and informative. Tel Central Reservations (263) 4-706077. P O Box CY826, Causeway, Harare.

WHERE TO EAT

Safari lodges provide all meals and drinks, as do all safaris; apart from these, there are no restaurants. Bring your own food and equipment. Makuti is the last place for (limited) stores and petrol before entering Mana Pools National Park.

HEALTH HAZARDS

Malaria, bilharzia and sunburn. Sunburn can lead to skin cancer, particularly on the ears, nose and forehead. Use a minimum factor 15 sun cream and wear a hat, preferably with a wide brim. Sun reflected off grass is half as powerful as full overhead sunlight, and off the water can also be damaging. Drinking water is suspect and don't drink the Zambezi. Be careful of hippos, crocodiles, buffalo and elephant.

USEFUL ADDRESSES AND TELEPHONE NUMBERS

AA (Karoi branch). Tel Karoi Tractor Services (263) 64-6337. Within Zimbabwe, dial 164-6337.

Air charter: *Executive Air* Tel (263) 4-304601, fax (263) 4-304328;

Immigration and Customs Control, Chirundu border. Tel (263) 63-7626. Within Zimbabwe, dial 163-7626.

Medical Air Rescue Service (MARS) Tel (263) 4-792304 or 791378. Within Zimbabwe dial (14) followed by 792304 or 791378. Fax (263) 4-721233. P O Box 7245, Harare.

National Parks, Central Reservations. Tel (263) 4-706077. P O Box CY826, Causeway, Harare.

National Parks, Marongora. Tel (263) 63-533. Private Bag 2061, Karoi.

Police emergency 99; changing soon to 999.

Safari Transfers Tel/fax (263) 4-302544; *United Air* Tel (263) 4-731713, fax (263) 4-575300.

LAKE KARIBA

Lake Kariba on the Zambezi River is an inland silvery sea, 282km (175 miles) long and up to 40km (25 miles) wide. With its bountiful shores of big game, its safari islands, superlative tigerfishing, houseboats, cruiseboats, catamarans and Mississippi-style paddle boats, it is no wonder that Lake Kariba is the playground of Zimbabwe. Locked in place behind the 128m (420ft) high and half a kilometre-wide (⅓ mile) wall, it forms Africa's third largest man-made lake. Overlooking its seemingly endless vistas and mountainous Matusadona rim is the town of Kariba with its tropical holiday hotels and harbour; each evening pontoon rigs head out from here into the waters to fish for *kapenta* sardines which, with tourism, form the economic mother lode of Kariba industry.

Big game-viewing by boat, especially along the Matusadona shore, is superb. You are quite likely to see game on the roads of Kariba village; elephant droppings, like flattened haystacks, are everywhere. The length of the lake and the shore is one long game-rich wilderness with pauses only for villages and the occasional *kapenta* harbour. Its wildness should not be underestimated; only giraffe and wildebeest are not found in Kariba. And zebra are seldom found in large herds. There is a big crocodile farm at Kariba, an Information Bureau at the dam viewpoint and a casino at the Caribbea Bay hotel. Small aircraft 'flight of the river god' flips can be taken over the dam and there are safari walking trails, sunset cruises and bird-spotting trips. A sailing regatta is held each May and the world tigerfishing tournament in October.

OPPOSITE: *Buffalo at Matusadona National Park.*
ABOVE: *Kariba Dam from Observation Point.*

KARIBA DAM

The massive concrete arch-wall of Kariba Dam, astride the high gorge of the Zambezi, does not seem big enough to contain Kariba, a lake longer than Wales. The dam wall, constructed between 1955 and 1959, is 579m (1 900ft) long and where it meets bedrock at its base, it is 24m (79ft) thick, tapering upwards to half of that where the road links Zimbabwe and Zambia. But when the turbines hum and the flood gates open, the whole structure still vibrates as if deep below the riverbed, *Nyaminyami*, the river god, has not forgotten or forgiven man for his temerity in damming this river. The best view of Kariba Dam is from the Information kiosk 1km (half a mile) up the winding road from the Shell garage.

The Zambezi, in parts, is 5km (3 miles) wide. At Kariba gorge the river's ferocious volume of water is compressed into a rock channel a mere 100m (330ft) across. Portuguese explorer Manuel Baretto was the first Westerner to see the turbulent gorge in 1667. David Livingstone and his brother shot the rapids 200 years later. It was just as violent when in 1955, contrary to the warnings of the local Tonga fishermen who said it would anger *Nyaminyami*, the Italian construction team began to choke the river with a million cubic metres (35.3 million ft3) of concrete and 10 000 tonnes of reinforced steel. The Zambezi replied by rising 30m (100ft) and hurling over 13 million litres (3.5 million gallons) through the gorge every second. The suspension bridges, the road between the two countries and the cofferdam were wiped out.

Then came another disaster: 17 men buried in one horrendous rush of cement. The bodies of the Italian workmen were sent back to their villages in Italy, their names inscribed with 69 others who perished, in the Church of Santa Barbara at Kariba Heights.

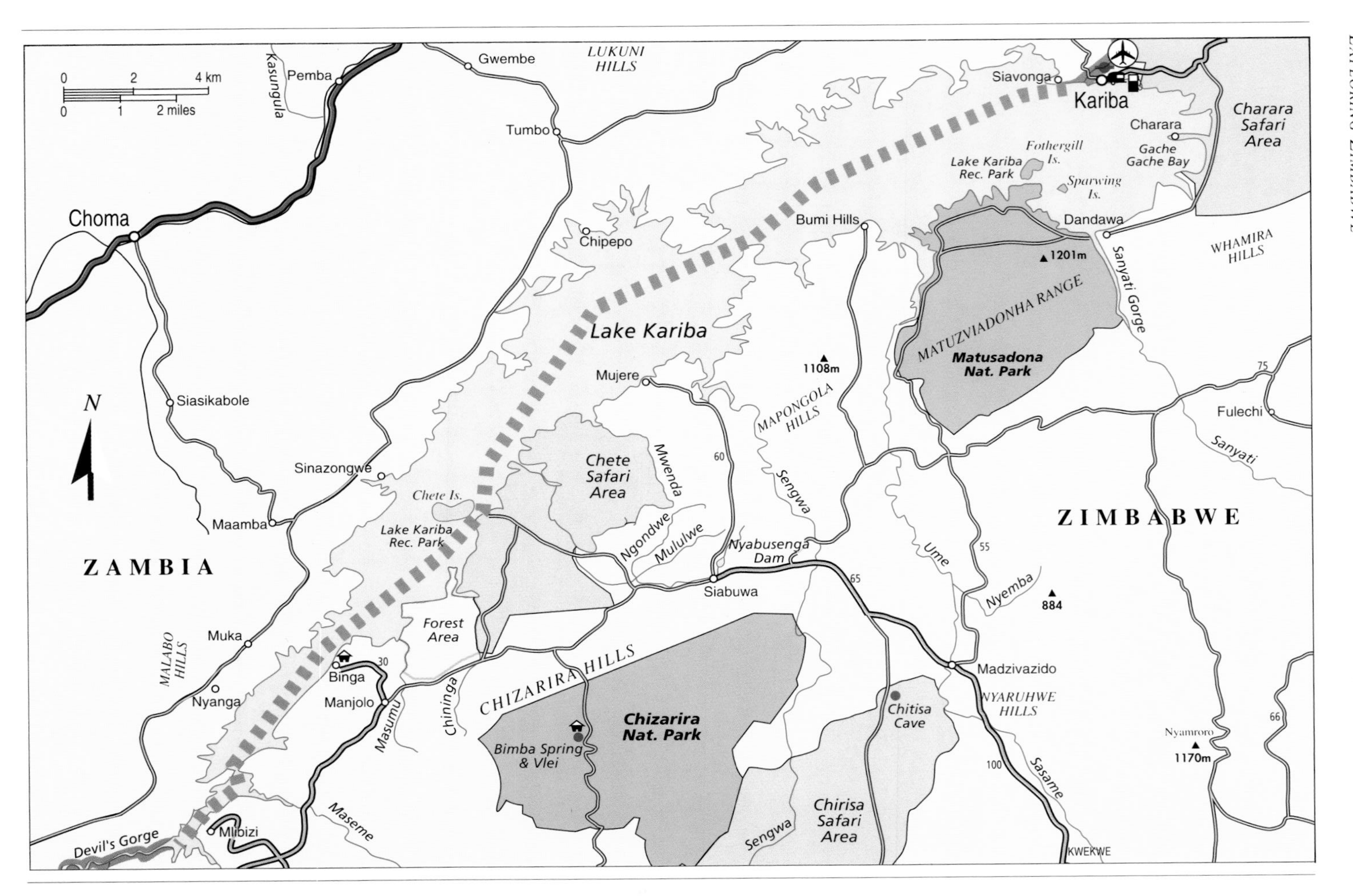
0 2 4 km
0 1 2 miles
Kasungula
Pemba
Gwembe
LUKUNI HILLS
Siavonga
Kariba
Charara Safari Area
Charara
Gache Gache Bay
Fothergill Is.
Lake Kariba Rec. Park
Sparwing Is.
Tumbo
Choma
Chipepo
Bumi Hills
Dandawa
WHAMIRA HILLS
1201m
Sanyati Gorge
MATUZVIADONHA RANGE
Matusadona Nat. Park
Lake Kariba
1108m
Mujere
N
Siasikabole
MAPONGOLA HILLS
75
Fulechi
Sanyati
Sinazongwe
Chete Safari Area
Mwenda
60
Sengwa
Chete Is.
ZIMBABWE
Maamba
Lake Kariba Rec. Park
Ngondwe
Mululwe
Nyabusenga Dam
Ume
55
ZAMBIA
Siabuwa
65
Nyemba
884
Forest Area
Muka
MALABO HILLS
30
Binga
CHIZARIRA HILLS
Madzivazido
Nyanga
Manjolo
Chininga
Chizarira Nat. Park
Chitisa Cave
NYARUHWE HILLS
Masumu
Bimba Spring & Vlei
66
Nyamroro
1170m
100
Sasame
Chirisa Safari Area
Maseme
Mlibizi
Devil's Gorge
Sengwa
KWEKWE

KARIBA VILLAGE

A series of sun-blasted green hills linked by winding mountain roads and trimmed with flowering cassias, jacarandas, bougainvillea and flame trees, rise steeply above Kariba Dam. Follow the main road (running from Makuti to Kariba) that goes past Polly's Ice-Cream Parlour to the junction and turn right. It leads to renovated hideaway houses, originally built for the dam construction workers, and to Kariba village itself atop the Heights where the views are spectacular.

At Kariba Country Club on the Heights, where visitors are welcome, it is much cooler than the harbour and townships where most of the people live. Bowls are played in the evenings and bingo at weekends. You can get breakfast and ices at the Christian-run Most High Hotel near the Operation Noah memorial, vegetables at the thatched Green Shop, cool drinks at the Little Shop, curios and crochetry at the viewpoint and fast food at Fish and Chip Paradise. In the Church of Santa Barbara, dedicated to the men who lost their lives in the construction of the dam, the Lord's Prayer is etched line by line in Latin in a circle of exquisite stained glass windows.

Kariba stretches 17km (10.5 miles) from the airport, past access roads leading down to bays, hotels, boat anchorages, and eventually to a choice of Andora harbour or the road across the dam wall. Elephant, baboons, even leopard, are regularly seen on these roads; the big pachyderms often fancy an evening walk up the main road to Hospital Hill. Little wonder that a thoughtful Wildlife Society sign as you approach the village informs you that Kariba is a game corridor for animals to reach the lake, source of water and forage, and that this delightful spot is the only town in Africa that 'lives with the animals'.

BELOW: *A fine display of crochet work at Kariba Heights where views of the lake stretch forever.*
RIGHT: *Kariba car ferry arriving at Andora.*

THE LAKE

People journey thousands of kilometres from South Africa to enjoy southern Africa's largest and wildest lake. To really appreciate Kariba and its close-up shores of big game, you should be afloat. Hundreds of boats of all shapes and sizes and each claiming to be the largest, latest or most luxurious, are available for charter. But the hype is unsophisticated, the welcome genuine. In fact, boats, barbecues, buffalo and beer epitomize the spirit of Kariba. And don't forget binoculars for the game-viewing and apocalyptic sunsets.

When first constructed, Kariba, with its characteristic shores of skeletal drowned trees, was the largest man-made lake in the

world. Some 5 200km² (1 930 miles²) of bush were flooded. The slowly rising waters trapped thousands of animals. Led by conservationist Rupert Fothergill, the animals were rescued in a dramatic mercy mission. Elephant and rhino were led to shore in this Operation Noah that fired the imagination of the world. About 5 000 creatures were eventually ferried to safety. A plaque at Kariba Heights records this quixotic exploit. Not so fortunate were 50 000 Gwembe Tonga who were resettled far from their riverside homes, causing a cataclysmic social upheaval.

The dam did, however, turn the inhospitable Zambezi Valley into a balmy holiday lake, its lush shores of *Panicum repens* grass ideal dry-season grazing for herds of elephant and buffalo whose numbers dramatically

KARIBA TIGER

The fighting tigerfish is a ferocious predator.

The tigerfish is hard-eyed, sabre-toothed and bony. And adored by fishermen. This silvery game fish with black stripes and flashes of orange on its fins, the 'water dog', will strike hook and line at magnum force, practically tearing the rod out of your hands. Moving like greased lightning, it will then do everything in its martial arts repertoire to bite through trace with interlocking teeth, devour swivels, snag your line on a drowned mopane, surge, backtrack, leap out of the water, even tailwalk across the waves to throw your spinner. No barracuda, sailfish, wahoo or dorado of Africa's coasts provides such sport as Kariba's tigerfish.

The largest tigerfish caught in Zimbabwe weighed 15.87kg (35lbs) and every year, usually in October, 300 teams of fishermen armed with stalinorgans of rods, tackle boxes, outboards, boats and crates of iced Zambezi beer, descend on Lake Kariba in the feverish hope of beating this record.

The Zimbabwe tigerfish tournament is described in the *Guinness Book of Records* as the largest freshwater angling competition in the world. It has been held every year since 1962 and attracts some 500 boats and 1 500 sportsmen and women. Support groups feed, forgive and sometimes outfish those who let them get away. Fortunately and unlike other fish, tiger don't seem to mind the noise these fishermen make in their boats, the jokes, the cursing and the popping of beer caps.

The creation of Lake Kariba caused an explosion of fish fauna while the introduction of the *kapenta* sardine provided superb additional nourishment for tigerfish, *Hydrocynus forskahlii*. Tiger are found in the Zambezi, Limpopo, Hunyani and for the lucky few in the Lowveld's Save, Runde and Pungwe rivers. They are not good eating although they make a tasty pickle if prepared soon after they are caught. That other predator, the fish eagle, loves them, however.

Every fisherman has his favourite technique for catching tiger but well-tried methods include spinners or large spoons, trolling at low speed, preferably in clear water, and the use of ball-bearing swivels. Drifting with live bait, such as a small bream, is good. A 5-10 kg (11-22 pounds) breaking strain line is preferred with a wire trace. Bring along a pair of pliers to remove the hook, or a tigerfish will willingly remove your finger. These days a 'catch and release' attitude is anglingly correct.

About 13 000 tonnes of *kapenta* are caught annually by up to 150 twinkling rigs on Lake Kariba. Fishing is done at night with lights to attract the sardines who, when the lights are extinguished, 'sound', or dive for the depths, right into big dish-nets. *Kapenta* are widely used as bait for catching tigerfish, particularly in shallow waters near submerged forests where many a hook and line is lost to the tree-twirling gyrations of tiger. The sardines are also used to 'chum', or sprinkle the water, a technique known as *doba doba* on Lake Kariba, to attract tiger.

The hush and calm of evening light across the lake is spectacular from Bumi Hills, one of Kariba's luxurious safari lodges.

increased, while the permanent shallows and drowned forests encouraged insects, then birds, hippo and crocodiles. In the waters that filled every hidden creek, backwater, river tributary and lagoon, tigerfish flourished on their new diet of introduced *kapenta* sardines, now a Zimbabwe food staple, and in turn, Kariba's sport fishermen, boats, harbours, taxidermists, ice-makers, bait shops and tall stories blossomed.

Old Kariba hands will tell you that there are no crocodiles in open, deep water but the occasional lone croc has been seen far out on the lake: be warned. The lowlands between the high escarpment and lakeshore is typical Zambezi Valley mopane scrub, woodland and scraggy *Combretum* jesse bush, the latter much loved by the narina trogon. The easiest access to the lake, where 42 species of fish thrive, plus jellyfish, sponges, prawns and mussels, is from the marinas at Caribbea Bay, Kariba Breezes or Lake View Inn.

ANDORA HARBOUR

To reach Andora Harbour, Kariba's busiest harbour, turn into Sable Drive off Lake Drive, then into Leopard Close near the Boathouse Restaurant. Here hippos snort in the waters, oxyacetelene torches sparkle on the shore and the noise of hammer on steel is constant. Andora Harbour has never quite outgrown its fishing village roots. Kariba man wears a baseball cap and grimy desert boots, has a dog in his open half-truck and a stuffed tigerfish over his office door. Signs in Kariba advertise hardware, tigerfish taxidermy and ice for sale, and there is the regular traffic of boats being backed into the water.

A floating fuel station serves the fishermen and a concrete ramp leads down to the *Sealion* car ferry that runs a 22-hour voyage the length of the lake. Hippos, indifferent to the engines and the bustle, periodically surface in Andora Harbour. It is all hot, noisy and colourful with birds and fruit-laden banana, pawpaw and mango trees everywhere. And a short walk to the Ten Star Bakery in nearby Mahombekombe high-density suburb means a perspiration bath.

Local life: a ferry docks at Msampa fishing village (top), while one of the dying customs is pipe smoking by Tonga women (above).

There are in fact two harbours: Andora and Chawara. Chawara is reached by driving via the power lines gravel road route, a distance of about some 15km (9 miles) from Andora Harbour. Here, the open, flat shore, grass-green to the water's edge, is a wild, wind-swept spot where terns tussle with the elements, waders delicately pick their way, and big-dish *kapenta* rigs jostle as they head out to sea. At Kariba, *kapenta* is king, but at least one woman has become a princess by making her fortune from the booming trade, and building one of the *kapenta* palaces that have mushroomed on the lovely hills and bays of Kariba village.

The people of Kariba

Kariba's population comes from all over the country. They speak Ndebele, Shona and English. But the people of the Zambezi Valley are the Tonga, particularly the river folk, the Gwembe Tonga. About 50 000 of them became exiles when the valley flooded 35 years ago, many relocated reluctantly near Binga, where their superb basket work originates and is now much copied.

Settled many kilometres inland far from their traditional homes and lifestyle based on fishing and subsistence agriculture, life for the Tonga people has not been easy in the hot dusty valley, where tsetse fly, heat and the cruel escarpment prevail. Even schools, boreholes and clinics have not compensated for a lost world. You will still occasionally find a Tonga woman, with her six front upper teeth removed and smoking the old-style calabash pipe but these customs, centuries in the making, are now dying.

The Tonga, historians believe, migrated south to the mouth of the Zambezi River 500 years ago, some settling upriver between Kariba and Chirundu. Although they had contact with Portuguese traders and were targeted by Ndebele raiders, their almost hunter-gatherer existence largely preserved them from contact with so-called civilization. Thus, their forced translocation was that much more of a devastating social upheaval.

MATUSADONA NATIONAL PARK

Many say that Matusadona National Park, lying between the Ume River and Sanyati Gorge on Kariba's southern shore and 25km (15 miles) from Kariba village, is the most beautiful of all Zimbabwe's parks. This is probably why half a dozen luxury safari lodges are sited on its baobab islands and secluded bays overlooking plains of lakeshore torpedo grass, loved by elephant and buffalo.

The 80km-long (50 mile) access road down to Matusadona off the gravel Karoi to Mlibizi 'highway' is rally calibre; the riverbed boulders would destroy a truck and a four-wheel-drive is essential. Canny fishermen,

ABOVE: *Houseboat game-viewing, Ume River.*
BELOW: *Elephants line Lake Kariba's shore.*

however, go by boat, leaving their wives to bring in supplies by landrover to rustic holiday lodges like Muuyu (Baobab).

Matusadona has a rich variety of game. Apart from buffalo and elephant, there are sable, klipspringer, eland and roan on the escarpment and uplands, while the lowlands have every large mammal, excluding giraffe, wildebeest and white rhino. Small groups of zebra occur here, while lion and leopard are plentiful. Cheetahs are being translocated into the park and so far a baby black rhino orphan resides in the park's Intensive Protection Zone (IPZ) and is being hand-reared by Parks and Wildlife Voluntary Service volunteers. On the lake shore it is estimated that there is one crocodile for every 200m (660ft), and hippo are plentiful. The shallow waters are home to ducks, goliath herons, geese, waders, kingfishers and one of Africa's finest (and noisiest) populations of fish eagles.

Matusadona ('constant dripping of dung') has many rivers that trickle through the escarpment mountains and over the gorges, and it is here that the non-stop cry of fish eagles can be heard as they swoop from sepulchral drowned trees to savage unwary tigerfish in the shallows. The water, skies and sudden upthrust of the Matusadona mountain skyline that frames and floats above the park, form a fluid cycle of pastel colours morning and evening as trees and mountains, lake and clouds meet, fuse and part.

SAFARI ISLANDS

Safari camps with luxurious thatched lodges dotted along the Matusadona shore, where the high mountains of the escarpment loom over them and big game graze at their garden fringes, are the jewels in Kariba's crown. But the changing level of the lake ensures that these safari islands are not always islands.

The first of these camps to be established was Fothergill Island Safari Lodge, named after the game-rescuing ranger. Its thatched rondavels and pool overlook a green manicured *panicum* plain where elephant lumber and lion hunt, an area ideal for a morning

TOP LEFT: *Fothergill Island Safari Lodge specializes in game walks but game-viewing at Kariba can also be done by boat (above) or even by air, flying over anchored houseboats (top right).*

game walk. Gache Gache ('gently, gently') is the newest camp with an upstairs view platform and big, round bar. *Ambuya* and *Sekuru*, powerboats of B-Line Lake Passenger Service, link Gache Gache with Kariba Breezes marina, a service that these torpedo-like boats provide for six other safari lodges around the Matusadona National Park. Also serviced are Spurwing Island, with its tents under thatch, described by Kon-Tiki's Thor Heyerdahl as a perfect place for animal lovers, Bumi Hills with its clifftop luxury west of Matusadona National Park and Tiger Bay luxuriating in lush green slopes and tropical fruit trees. A huge dinosaur, *Volcanodon karibaensis*, that lived 150 million years ago, was an early Bumi Hills guest; fossil remains of this beast were found on an adjacent island.

Floating wilderness rafts up the Ume River, Sanyati Lodge perched on a rocky outcrop over the Sanyati Gorge, Musango, Katete and several others, all compete with each other and all offering excellent accommodation, trained guides, fishing, boating, game trails, birdlife expertise and huge if not *haute cuisine* meals. Several have airstrips, making the transfer from Kariba airport a ten minute flip which inevitably includes a pre-landing pass over the runway to shoo off game.

SANYATI GORGE

High in the Zambezi escarpment, the Sanyati, having begun its journey 350km (220 miles) away, is already a powerful river. The long, single-lane Sanyati Bridge crosses it, providing the necessary link between highveld and the twisting four-wheel-drive descent into the Matusadona National Park. The Sanyati spent many millions of years fighting its way down to the Zambezi. It follows a line of erosion 300 million years old but only in the last 100 million has it worked its way through the resistant gneiss of the uplifted Matusadona range to produce the Sanyati Gorge, a high-cliffed, moody wilderness, haunt of tigerfish, fishermen and crocodiles.

The Sanyati is the largest river to flow into Kariba's eastern basin. Together with Kariba's back-up flooding, it has created a deep, silent fjord half a kilometre (a quarter mile) wide at its mouth. Here, where the cliffs seem to hang suspended above you, the cry of a fish eagle echoing off water and rock in this ravine, is eerie. But its aura of ghostly hideaway is ameliorated by the occasional sun-stepped waterfall cascading 500m (1 640ft) down the mountainside and the familiar grunt of hippo. Zimbabwe sport fishermen speak in hushed, reverential, tones about the Gorge, quietly exchanging insider knowledge about this eldorado of tigerfish and bream.

When Lake Kariba filled 35 years ago and whenever the level of the lake has fallen, minor earthquakes varying in magnitude from 2.8 up to 4.9, even 5.9 on the Richter scale, and brought about by the changing stress on the lake floor, have occurred near the Sanyati Gorge mouth. The Zambezi region from Kanyemba to Hwange is carefully monitored as it has the potential of a magnitude 6 earthquake once every 50 years that could damage Kariba's hydroelectric generating facilities although, it would seem, not the dam itself. The Sanyati Gorge is a fast, 20 minute speedboat ride from Spurwing and Fothergill islands.

KUBURI WILDERNESS AREA

Near Kariba airport and 56km (35 miles) from Makuti, a gravel road leads down to both the National Parks' Nyanyana Camp and Kuburi, a wilderness area covering

Impala drinking at their local.

37 700ha (93 178 acres) of Kariba lakeshore and rugged hinterland. It stretches from Kariba village in an arc framed by the Zambezi River Gorge on the one flank, and the Charara and Hurungwe Safari Areas on the other. Incorporating the Kuburi Range, this rough-hewn country ranges from *Brachystegia* woodland on the rocky escarpment to skinny mopane trees on the hot valley floor, plus a sprawl of hideaway bays, lagoons and islands on the long, shelving lakeshore.

Kuburi Wilderness Area is managed by the Zimbabwe Wildlife Society who, among other environmental efforts, specialize in

MISSISSIPPI PADDLE STEAMER

The *Southern Belle* floats high-stacked white and gorgeous in the cloud-framed waters of Chawara Harbour beneath the Kuburi Hills. She has 20 *en suite* cabins, luxury suites, a 44-seater restaurant with maroon drapes and chandeliers, a splash pool, a dance floor of seligna wood, a Victorian lounge, pale green and cream with potted palms, a 4m-wide (13ft) staircase from where speeches are made about the southern grandaddy comfort of tigerfish, a fully equipped stage (plus grand piano), lace balustrades and promenade deck.

A 58m (190ft) twin-hulled vessel, *Southern Belle* is 16m (54ft) wide, multi-decked and weighs 300 tonnes. She has a crew of 30, sits on twin steel floats and has a sophisticated world-wide communications capacity. Her skipper at time of writing, moustachioed

The Southern Belle, *princess of Kariba.*

Captain Andy Van Niekerk, ex Royal Navy, has had 20 years experience on Lake Kariba. The *Southern Belle* is powered by two 250hp Cummings diesel engines, the red and white 'paddle wheels' being fire escapes.

caring for habitats close to and threatened by urban settlements. Kuburi incorporates the airport, crocodile and banana farms, the Zimbabwe National Anglers Union Headquarters (whose bar is claimed to be the longest in the world), and a variety of safari and fishing lodges in the Charara River area. But 90% of it is an untouched, hot, rocky bushland quilted with a dozen torturous rivers where game abound. Let Kariba-based Tracker Safaris show you around. Chirembgwe, their reed and thatch bushcamp where hyaena have chewed the fridge, is not the normal chardonnay and chocolate-on-pillow safari lodge. But here you will learn to identify the whirring 'skiz-skiz-too-puddly' duet of red-faced blackcollared barbets and be told that froghopper insects suck the sap of the *Lonchocarpus* tree at breakneck speed, secreting water so rapidly that standing beneath this 'rain tree', you actually get wet.

A thatched view platform on stilts overlooks flooded loops of the lake in Kuburi where fish eagles swoop, hippos grunt, crocodiles bask and glossy ibis birds peck in stately pride on the wide banks. Behind the hide, impala frolic among mopane trees that have a built-in warning system activating nasty-tasting tannin when one branch is being over-browsed, forcing the antelope to move onto other branches.

Lomagundi Hunters Association has built an ecological summer school for children in Kuburi, where Kariba residents voluntarily patrol the shore to prevent fish poaching.

CHIZARIRA NATIONAL PARK

Chizarira National Park is best reached by four-wheel-drive vehicle from Hwange or the Victoria Falls, the latter a drive of some 372km (186 miles) of which the last 90km (55 miles) is on gravel. By road from Harare the quickest (530km; 350 mile) route is via Kadoma and Gokwe, or Karoi. From Bulawayo it is 500km (300 miles).

Chizarira, perched on the edge of the Zambezi valley escarpment, is a majestic mountainous wilderness, possibly the most remote park in Zimbabwe and difficult to access. The drop-off to the Zambezi Valley is often a sheer 600m (1 968ft) with superb long-distance views across the valley to Lake Kariba, 50km (30 miles) away. One of Zimbabwe's largest parks at 1 910km^2 (737 miles^2), it is also one of the least known.

And for those who are patient and keen of eye (and ideally, guided) there is game aplenty: elephant, buffalo, tsessebe, roan and sable antelope, particularly during the dry season when the park's bountiful mountain rivers, springs, pans and natural catchment area attract a broad spectrum of game.

Walking is the normal method of seeing the game in Chizarira, and the bird life includes the rare Livingstone's flycatcher with its yellow and ochre fantail, crowned eagle, the noisy goldentailed woodpecker and in the gorges, even the rare taita falcon. With its powerful scream and orangy-yellow claws, it catches and snacks on swifts and bats.

Chizarira's name comes from the Tonga word meaning 'barrier'. It has unique vegetation and ecozones, ranging from highveld *Brachystegia*, or msasas, in the north, to lowland mopane trees with their butterfly leaves that shy away from the sun. The highest

Remote and rugged, Chizarira is perched on the edge of the Zambezi Valley escarpment.

A Kariba denizen: a young Nile crocodile.

mountain, Tundazi, is in the far northeast. A climber's and backpacker's dream, the 1 370m-high (4 495ft) mountain, according to the local Tonga people of the Zambezi, is the legendary home of an immense serpent. When the mountain is shrouded in rain, that is all too believable. In the south, the Busi Sand River with its apple-ring thorn trees forms the boundary. Most of the park, however, consists of harsh miombo scrub.

National Parks operate six camps and five walking trails in Chizarira, while safari companies, such as the Victoria Falls-based Zambezi Wilderness Safaris, will package a visit for you based on their attractive Chizarira Wilderness Safari Lodge. Sited like a black eagle's eryie on the escarpment rim beneath mountain acacia trees, it is the only permanent camp in the park. There is an airstrip 15km (9.5 miles) from the Lodge.

Of holidays, hot springs and hunting

Most visitors to Kariba will see the dam, the crocodile park, the Church of Santa Barbara, buy a *Nyaminyami* walking stick and stay at one of the luxury safari lodges on the

FISH EAGLE: SYMBOL OF KARIBA

The ermine-shouldered fish eagle silhouetted in full-throated cry against the Matusadona sky is synonymous with Lake Kariba. Its haunting kyo-kyo-kyo, high and liquid, infiltrates each hidden bay and remote lagoon.

The fish eagle (*Haliaeetus vocifer*) means, appropriately, vociferous. These noisy eagles are usually seen in loving pairs, the male perched in a tree yelping stridently for his mate, she answering while still in the air; the quintessential call of the African wild. The fish eagle, with its white hood atop dark brown feathers, hooked yellow beak and yellow claws, is one of Zimbabwe's 20 eagle species.

Seeing the flash of tigerfish in the waters below, this elegant bird, talons outstretched, makes its pass, raking the waters and snatching its prey. With the fish wriggling helplessly in its talons, the fish eagle turns like a jump jet, pulls up rapidly and returns to its perch to rip at the feast before him. This eagle's nest looks slightly ridiculous, high, huge and a mess of twigs and branches, a great untidy bowl above lake and grass shore. Two rough white eggs are normally laid each year, the less noisy female doing the incubating which takes a month and a half. After hatching, the young birds only start learning to hunt for themselves after 60 days. They remain hungry and noisy in the nest, devouring every scrap of fish delivered to them, as well as such tasty morsels as unwary egrets and cormorants.

The immature fish eagle has a streaky appearance and prefers smaller backwaters and ponds. These eagles live all over Africa as far north as the Sahara and even occasionally at the seashore. They feed mainly on dead fish, will even attack flamingoes and have no compunction in buzzing other fish-eating birds to rob them of their catch.

The fish eagle is one of the largest eagles.

TOP: *The views are always panoramic from Kariba's many safari lodges.*
ABOVE: *Crowned hornbill, a common resident.*

Matusadona shore. Others may choose to cruise in a houseboat hunting for tigerfish. A few will backpack in Chizarira's wilderness. Relatively few, however, know of the variety of alternative holiday options along the shores of this 282km-long (175 miles) lake.

For those with a sense of adventure and a reasonably strong car, the old 'Hostes Nicole' trail, 8km (5 miles) north of Karoi that traces the lake is an interesting option. It runs the length of Lake Kariba, some 50km (30 miles) south of it, from east to west. A catamaran sailing boat, motorboat, cruiseboat, keelboat or luxury houseboat, all of which can be chartered at Kariba and prebooked through numerous safari agents, widens the choice enormously.

Charara, Masango and Gache Gache bays to the east of Kariba village have dozens of hideaway nooks and islands. Be careful that your outboard propeller doesn't get damaged on dead trees and before you jump ashore, remember that game is everywhere. This particularly applies to the hundreds of bays, backwaters, islets and creeks that twist around the shoreline of Matusadona National Park. And if the wind blows up, which it can quite suddenly, dive for cover behind an island as the waves can be quite frightening, and the occasional hailstorm battering. Never 'go to sea' without checking life jackets, fuel, water and auxiliary motor. Radio and compass should be standard equipment.

Further down the southern shore past the clifftop Bumi Hills lodge, lies Chalala lagoon and village, populated by *kapenta* fishermen and their rigs, and where the tiny fish are laid out on racks to dry in the sun. Chalala also has its own airstrip. Chalala leads into Sibilobilo lagoon with its ring of islands between which game, including elephant, like to swim. When elephant swim, they appear to be walking submerged through the water, trunk held high. Some have been known to go 30km (19 miles) right across the lake and on one occasion, an exhausted elephant had to be helped along by rangers. Kota Kota Narrows, situated between two islands, comes next. The big *Sealion* car ferry squeezes slowly through these Narrows on its 22-hour journey from Kariba to Mlibizi.

Near Kota Kota narrows is one of the country's 30 known hot springs. Others, whose geyser bursts heat up to 97 °C (207 °F), bubble away beneath the waters of Lake Kariba which, due to its alternating weight of water, is an area prone to small earthquakes. The lake now opens into the wide Sengwa Basin. It has long been a University of Zimbabwe Wildlife Research Centre, with pioneering work studies on elephant.

Chete ('the end') is, at 10km (6 miles), the largest island in Lake Kariba. Sited two thirds of the way down the lake, it is only 400m (1 312ft) from the Zimbabwe shore but belongs to Zambia, 15km (9.5 miles) away.

Zambia is hoping to make this area and the village of Sinazongwe its holiday equivalent of Kariba's eastern basin, with a border post at, and ferry from, Binga (the second largest town on the lake) and linked by a new 50km-long (30 mile) lakeshore road to Sinazongwe. Animals not seen in Zimbabwe, such as lechwe, will be translocated onto Chete Island where there will soon be a tented safari camp. Several Zimbabwe companies now offer Zambia safari options along the Zambezi. Chete mainland in Zimbabwe is a safari hunting area. Sport hunting is a major factor in the country's tourism industry, so valuable, in fact, that it is probably the reason why so much of Zimbabwe's game has been preserved. Working via the Campfire Project, local people are increasingly benefitting from 'selling' hunting rights, for

The car ferry journeys the length of the lake.

example the right to hunt an elephant, to a hunting concessionaire. The return is enormous and encourages subsistence villagers to protect wildlife resources. Behind Chete Safari Area, on the edge of the escarpment, is Chizarira National Park.

Binga, a small village set among low hills and originally built as an administrative centre for Tonga resettlement when Kariba flooded, has a harbour and is a fishing resort. It lies 230km (143 miles) from Kariba Dam with a good 180km-long (110 mile) tar road to Hwange Main Camp. It has a camp site, crocodile farm, hot springs and the attractive Kulizwe Lodge, ideal for visiting fishermen.

To the west, where the Sebungwe River flows down from the Chizarira escarpment into the lake, the narrows dividing Zimbabwe and Zambia are only 200m (660ft) wide. From here the lake becomes increasingly narrow with lush banks encroaching from both sides, and it is only a 25km-cruise (15 mile) to Mlibizi, the western terminus of the lake.

Mlibizi lagoon, together with Msuna and Deka Drum up the nearby Zambezi River, are favourite fishing spots with access roads to both. Devil's Gorge, a few minutes by boat from Mlibizi, is the Zambezi's entry point into the lake, 100km (62 miles) downstream from Victoria Falls. The Mlibizi Hotel will provide fishing tackle, bait, boats, ghillies, deepfreeze facilities for trophy tiger and even arrange to have them mounted. From Mlibizi it is 130km (80 miles) to Hwange National Park and 250km (160 miles) to Victoria Falls.

INTERESTING PLACES EN ROUTE

- Fambidzanai Training Centre is 18km (11 miles) from Harare (4 Dovedale Road, Stapleford, Mount Hampden airport area) where African cloths and organically grown vegetables are produced.
- Crossing the mineral-rich Mvurwi Range, 70km (45 miles) from Harare, with lovely msasa trees and views, is the Great Dyke Mountain Pass. The Great Dyke, with its ores, gold and precious gems, is nearly 500km long (300 miles), cutting right across Zimbabwe.
- Mazvikadei Dam is 90km (55 miles) from Harare; just beyond Banket, turn right for 25km (15 miles). The birdlife is prolific on this large lake whose wall across a steep gorge is the highest after Kariba.
- Sited 8km (5 miles) beyond the farming centre of Chinhoyi, some 115km (71 miles) from Harare on the main road, the Chinhoyi Caves are interconnected and artificially lit limestone stalactite caverns. One of these caverns, the blue 90m (300ft) 'sleeping pool', collapsed and is open to the sky. It is also known as Chirorodziva ('Place of the Fallen'), after those who were killed and thrown into the depths by Zulu impis. There is a small recreational park, hotel and camp site while the nearby Lions Den area is famed for its biltong.

ADVISORY: LAKE KARIBA

CLIMATE

Kariba is the hottest place in Zimbabwe. In late November 1994 it was announced on CNN World Report that Kariba was that day, at 57 °C (130 °F), the hottest holiday resort in the world. It often hovers at 40 °C (105 °F) in the months of October through February. Ice, pool dips and air-conditioning are necessities, and when it's really hot, water and wet towels are carried around. When the Italian workmen were building the dam, they even had to keep their tools in buckets of water. But it is cooler at night with welcome lake breezes, particularly in the mid-year winter months.

On the lake it can be scorching, although it has also been known to hail. Sudden dramatic thunderstorms can create 3m (10ft) waves. There are never less than seven to eight hours of sunshine daily although in December, January and February it will rain one day in two.

The altitude ranges from 366m (1 200ft) in the Zambezi River gorge, 440m (1 444ft) at Andora harbour and 800m (2 625ft) up at the Heights.

BEST TIMES TO VISIT

June and July (winter) are the coolest, but even at higher altitudes such as Kariba Heights, the Zambezi Valley is always hot, particularly in October. Nights cooled by a breeze are pleasant on a houseboat. December to January can be rainy.

MAIN ATTRACTIONS

A few nights on a Matusadona safari island with their teeming wildlife should not be missed. Tigerfishing enthusiasts will know what to do and for beginners, most resorts will have tackle.

Sailing safaris on the lake in either a twin-hulled catamaran or monohull, sleeping at night close to shore, is a unique experience. Kariba car ferries cruise the length of the lake, enabling you to go on to Victoria Falls and Hwange, or Harare.

A walking trail in Chizarira National Park will be a special experience for those who love wilderness and solitude. In Kariba village itself, a visit to the dam wall viewpoint, the Church of Santa Barbara on the Heights, or a sundowner at one of the hotels overlooking the lake as the *kapenta* rigs set sail, are all highlights.

TRAVEL

By Air There are daily flights to Kariba village from Harare, Hwange and Victoria Falls. Airstrips are dotted along the lake, including Fothergill Island Safari Lodge, Bumi Hills, Chizarira and Binga, and there are numerous private air charter operators. These are usually Harare-based.

By Road To get to Kariba, you travel north from Harare on a good metal road for 290km (111 miles), turning left at Makuti and the Clouds End Hotel for the last winding 75km (45 miles). The gravel road 8km (5 miles) north of Karoi that runs along the edge of the escarpment 50km (30 miles) from the Lake can be negotiated by two-wheel-drive vehicles. However, this cannot be done on the drop-off roads such as those down the escarpment to Matusadona, Chete Safari Area or up to Chizarira National Park, all of which have some of the wildest riverbed boulder tracks in the country and definitely require a 4 x 4. The distance from Karoi to Hwange Main Camp on this route is over 500km (310 miles). There is a good tar road from Hwange Main Camp to Mlibizi, a distance of 130km (80 miles).

A 50km-long (31 miles) gravel road from Hwange town leads to the Deka Drum fishing resort above Devil's Gorge on the Zambezi, and Msuna Camp. Petrol and supplies are available at every town from Harare to Kariba, as well as at Binga, Mlibizi, three Hwange National Park camps and Hwange town. A good tar road leads to Bulawayo 276km (172 miles) south of the Kamativi and Mlibizi turn-off. There are no trains to Kariba; a regular car ferry service exists on the lake and one to Binga.

By Water A sailing boat is the perfect way to see the game on the shores of Lake Kariba, the equivalent in silence, peacefulness and lakeshore approachability to a canoe trip on the Zambezi. It is possible to navigate practically the whole 2 700km (1 678 mile) Zambezi, including Lake Kariba, by canoe. It will, however, involve portage sectors at the Victoria Falls, Batoka Gorge, and the Kariba and Cahora Bassa dam walls.

GETTING AROUND

Sail safaris

Sail Safaris Light Tiki 30 catamarans. Mothership accompanies flotilla on week-long lake safaris. Tel (263) 4-335120, fax (263) 4-339483. Kasisi Gardens, 37 Oxford Road, Avondale, Harare, or c/o *Europcar*, Cutty Sark Hotel, Kariba, tel (263) 61-2321, fax (263) 61-2575.

Yacht Safaris 6.6m (22ft) sloop rigged keel cabin cruisers. First day training, then set sail in six yacht pack. *Kariba Yacht Safaris*, Cutty Sark Marina, tel (263) 61-2983, telex Kariba 41298 CUTTY. P O Box 80, Kariba.

Luxury motor cruisers

MV Southern Belle: Tel (263) 4-794377, fax (263) 4-795344. P O Box A131, Avondale, Harare.

Barbelle 18m (60ft) twin pontoon hull. Multi-deck. Fishing tackle, tender boat with outboard. *Hungwe Tours and Safaris*, tel (263) 4-733087, fax (263) 4-733009.

Concorde 27m (90ft) monohull. 300 bottle wine rack. Microwave. Bermuda deck. Washing machines. Phone, fax and video. Air curtain air-conditioning. 2 x turbo charged V8 Cat 640hp engines. Helicopter pad. Tel c/o Kariba Cruises (263) 61-2839, fax (263) 61-2885. P O Box 186, Kariba.
Kamba 22m (71ft) monohull. Video. TV. Stereo. Luxury showers. Large dining area. Run Wild Safari Consultants, tel (263) 4-792333, fax (263) 4-792342. P O Box 6485, Harare.
Mirimba 17m (55ft) monohull. Sleeps ten. Two x 3208 Cat diesel engines. Tel (263) 4-667502, fax (263) 4-664392. P O Box ST313, Southerton, Harare.
Salon Privé 18m (60ft) monohull. Four air-conditioned cabins. Three decks. Tel (27) 11-8834534. P O Box 78719, Sandton 2146, South Africa.
Catalina 33m (107ft) catamaran. Pool-deck. 2 x double beds in each *en suite* stateroom. Tel/fax (263) 9-79627. P O Box 9099, Hillside, Bulawayo.

Houseboats

Houseboats are usually multi-decked, cruise at a stately pace and float on torpedo-like steel pontoons, the hallmark of Lake Kariba shipbuilding.
Kariba Houseboats For a full selection of available vessels. Tel/fax (263) 61-2922/3. P O Box 129, Kariba.
Belinda 17m (55ft). Solar panel heating. Three-man crew. Cage pool. Four cabins. Tel (263) 4-335486/790447. P O Box ST172, Southerton, Harare.
Karibezi 21m (70ft). 18 passengers. Long distant engines. Three tender boats. Top deck bar. Tel (263) 68-8, fax (263) 4-720711. P O Box 61, Chakari.
Sanjika Sleeps 10. Passengers often sleep on deck. Swimming croc-proof cage-pool lowered into water. Tel (27) 11-4862140. P O Box 16932, Doornfontein 2108, South Africa.
Sunseeker 21m (68ft) double decker. Three wooden pannelled cabins. Experienced crew. Tel c/o Kariba Cruises (263) 61-2839, fax (263) 61-2885. P O Box 186, Kariba.
Tygers Eye 17m (56ft). Jacuzzi. Three cabins. Husband and wife crew. Tel (263) 61-2839, fax (263) 61-2885. P O Box 186, Kariba.

Open motorboats

If you are bringing your own open motorboat, the following (among others) are suitable for Kariba: **Nikikraft**, with rear and front self-draining line wells and built in cooler compartments; **Raker X16 Ruffnek**; and **Sabre Bow Rider**, with easy access to the nose area of the boat.

TOURS AND EXCURSIONS

Crocodile Farm (Lake Crocodile Park) 20km (12.5 miles) from Kariba. Airport Road. Tel (263) 61-2822.
Flights Scenic over dam and lake. Contact United Air. Tel (263) 61-2305.
Photographic Safaris Contact Chris Worden Tel (263) 61-2321.
Village Tours Contact United Touring Co. Tel (263) 61-2321.
Walking Safaris (in Chizarira): *Backpackers Africa* Tel (263) 13-4424 (Victoria Falls); *Kingdom Safaris* (minimum two nights). Tel/Fax (263) 61-2777; *Tracker Safaris* (Kariba, Kaburi area). Tel (263) 61-2255.

Canoe safaris

Kingdom Safaris Departures each Friday from Kariba Gorge, two to four nights along Zambezi River. Tel and fax (263) 61-2777. P O Box 255, Kariba.
Lake Wilderness Safaris Combined houseboat and canoe game safaris. Tel (263) 61-2645. P O Box 113, Kariba.
Sobec Canoe Adventures 'Taita' three days from Kariba Dam wall. Tel *Run Wild* (263) 4-792343, fax (263) 4-792342. P O Box 6485, Harare.

ACCOMMODATION

Kariba Hotels

Caribbea Bay Long resort hotel in mock Mexican village style overlooking big marina. Zimbabwe Sun Group. Features: * Water-skiing. * Multi split-level sports facilities. * Small casino. Tel (263) 61-2453, fax (263) 61-2765. P O Box 120, Kariba.
Cutty Sark Attractive rooms with a view almost on the edge of the water. Candlelit dining room. Pub overlooks trees and lake. Features: * Sail Safaris and Europcar office. * Pool. * Safari shop. Tel (263) 61-2321, fax (263) 4-753038. P O Box 80, Kariba.
Kariba Breezes Part of Shearwater group. Two lovely tiered pools beneath tall ilala palms overlooking lake and Matusadona mountains. Young, go-ahead hotel, favourite with canoe crews. Dave's Restaurant. Features: * Marimba band and pub. * Parasailing. * 80 delegate conference facility. * Popular marina. * Canoeing Centre. Tel (263) 61-2433, fax (263) 61-2467. P O Box 3, Kariba.
Lake View Inn Part of Zimbabwe Sun Group. Panoramic patio high above pool, trees and lake, ideal for fairytale dinners. Features: * Crotchet ladies and walking stick carvers in the carpark. * UTC office. * Hertz office. Tel (263) 61-2411, fax (Zimbabwe Sun Central Reservations) (263) 4-736646. P O Box 100, Kariba.
Most High Hotel Family hotel. Kariba Heights. Budget priced. Views over lake only excelled by Kariba Club. Features: * Operation Noah Monument, village and the Church of Santa Barbara nearby. * Big breakfasts for backpackers. Tel/fax (263) 61-2964. P O Box 88, Kariba.

Zambezi Valley Hotel High-density suburbs Kariba village. Lively and much enjoyed by young canoeists. Tel (263) 61-2926. P O Box 105, Kariba.

Safari Lodges

Chizarira Wilderness Lodge (Chizarira National Park). Only lodge in this remote park. Thatched cliff-edge luxury overlooking Zambezi Valley and Lake Kariba. Independent Wilderness Safari Group that includes Ilala Lodge at Victoria Falls. Features: * Eight stone and thatch lodges *en suite*. * Pool built into rocky outcrops. * Specialized game walks. *Zambezi Wilderness Safaris*, tel (263) 13-4637, fax (263) 13-4417. P O Box 18, Victoria Falls.

Fothergill Island Safari Lodge (Matusadona National Park). Ground level electric game fence surrounds the 25 thatched Tonga style lodges overlooking 400ha (989 acres) expanse of grass shore and plenty of game. Zimbabwe Sun Group. Features: * Airstrip and marina. * Open to sky *en suite* facilities. * Pool. Tel (263) 61-2253/2378, fax (263) 61-2240. Private Bag 2081, Kariba.

Spurwing Island (Matusadona National Park). Eleven walk-in tents under thatch. 'Out of Africa' style. Game-rich island named after the lovely spurwing goose. Features: * Double-storey thatched pub and game-viewing platform. * Pool. * Unobtrusive electric game fence, shin-high. (Introduced here and at Fothergill following incidents when guests, new to the bush, occasionally walked into buffalo and elephant). * 3-day game trails. Tel (263) 61-2466, fax (263) 61-2301. P O Box 101, Kariba.

Water Wilderness (Ume River, Matusadona National Park.) Four floating self-contained houseboats, like log cabins on pontoons. With 'mother ship', professional guide and catering staff. Zimbabwe Sun Group. Features: * Airstrip at nearby Bumi Hills Safari Lodge. * Canadian canoe with each houseboat. * Solar heating. * Secluded river bay. Tel (263) 61-2353, fax (263) 61-2354. P O Box 41, Kariba.

Mlibizi Hotel (Mlibizi). Ideal for overnight stops prior to or after disembarking from the Kariba ferry lake-long cruise. Lake front bungalows and 10ha (25 acres) of lush lawns overlooking the lake's headwaters lagoon. Features: * Devil's Gorge (Zambezi River) nearby. * Tigerfishing. * Sparkling pool. * Lakeside bar. Tel (263) 15-271 (Binga), fax (263) 15-271. P O Box 298, Hwange.

Other safari lodges at Kariba include the luxurious **Bumi Hills** (tel (263) 61-2353, fax (263) 61-2354), the excellent **Musango** tented camp near Tashinga (tel (263) 4-796821, fax (263) 4-796822), the new Zimbabwe Sun **Katete Safari Lodge** (tel (263) 4-736644, fax (263) 4-736646), **Sanyati Lodge** (tel (263) 4-734043, fax (263) 4-750785), **Tiger Bay** for fishermen (lovely open chalets) (tel/fax (263) 4-792617), **Gache Gache**, brand-new, for birders and part of the Landela Group (tel (263) 4-734043, fax (263) 4-750785), and **Kulizwe Lodge** at Binga (ideal for fishermen) (tel (263) 15-286). There is a variety of self-catering chalets (often called Safari lodges) particularly in the Charara area within driving distance of Kariba Town.

Bush and Safari Camps

Chirembgwe Bush Camp (Kuburi Wilderness). Kariba-based Tracker Safaris run this 4-chalet reed and thatch camp, each named after an antelope and sited under giant baobabs in Kuburi. Features: * Game trails. Guides have excellent knowledge of birds and trees. * Chess set for evenings. Tel (263) 61-2255/2663. P O Box 11, Kariba.

Msuna Fishing Camp Msuna Lodges. Tel (263) 9-77029, fax (263) 9-77000. P O Box 1235, Bulawayo.

Deka Drum Fishing Resort with camping and caravan facilities, where the Deka and Zambezi rivers meet, 35km (20 miles) west of Lake Kariba headwaters. Tel (263) 81-250524. P O Box 2, Hwange.

Hogwe Safari Camp (Omay and Matusadona). New and exceptionally remote John Stevens camp in the rugged hills of the Zimbabwe escarpment on the edge of Matusadona National Park. Six people only. Features: * Gauzed canvas tents, camp cots, long drops, bucket showers, paraffin lamps. * Minimum 3 nights. * Part of camp proceeds refunded to local Omay villagers under Campfire scheme. Tel Bushlife (263) 4-496113, fax (263) 4-498265. P O Box CH 84, Chisipite, Harare.

National Parks, Wildlife Society, Camping, Self-Catering

Caribbea Bay Hotel camping park, Kariba shoreline. Tel (263) 61-2453.

Mopani Bay Camping and Caravan Park, Kariba village. Tel (263) 61-22313. P O Box 130, Kariba.

Moth Cottages and Camp Site Kariba village near Andora harbour. Tel (263) 61-2809. P O Box 67, Kariba.

Tamarind Lodges Kariba Village. Attractive stone cottages. Self-catering. Recommended. Tel (263) 61-2697. P O Box 1, Kariba.

Chizarira National Park, six camp sites, some with sleeping shelters. Same address as National Parks below or tel (263) 9-63646. P O Box 2283, Bulawayo.

Kuburi Wilderness, Wildlife Society camp site. Near Chaware harbour. Bookings Wildlife Society, Harare. Tel (263) 4-700451. P O Box HG996, Highlands, Harare. For information, tel (263) 61-2705 Kariba.

Nyanyana National Parks Camp Site Kuburi Wilderness. Tel (263) 61-2337/557. Private bag 2002, Kariba.

National Parks Rustic, one party only lodges, Matusadona National Park, known as exclusive camps. Plus other camping sites. Reservations: National Parks, tel (263) 4-706077. P O Box CY826, Causeway, Harare.
Ruzi Island Four twin-bedroomed chalet with overhead fans at Ruzirukuru Bay, on shore of Chete Safari Area halfway between Mlibizi and Kariba village. Tel (263) 53-2246.
Camping is available at Binga, Mlibizi, Msuna and Deka, snd in all National Parks. Do not, however, follow the advice of some who say you can camp anywhere. You cannot. Not only is it against the law, but you are also likely to be eaten by a lion or hyaena.

Note: Like Victoria Falls, Zimbabwe shares Kariba with Zambia, a country that offers excellent safari lodge facilities. Chete Island, Zambia, in the middle of Lake Kariba, may soon have a new safari camp run by the man who pioneered Fothergill Island Safari Lodge. These and other new camps are likely to be advertised in Zimbabwe's monthly *Africa Travel News* magazine.

WHERE TO EAT

Nearly everyone eats at the hotel or safari lodge in which they are booked. The luxury safari lodges serve excellent, big, if not *haute cuisine*, meals. The cooking at the hotels is geared for people whose minds are on fishing, not eating. Kariba is not Taki's cup of tea, more Hemingway country. But the service is always in *droit de seigneur* chateau style and always comes with a smile even if the fish has the wrong sauce. And the cabernet has been chilled.

You can buy ice-creams and get good breakfasts at the **Most High Hotel** and at the village atop the Heights, there is the **Fish 'n Chips Paradise**. The **Kariba Country Club** nearby welcomes visitors to their inexpensive yet tasty meals and barbeques. They have the best lake view of all. The **Boathouse Takeaways and Restaurant** is near the entrance to Andora harbour and Kariba ferry terminal.

HEALTH HAZARDS

You can easily come across an elephant, buffalo or leopard right outside your hotel or between your room and the lake shoreline. Take great care. Wild animals walk happily around the Heights suburb, especially at night. You should be even more careful at a safari camp although some have low electric tripwires to discourage game.

Take prophylactics for malaria. Bilharzia is a risk, so avoid going into water unnecessarily. Ticks may cling to you while walking in the bush; brush yourself off after walking.

ANNUAL EVENTS

Tigerfishing Tournament. International and annually since 1962. Up to 300 teams and 500 boats participate. For more information contact *The Master Angler*, tel (263) 4-885660, fax (263) 4-750525.

USEFUL ADDRESSES AND TELEPHONE NUMBERS

Note: When dialling within Zimbabwe dial 161, then the Kariba number.

AA Tel (263) 61-2697.
Air Zimbabwe (airport). Tel (263) 61-2914/2913.
Banks: *Barclays* Tel (263) 61-2303; *Standard Chartered* (263) 61-2207.
B-line Lake Passenger Service for getting across the lake and to safari islands. Tel (263) 61-2473. P O Box 15, Kariba.
Boat Maintenance Contact *Jay's Engineering* Tel (263) 61-2538. P O Box 76, Kariba.
Houseboat and general boat hire Contact *Kariba Cruises* Tel (263) 61-2839, fax (263) 61-2885. P O Box 186, Kariba.
Kariba Ferries Harare Central Booking. Tel (263) 4-614162, fax (263) 4-614161. P O Box 578, Harare. Kariba, tel (263) 61-2460.
Kariba Publicity Association Tel (263) 61-2328. P O Box 86, Kariba.
Lake Safety and Lake Captain Lake Navigation Control. Tel (263) 61-2289. P O Box 10, Kariba.
Master Angler, tel (263) 4-885660, fax (263) 4-883214. P O Box BW550, Borrowdale, Harare.
Medical Doctor Tel (263) 61-2819 or District Hospital, (263) 61-2382.
Wildlife Society, Kariba Branch. Tel (263) 61-2538 or *Kuburi Wilderness*, tel (263) 61-2705.
The Little Shop Books, gifts and hairdresser. Tel (263) 61-2887. P O Box 44, Kariba.
Post Office Tel (263) 61-2390.

PART THREE

VISITOR'S DIGEST

Zimbabwe is an easy country to visit, particularly if you are English-speaking. Even if your mother tongue is another language, Zimbabweans are not complicated people and their country with its high sunny skies reflects this courtesy and their willingness to assist visitors. So remember, Zimbabweans drive on the left, work on the metric system and their institutions are rather British. Consult the following digest for useful tips on everything from arriving at Harare safari city, to white-water rafting at the Victoria Falls, to learning the language. And have a grand holiday.

LEFT: *The impressive Chilojo Cliffs in Gonarezhou National Park.*
ABOVE: *White-water rafting, Victoria Falls.*

VISITOR'S DIGEST

TELEPHONE TIP

All telephone codes within Zimbabwe start with the number (1) e.g. Harare (14), Victoria Falls (113). This first one (1) is dropped if you are ringing from outside Zimbabwe. The city or area code is never used if you are in that city or area. Be patient on the phones; many numbers have recently changed in Zimbabwe and many companies do not yet have adequate exchanges for the traffic volume.

ENTERING ZIMBABWE

PASSPORTS All visitors need a passport that is valid for at least 6 months.

VISAS Visas are not required for E.U. (European Union) or Commonwealth visitors but are necessary for nationals of some 40 other countries including, at time of writing, South Africa. They are obtainable from Zimbabwe Diplomatic Missions, and where Zimbabwe has no representation, contact the British High Commission in your country or write to the Chief Immigration Officer.

Visas are valid for three months and can be renewed as Temporary Residence Permits by the Chief Immigration Officer, Private Bag 7717, Causeway, Harare, tel (263) 4-791913, Linquenda House, Baker Avenue, between 1st and 2nd Streets.

Bulawayo enquiries: tel (263) 9-65621; *Victoria Falls* (if you are arriving from Zambia, Namibia or Botswana): tel (263) 13-4237; *Mutare* (from Mozambique): (263) 20-62322; *Beitbridge* (from South Africa): tel (263) 86-211; *Chirundu* (from Zambia): tel (263) 637-626; *Plumtree* (from Botswana): tel (263) 80-571; *Kariba* (from Zambia): (263) 61-2323; *Nyamapanda* (from Mozambique and Malawi): tel (263) 72-551 in Mutoko.

You will also require a return air ticket, your own car, or sufficient traveller's cheques or foreign currency to finance your travel in and exit from Zimbabwe. Students without these funds should have proof of accommodation offered by friends. Authorization of the Chief Immigration Officer is needed for any visitor who wishes to take up work or residence. Zimbabwe is a convenient place to obtain visas for other African countries.

HEALTH REQUIREMENTS Malaria, bilharzia and Aids are hazards in Zimbabwe. Travellers from South Africa or coming direct from Western countries need no inoculations. There is no malaria on the highveld in winter, but it does occur in summer in certain areas. A course of malaria prophylactics is generally advisable for all non-African visitors and for all visitors intending to visit areas such as the Victoria Falls, Kariba, Mana Pools and Hwange.

Water can be drunk from any tap in the cities and in most visitor areas. Keep away from river and dam water which is often bilharzia-infected. Zimbabwe was the third country in the world to screen donor blood for Aids (a few months ahead of the United Kingdom). Always take precautions against the persistent overhead sun. In the winter months, the big-game areas can be dusty.

CUSTOMS There are no longer any financial restrictions. Visitors may bring in gifts to the value of Z$2,000 duty-free which may include 5 litres of liquor, two of which may be spirits; 55% duty is charged for gifts over this value and 65% on radios, TVs and certain electrical items. Importing a pet is very difficult; you must write to the Director of Veterinary Services, P O Box CY66, Causeway, tel (263) 4-791355, fax (263) 4-720879.

TEMPORARY IMPORT PERMITS These are required for personal firearms, cars and boats, and are issued at the port of entry; they must be surrended when leaving.

CLOTHING Lightweight clothing in neutral colours is suitable for the bush (including a long-sleeved shirt for protection from the sun and long pants against mosquitoes in the evenings). Pack a hat, sunglasses and strong shoes for walking. You'll need a warm jacket for winter evenings.

The occasional city restaurant may require smart-casual dress and even a tie. Take a raincoat for the Victoria Falls rain forest. If you are joining an organized safari of any kind, the amount of luggage you are permitted to take with you is restricted, particularly in a small aircraft or canoe. Limit yourself to a soft, preferably waterproof, carryall or bag of 10kg (22 pounds) on these occasions.

ARRIVING BY AIR Some 30 international carriers have flights to Zimbabwe. Harare and Victoria Falls are the main entry points by air. Harare is serviced by the following airlines (among others):

South African Airways, tel (263) 4-738922; **Comair**, tel/fax (263) 4-739879; **Kenya Airways**, tel (263) 4-792181; **British Airways**, tel (263) 4-794616; **Lufthansa**, tel (263) 4-793861.

Air Zimbabwe has offices in some 25 cities worldwide, including:

Amsterdam The Netherlands. Air Agencies Holland, Freightway Building, Flamingweg1 Room 316, P O Box 7633, 11182J Schiphol Airport, Amsterdam. Tel (020) 604 1844, fax (020) 604 1634.

Dubai United Arab Emirates. National Travel and Tourist Agency, Al Makhtoum Street (opposite Dubai Airline Centre), P O Box 298. Tel (4) 27 2222/ 521500, fax (4) 527868.

Houston U.S.A. Sita World Travel Inc. 9001 Airport Blvd Suite 202, Houston. Tel (713) 943 2279, fax (713) 626 1905.
Johannesburg South Africa. P O Box 9398, Johannesburg 2000, Carlton Centre, Commissioner Street. Tel (011) 331 1541, fax (011) 331 6970.
London England. Colette House, 52/55 Piccadilly, London W1V 5AA. Tel (0171) 491 3783, fax (0171) 355 3326.
Nairobi Kenya. Chester House, Koinange Street, Nairobi, P O Box 41127. Tel (2) 339522/4, fax (2) 331983.
New York U.S.A. Sita World Travel, Inc. 767 Fifth Ave, GM Plaza Building, New York, N.Y. 10153. Tel (212) 980 8010, fax (212) 759 0184.
Perth Australia. South Pacific Express, Suite 5, Level 7, City Arcade Tower Block, 207 Murray Street, Perth. 6000. Tel (09) 321-3751, fax (09) 321- 1081.
Sydney Australia. South Pacific Express, Level 17, 456 Kent Street, Sydney, NSW 2000. Tel (02) 264 7346, fax (02) 264 7046.
Air Zimbabwe offices are also found in Belfast, Copenhagen, Dar-Es-Salaam, Durban, Gabarone, Lilongwe, Lusaka, Milan, Nicosia, Oslo, Rome and Sun Valley CA.

The US$20 departure tax from Zimbabwe airports is not usually included in your air ticket.

INTERNAL AIR SERVICES Air Zimbabwe operates internal services to Bulawayo, Victoria Falls, Kariba, Hwange National Park, but not to Mutare or Masvingo (Great Zimbabwe). However, there are scheduled small aircraft flights to Masvingo and Buffalo Range in the Lowveld with reservations through **Air Zimbabwe**, tel (263) 4-575021/ 737011, or United Air, tel (263) 4-575016/ 731715.

Air charter companies include: **Executive Air**, tel (263) 4-302248, fax (263) 4-302041; **United Air**, tel (263) 4-575016, fax (263) 4-575300; **Zambezi Air Services**, tel (263) 4-302076, fax (263) 4-304871; **Bush Pilots**, tel (263) 73-2567, fax (263) 73-2612; **Air Tabex**, tel (263) 4-790225, fax (263) 4-704457.

Airport buses: Regular buses leave from Harare, Bulawayo and Victoria Falls airports. Safari operators usually provide this service in Hwange, Kariba and Masvingo, as do some hotels in the larger cities.

ARRIVING BY RAIL Zimbabwe is linked by rail with its neighbours South Africa, Zambia, Botswana and Mozambique. A weekly (return) sleeper runs between Harare and Johannesburg via Beitbridge. For reservations, tel Harare (263) 4-73393306/ 73393307, or Bulawayo, tel (263) 9-322210/322310.

Rail Safaris in Bulawayo operate a twice-monthly old-fashioned steam train safari between Bulawayo and Victoria Falls. Tel/fax (263) 9-75575, P O Box 2536, Bulawayo.

ARRIVING BY ROAD The superb road network connects Zimbabwe with all its neighbours, making it possible to drive from Cape Town, Windhoek, Beira, Gabarone, Blantyre, Lusaka or Nairobi. The roads linking the cities with Victoria Falls, Hwange and the Eastern Highlands are all good tar roads. Hitchhiking is fine. Access to Matusadona, Mana Pools, Chizarira and Gonarezhou should only be undertaken in four-wheel-drive vehicles. There are border posts at Beitbridge, Victoria Falls, Chirundu, Plumtree, Kazangula, Mutare (Forbes), and Nyamapanda, and are normally open 06h00-18h00 daily but longer during peak holiday periods.

You will need to produce a police clearance certificate (cross border theft is frequent), your vehicle registration book and vehicle insurance. To be sure, check with the AA before departure in the event of any change in regulations such as the possible need for a Zimbabwe third party insurance or a triptique. If your vehicle is borrowed, you should carry a Letter of Authority from the owner.

MONEY

CURRENCY The Zimbabwe dollar is divided into 100 cents. Notes are in denominations of Z$100, Z$50, Z$20, Z$10, Z$5 and Z$2, and coins in 1c, 5c, 10c, 20c, 50c and Z$1.

CURRENCY REGULATIONS Money can be exchanged at the airport, hotels, banks and *bureaux de change*. Until recently there was a flourishing black market in currency, but with market liberalization this has all but disappeared as there is sufficient forex available through normal channels. There are no restrictions on the amount of traveller's cheques or foreign cash visitors can bring in or take out of the country. No-one may take more than Z$500 in cash out of Zimbabwe and residents are restricted to an annual holiday allowance equivalent to US$5000 per person.

BANKS Normal banking hours are 08h00-15h00 on weekdays (Wednesdays half-day closing at 13h00) and on Saturdays 08h00-11h00. Suburban banks have shorter hours. Major banks, including Barclays, Standard Chartered, Zimbank (and a variety of building societies who offer some banking facilities), have branches in all the major centres and holiday destinations.

SERVICE CHARGES Hotels and restaurants do not levy service charges. Banks usually charge 2% on travellers' cheques.

CREDIT CARDS International credit cards are acceptable at hotels and restaurants, but not every shop is used to them, especially in smaller centres.

TIPPING Tips at around 10% are much appreciated everywhere and in most situations.

ACCOMMODATION

All of Zimbabwe is serviced by good, reasonably priced accommodation, which ranges from rustic National Parks chalets to luxury safari lodges. The latter are available at all the holiday destinations, and even in Harare and Bulawayo where game parks exist close to these cities. A wide range of hotels can also be found throughout the country, particularly in the cities. Accommodation in each region is described in the advisories.

SAFARI LODGES There are many safari lodges throughout the country, usually in or near wildlife areas; all are highly recommended. A good guide to choosing a safari lodge is to ask how many chalets or units they have. Normally the fewer the units, the smaller the lodge, the better your holiday. Apart from other factors, the guides have more time to explain the wild to you.

The following organizations, among others, will suggest alternatives: **Shearwater Adventures**, tel (263) 4-757831, fax (263) 4-757836; **Safari Consultants**, tel (263) 4-758841, fax (263) 4-756602; **Safari par Excellence**, tel (263) 4-720527, fax (263) 4-722872; **Phileas Fogg Travel**, tel (263) 4-786491, fax (263) 4-746152.

HOTELS Hotels are graded one to five stars, somewhat optimistically in the higher ranges. The largest and most expensive are the **Zimbabwe Sun Hotels**, tel (263) 4-736644/707759, fax (263) 4-734739, followed by **Cresta Best Western Hotels**, tel (263) 4-703131, fax (263) 4-794655, and **Rainbow Hotels**, tel (263) 4-733781, fax (263) 4-790585.

KARIBA HOUSEBOATS *See* the **Kariba Advisory** on pages 172-175, or tel **Kariba Cruises**, (263) 61-2839, fax (263) 61-2885; **Kariba Houseboats**, tel/fax (263) 61-2922, or **Rhino Rendezvous**, tel (263) 4-735912, fax (263) 4-791348.

MOTELS These motels cater for the needs of motoring visitors and their families and are found at strategic points along the main visitor routes. The motels (some are called hotels) are usually reasonably priced. They are normally equipped with a pool, a steakhouse-type restaurant and cater for children informally.

Beitbridge to Harare: **Lion and Elephant** (80km; 50 miles) at Bubi River, tel (263) 14-336.

Beitbridge to Bulawayo: **Tod's Guest House** (120km; 75 miles) West Nicholson, tel (263) 16-5403.

Chipinge to Beitbridge: **Tambuti Lodge** (250km; 160 miles), Chiredzi, tel (263) 31-2575.

Beitbridge to Mutare: (Luxury) **Hot Springs Resort** (500km; 300 miles) tel (263) 26-361.

Bulawayo to Victoria Falls: **Gwaai River Lodge** (240km; 150 miles), tel (263) 18-355.

Bulawayo to Harare: **Fairmile Motel**, Gweru (165km; 102 miles), tel (263) 54-4144.

Mutare/Nyanga to Harare: **Crocodile Motel** (90km; 55 miles) at Rusape, tel (263) 25-2404.

Harare to Chirundu/Mana: **Cloud's End** (390km; 240 miles), Makuti, tel (263) 63-526.

Kariba to Harare: **Orange Grove Motel** (250km; 160 miles), Chinhoyi, tel (263) 67-22785.

COUNTRY GETAWAYS As distinct from safari lodges at Hwange, Kariba, Gonarezhou, Zambezi Valley or Victoria Falls, country getaways are usually in the Eastern Highlands. They are small, cosy, cottagey hotels with excellent food and log fires. *See* the **Eastern Highlands Advisory** on pages 130-131.

SELF-CATERING AND NATIONAL PARKS National Parks have rustic, self-catering but fully equipped chalets in nearly all the country's wilderness areas. The National Parks accommodation has to be booked well in advance (although one night is often possible on arrival), and is much sought-after in areas such as Victoria Falls, Hwange, Kariba (Matusadona shore), Mana Pools, Nyanga, Gonarezhou, Mutirikwi (Great Zimbabwe), Lake Chivero (20 minutes from Harare) and the Matobo National Park. For reservations, tel (263) 4-706077, P O Box CY826, Causeway, Harare.

All the private cottages in Nyanga, Bvumba and Chimanimani Eastern Highlands are self-catering and ideal for an inexpensive family holiday.

GAME FARMS AND RANCHES Mostly members of the Wildlife Producers' Association, they have fully equipped cottages available to visitors. These are marketed through various travel and safari agents or write to P O Box 952, Harare.

CAMPING/CARAVANNING There are sites in all the wilderness and holiday areas and in the main towns. The AA can provide further information, or contact the **Caravan Club of Southern Africa** in Johannesburg, tel (27) 11-7893202, P O Box 50580, Randburg 2125, South Africa.

BACKPACKING This is a relatively new phenomenon to Zimbabwe but one that has caught on. Among other places, there are inexpensive and decent backpacker facilities at Victoria Falls town, Bulawayo, Hwange National Park camp sites (but no hitching is allowed in the parks), Kariba village, the Eastern Highlands (the best are here), Harare and Mutare. You will usually find people helpful and considerate on the road. Single women should be sensible but there is relatively little violent crime in Zimbabwe. Keep your pack near you and keep it light. Good luck.

Pets Pets are not allowed into any National Park under any circumstances. There are no kennel facilities near the parks but there are kennels in Harare and Bulawayo (*see* **Customs** on page 176).

TRAVEL WITHIN ZIMBABWE

ROAD TRAVEL In Zimbabwe one drives on the left and gives way to the right at all intersections where there are no 'robots' or traffic lights. The speed limit on open roads is 120kph (75mph) for cars. Effective electronic speed traps and highway patrols obligingly permit you to pay your fines on the spot. Vehicle- and licence-checking road-blocks occur on the main highways, particularly over holidays. Drive defensively; city drivers, especially Emergency Taxis, will pull over suddenly to pick up passengers. Long-distance rural buses can be equally reckless.
Warning: In Harare, the road past the President's house (Chancellor Avenue, Extension of Seventh Street) is closed at night from 18h00-06h00, the road-blocks manned by armed soldiers.

DRIVER'S LICENCE Always carry your licence with you, which should have a photo on it. An international licence is recommended but not essential.

PETROL Cities, towns and main highways are well served by filling stations, the more remote areas less so. Petrol (and particularly diesel) is a little cheaper than, for example, South Africa or the United Kingdom. Some filling stations stay open 24 hours a day; others (usually) from 06h00-18h00. Repair services are available usually up to 17h00 Monday to Friday but not at weekends. Pump attendants check your car's fuel, oil, tyres and so on – there is no self-service in Zimbabwe.

Petrol is sold in litres. Tubeless tyre repairs and wheel-balancing facilities are usually found only in one or two places in the largest cities. Spares are now widely available as are tyres, although steel belted radials are not the norm. There is only one type of petrol in Zimbabwe, called 'blend', petrol mixed with sugar cane ethanol.

MAPS AND BOOKS The **AA** produces a good map. More detailed ones are available from the **Government Surveyor** at Electra House, Samora Machel Avenue in Harare, tel (263) 4-794545; and in Bulawayo on 2nd Floor, Tredgold Building, tel (263) 9-62816. City maps of Harare and Bulawayo and road atlases and maps published under the *Globetrotter* series are sold in bookstores.

ROAD SIGNS These are international. The wording, if any, is in English, but additional local ones include warning 'picture signs' of cattle, elephant, wild dog or kudu. Be especially wary when you see the cattle sign, or anywhere where the side of the road is unfenced, such as in rural areas. Cattle and sheep do not move aside, but goats quickly respond to hooting. Beware of 'Hump Ahead' (a raised section of tarmac making a hillock) signs, and slow down drastically and quickly. Driving at night in the country is not recommended because of animals and inadequate road markings. Trucks and buses usually belch fumes of diesel smoke.
Remember: The standard of driving in Zimbabwe is not very good. Always maintain a defensive driving approach.

AUTOMOBILE ASSOCIATION Membership of the AA is desirable; the main office is located at Fanum House, Samora Machel Ave, Harare, tel (263) 4-752779. There are AA representatives in most of Zimbabwe's cities. The AA also advises on touring and hotels, provides maps and sells travel items.

Bulawayo: (263) 9-70063; *Mutare:* (263) 20-64422; *Gweru:* (263) 54-4251; *Victoria Falls:* (263) 13-4764; *Kariba:* (263) 61-2697; *Hwange Town:* (263) 81-2275; *Chiredzi* (Lowveld): (263) 31-2897; *Masvingo* (Great Zimbabwe): (263) 39-62563.

CAR HIRE Companies including Europcar, Hertz, Budget and Avis serve the airports and are well represented in cities and major holiday destinations such as Kariba, Hwange, Victoria Falls and Mutare (Eastern Highlands). Vehicles available range from small Japanese cars, to 1-tonne pick-up trucks, all chauffeur-driven if required. Tariffs vary widely according to the type of vehicle and a kilometre or unlimited kilometre charge is levied. For one-way rentals there are often drop-off charges. Sales tax is included in the rates and credit cards are accepted. **Europcar:** Tel (263) 4-752559/752660, fax (263) 4-752083; **Avis:** Tel (263) 4-751542, fax (263) 4-750526; **Hertz:** Tel (263) 4-793701, fax (263) 4-756060; **Budget:** Tel (263) 4-724800, fax (263) 4-724645; **Rent-a-Camper:** Tel (263) 4-752411, fax (263) 4-791188; **Fleet Contracts:** Tel/fax (263) 4-336640.

LONG-DISTANCE DRIVING There are roadside rest points (lay-byes) on all major routes. These are developed and often shady areas equipped with a table, benches and a refuse bin. For long journeys through remote regions and over rough road surfaces, a basic checklist would comprise: Route maps, a jack, tyre levers, pump and tube, wheelbrace and good set of tools; spare wheel in good condition, spare fan belt, fuses; brake fluid, jump leads, reflective triangle, tow rope, electric torch, spare set of car keys, car instruction manual; 5-litre can of water; fire extinguisher and first-aid kit (and for camping a snake bite kit).

Really careful travellers would also carry spares that includes a set of contact-breaker points and condenser; radiator hose and clips; tyre valves; insulating tape; insulated electric wire; 'in line' fuel filter and a selection of nuts, bolts, washers and split pins. Don't forget your Identity Document or passport, driver's licence, medical aid card or similar, travellers' cheques and a separate copy of the cheque numbers, and your AA membership card.

PUBLIC TRANSPORT This is irregular in the cities and often crowded. Long-distance and colourful rural buses ply every road. In Harare they usually leave from Mbare Musika station, and from Renkini terminus, Mzilikazi suburb or Lobengula Street/ Sixth Avenue in Bulawayo. Taxis are available at airports, railway stations, the larger hotels, from ranks in various points of Harare, Bulawayo, Mutare and Victoria Falls, and from one-car companies in some of the holiday areas. They are listed in the yellow pages of the telephone directories.

Taxis These vary from museum-pieces to brand-new sedans, nearly always fitted with meters. *Harare:* A1 Taxis, (263) 4-706996; Rixi Taxis, tel (263) 4-753080; Pfumo, tel (263) 4-662008; *Bulawayo:* Rixi Taxis, tel (263) 9-60666; *Mutare* Taxi Rank, (263) 20-63166; *Victoria Falls* Taxi Services, (263) 13-4743.

Emergency taxis (ET's) These are ancient Peugeot station wagons into which people are packed. They are usually held together by goodwill, bubblegum and reggae music. They stop anywhere (often without warning), obey no rules and are cheap.

Commuter omnibuses These are newish 13-seater microbuses (upmarket versions of E.T.'s). They are fast mavericks of the road and today's method of urban transport for civil servants and office workers. They stop anywhere – just flag them down.

Coach travel Coach services link the country's main centres. Try *Silverbird*, tel (263) 4-794778; *Express Motorways* (Manica Travel Services) in Harare, tel (263) 4-703421, fax (263) 4-705590; in Bulawayo tel (263) 9-62521, fax (263) 9-62906. *Blue Arrow* (United Transport Group) runs to Mutare and Bulawayo daily, and twice weekly to Victoria Falls. Tel Harare (263) 4-729514-8, fax (263) 4-729572, or Bulawayo, tel (263) 9-65548, fax (263) 9- 65549.

WOMEN TRAVELLERS The threat of sexual assault is no greater in Zimbabwe than in Western Europe, just be sensible when alone and at night. Hitch-hiking, especially alone, is not a very good idea. Zimbabwe, like many countries, is chauvinistic but this is usually accompanied by old-fashioned courtesy, especially in the rural areas. There are no taboos about single women.

BICYCLES/MOUNTAIN BIKES These can be hired from *Bush Trackers* at the Bronte Hotel in Harare, tel (263) 4-303025; Victoria Falls opposite the Craft Village, tel (263) 13-4424; Mutare: Bhadella Arcade in Main Street, tel (263) 20-64844 and *Ikes* (motor) *Bikes* in Kariba, tel (263) 61-2839..

BREAKDOWNS Contact the nearest AA office. No highway emergency phones exist in Zimbabwe.

TRAVELLING BY RAIL Regular daily services link Bulawayo and Victoria Falls, Bulawayo and Harare, and Harare to Mutare. For reservations contact: *Johannesburg:* (27) 11-773 2944; *Bulawayo:* (263) 9-322210; *Harare:* (263) 4-73393603; *Mutare:* (263) 20-62801; *Victoria Falls:* (263) 13-4391.

For twice monthly rail safaris by old-fashioned steam train to Victoria Falls from Bulawayo via Hwange, tel *Rail Safaris* (263) 9-75575.

TRAVELLING BY AIR *Air Zimbabwe* is the main scheduled carrier at present, although this is changing. It is an efficient airline with an excellent safety record and good in-flight service standards. Aircraft are usually Boeing 737's or smaller Fokker 50's. Regular and daily return flights leave from Harare to Victoria Falls, Hwange, Kariba and Bulawayo.

Several weekly flights on smaller 12/20 seater aircraft are scheduled to Masvingo (Great Zimbabwe) and the Lowveld (Gonarezhou) on Mondays, Wednesdays and Fridays, and from Bulawayo to Kariba twice weekly, operated by the private *United Air Company*, part of the United Touring Group. Contact *Air Zimbabwe* or *United Air*.

Zimbabwe Express Airlines operates 77-seater BAe 146's jet flights to Kariba and Victoria Falls, tel (263) 4-737117, fax (263) 4-720124. Excellent air charter companies are also available (*see* **Air Charter** on page 177).

Air Zimbabwe: Harare, tel (263) 4-575021; Bulawayo, tel (263) 9-69732; Victoria Falls, tel (263) 13-4316/4518.

HANDICAPPED TRAVELLERS As a result of Zimbabwe's long *chimurenga* (liberation) war nearly 20 years ago, ramped sidewalks/pavements were built in the main centres. Hotels and some cinemas have facilities for wheelchairs.

TOURISM AND PUBLICITY OFFICES

Zimbabwe tourist offices abroad:

Germany: An Der Hauptwache, 7 60313, Frankfurt/ M, tel (49) 69-9207730, fax (49) 69-9207731/5;

South Africa: Upper shopping level, Carlton Centre, Commissioner Street, P O Box 9398, Johannesburg 2000, tel (27) 11-3313137, fax (27) 11-3316175;
United Kingdom: 429 The Strand, London WC2 ROSA, tel (44) 171-8367755, fax (44) 171-3791167;
United States of America: Rockfeller Centre, Suite 1905. 1270 Ave of the Americas, New York 10020, USA. Tel (1) 212-3321090, fax (1) 212-3321093.
Zimbabwe Tourist Development Corporation:
Bulawayo: Ground Floor, City Council, Tower Block, cnr Robert Mugabe Way/Leopold Takawira. P O Box FM150, Famona, Bulawayo. Tel/fax (263) 9-72333;
Harare head office, Three Anchor House, Floor 7, Jason Moyo Ave (between 1st and Angwa), tel (263) 4-758712/758714/28/30, fax (263) 4-793669. P O Box CY286, Causeway, Harare.
Victoria Falls: Zimbank Building, Livingstone Way. P O Box 103, Victoria Falls. Tel (263) 13-4380/76, fax (263) 13-4380.
Zimbabwe Council for Tourism: 9th Floor, Travel Centre, corner of 3rd Street and Jason Moyo Avenue, Harare. Tel/fax (263) 4-794015/6. P O Box 7240, Harare.
Zimbabwe Association of Tour & Safari Operators and the Zimbabwe Professional Hunters & Guide Association: 9th Floor, Travel Centre, P O Box UA191, Union Avenue, Harare. Tel (263) 4-733211, fax (263) 4-794015.
Visitors and publicity bureaux:
Bulawayo Opposite the City Hall carpark, next door to Jairos Jiri Craft Shop, between Takawira/ 8th Avenue. Tel (263) 9-60867, fax (263) 9-60868;
Harare Unity Square, Second Street/Jason Moyo Ave. Tel (263) 4-705085/6/7;
Masvingo (Great Zimbabwe), just south of town and railway crossing on the Beitbridge road. Tel (263) 39-62643;
Mutare Cnr Robert Mugabe/ Herbert Chitepo, tel (263) 20- 64711;
Victoria Falls Cnr Parkway/Livingstone Way, tel (263) 13-4202. 'Kariba Dam' wall observation point, tel (263) 61-2328.

GAME AND NATURE RESERVES Zimbabwe has 11 national parks, 16 safari hunting areas and 13 recreational parks, usually centred around lakes and large dams, plus several small game or botanical sanctuaries. In addition there are many privately owned game reserves and wilderness conservancies, one in the Lowveld covering 343 910ha (850 000 acres). Game ranching combined with wildlife safaris is a way of life in Zimbabwe.

WILDLIFE / CONSERVATION ORGANIZATIONS
National Parks and Wildlife Management *Harare* Botanical Gardens, Borrowdale Road/Sandringham Drive, tel (263) 4-726089, or (263) 4-706077, P O Box CY140, Causeway, Harare. *Bulawayo* Tel (263) 9-63646. Corner 11th Street/ Herbert Chitepo Avenue, P O Box 2283.
The Wildlife Society of Zimbabwe Mukuvisi Woodlands, Glenara Ave South. Tel (263) 4-700451, PO Box HG996, Highlands, Harare.
The Zambezi Society Mukuvisi Woodlands, Glenara Ave South, tel (263) 4-731596, P O Box HG774, Highlands, Harare.
Environment 2000 Tel (263) 4-303958. P O Box A639, Avondale, Harare.
National Trust of Zimbabwe Tel (263) 4-339175, P O Box 709, Harare, 15 Cheshire Road, Avondale.
Monuments and Museums Tel (263) 4-707202, P O Box CY1485, Causeway, Harare.
National Parks (Public Relations Officer) Tel (263) 4-707624, P O Box CY140, Causeway, Harare.
Centre of Applied Social Sciences University of Zimbabwe, tel (263) 4-303211, P O Box MP 167, Mount Pleasant, Harare.

SAFARI OPERATORS

There are some 250 members of the Zimbabwe Association of Tour and Safari Operators (ZATSO) in the country covering canoeing, backpacking, walking, white-water rafting, touring, game lodges, fishing, birding safaris, tree safaris and hunting safaris.

General

Abercrombie & Kent Tel (263) 4-759930, fax (263) 4-759940, P O Box 2997, Harare.
African Adventures Tel (263) 4-725213, fax (263) 4-725224, P O Box A88, Avondale, Harare.
Dabula Safaris Tel/fax (263) 13-4453 or 4609, P O Box 210, Victoria Falls.
Hungwe Safaris Tel (263) 4-733087, fax (263) 4-733009. P O Box 5438, Harare.
Nemba Safaris (Hwange) Tel (263) 18-375 (or dial 0 and ask for 03533). P O Box 4, Gwaai.
Phileas Fogg Travel Tel (263) 4-786491, fax (263) 4-746152.
Run Wild and **Twin Springs Safaris** (Kwekwe) Tel (263) 4-792333, fax (263) 4-792342. P O Box 6485, Harare.
Safari par Excellence Tel (263) 13-2051, fax (263) 13-4510, P O Box 44, Victoria Falls.
Shearwater *Harare* Tel (263) 4-757831- 4, fax (263) 4-757836 P O Box 3961; *Victoria Falls* Tel (263).113.4471, P O Box 125, Victoria Falls; *Johannesburg* Tel (27) 11-8046537, fax (27) 11-804 6539), P O Box 3961, Harare.
Sotani Safaris (Bulawayo-based) Tel (263) 9-77029, fax (263) 9-77000. P O Box 1235 Bulawayo.
Sunlink International Tel (263) 4-708307, fax (263) 4-728744, Murandy Square, Newlands, Harare.
Tundazi Safaris Tel/fax (263) 4-744618, P O Box 557, Harare.

United Touring Tel (263) 4-793701, fax (263) 4-792794, P O Box 2914, Harare.
VFR Tours (Hwange and Chivu) Tel (263) 4-793996/790342, fax (263) 4-791188, P O Box 4128, Harare.
Wild Africa Safaris Tel (263) 4-738329, fax (263) 4-737956, P O Box 1737, Harare.

Sail safaris

Kariba Cruises Tel (263) 61-2839, fax (263) 61-2885. P O Box 186, Kariba.
Sail Safaris Tel (263) 4-335120, fax (263) 4-339483, or Kariba, tel (263) 61-2321, fax (263) 61-2575.

Canoe safaris

Shearwater Canoeing Safaris Tel (263) 4-757831, fax (263) 4-757836, P O Box 3961, Harare. In Kariba, tel (263) 61-2459, P O Box 229, Kariba.
Sobek Tel (263) 4-795841, fax (263) 4-795846, P O Box 6485, Harare. In Zambia, tel (2603) 321432, fax (2603) 323542, P O Box 60957, Livingstone.
Zambezi Canoe Safaris Tel (263) 13-2058/9, fax (263) 13-2058. Private Bag 5931, Victoria Falls.

Birding safaris

Peter Ginn Tel (263) 79-430017 or 20902, fax (263) 79-23411, P O Box 44, Marondera.

Hotels

Rainbow Tourism Tel Harare (263) 4-733781, fax (263) 4-790585.

Zambezi Valley

Buffalo Safaris (Zambezi) and **Lake Wilderness Safaris** (Kariba) Tel (263) 61-2645, P O Box 113, Kariba.
Flip Nicholson Safaris Tel/fax (263) 4-738143, P O Box UA501, Union Avenue, Harare.
Wild Getaway Safaris (Kariba) Tel (263) 61-22413, P O Box 2, Kariba.

Overland safaris

African Overland Expeditions Tel (263) 4-756219, fax (263) 4-790679. P O Box CY1519, Causeway, Harare.

Package holidays

Air Zimbabwe (Flame Lily) Tel (263) 4-794481/575021, P O Box AP1, Harare Airport.

Tourism services

Tourism Services Zimbabwe. Tel (263) 4-733771/3, fax (263) 4-733770. P O Box 2281, Harare.

Study tours

GD Travel & Tours Tel (263) 4-794031, fax (263) 4-723888, P O Box 1010, Harare.

Walking safaris

Backpackers Africa Tel (263) 13-4424, fax (263) 13-4510. P O Box 108, Victoria Falls.
Central African Wilderness Tel (263) 13-4527/4637, fax (263) 13-4417. P O Box 288, Victoria Falls.

Photographic safaris

Jed Robinson Safaris Tel Bulawayo (263) 9-75406, fax (263) 9-77300.

White-water rafting

Far and Wide Nyanga Tel (263) 29-26329. P O Box 14, Juliasdale.
Frontiers Tel (263) 13-4772/5800, fax (263) 13-5801, P O Box 117, Victoria Falls, or Harare, tel (263) 4-732911, fax (263) 4-704759, P O Box 4876.
Shearwater Adventures Tel (263) 4-757831, fax (263) 4-757836, P O Box 3961, Harare. Tel (Victoria Falls) (263) 4-13-4471.

River cruises

Kalambeza Safaris Victoria Falls Tel (263) 13-4480, fax (263) 13-4644, P O Box 121, Victoria Falls.

BUSINESS AND TRADE

Zimbabwe National Chamber of Commerce Tel (263) 4-753444. Equity House, Rezende St, Harare. Bulawayo: Tel (263) 9-70336/69769. P O Box 1292.
Chamber of Mines Tel (263) 4-750942, P O Box 712, Harare.
Confederation of Zimbabwe Industries (CZI) Tel (263) 4-739833/9, P O Box 3794, Harare. Bulawayo: Tel (263) 9-60642. P O Box 2317, Bulawayo.
Tobacco Trade Association Tel (263) 4-791288, P O Box ST 180, Southerton, Harare.
Horticultural Promotion Council Tel (263) 4-791881, fax (263) 4-750754. P O Box 1241, Harare.
Travel Trade Information *Africa Travel News*, tel (263) 4-752411, fax (263) 4-791188; *Travellers Times*, tel (263) 4-794106, fax (263) 4-786954.

Zimbabwe's annual International Travel Trade Expo is normally held in Harare in February.

GENERAL INFORMATION

BINOCULAR REPAIR *Rhodes Survey Repairs*, tel (263) 4-726874. 208/ 210 Dublin House, Mbuya Nehanda Street/Albion Road, Harare.

BOOKS TO BRING Suggested books to bring to Zimbabwe are: Roberts' *Birds of Southern Africa*, Newman's *Birds of Southern Africa*, and *Sasol Birds of Southern Africa* (all published in South Africa). The Bundu Series, published in Zimbabwe, covers every wildlife subject, e.g. *Birds of the Highveld* by Peter Ginn, and *Snakes of Zimbabwe* by D G Bradley and E V Cook. *Land Mammals of Southern Africa* (a field guide) by Reay H N Smithers, published in South Africa. *Wild Flowers of Zimbabwe* by D C H Plowes and R B Drummond. *Rhodesian Wild Flowers* by Margaret H Tredgold. *Trees of Southern Africa* by Keith Coates Palgrave. Other local publishers and/or book sellers are:

Mambo Press, Gweru, tel (263) 54-4016, fax (263) 54-51991;

Baobab Books, tel (263) 4-706279, fax (263) 4-702071, and **Zimbabwe Publishing House**, tel (263) 4-497555, fax (263) 4-497554.

CAMPING EQUIPMENT can be hired or bought from Rooney's Hire Service, tel (263) 4-792724, fax (263) 4-733089, or from Feredays, tel (263) 4-751687, fax (263) 4-728316 in Harare. In Bulawayo try Eezee Kamping, tel (263) 9-62105, 95 George Silundika St, between 9th/10th Avenues.

CARAVAN/TRAILER HIRE In Harare *Campavan*, Pendennis Road in Northwood, tel (263) 4-301842.

CHURCHES AND RELIGIONS Church services of the various Christian and other denominations are often advertized in the press or in the monthly booklets produced by the individual cities' publicity bureaux. Other religions include Jewish, Hindu, B'Haai and Moslem.

Useful numbers in Harare are *Christian*: Anglican Cathedral, tel (263) 4-702251, Baptist Central, tel (263) 4-664405, Catholic Cathedral, tel (263) 4-720441, Methodist, tel (263) 4-724069, Seventh Day Adventist, tel (263) 4-601631. *Jewish*: Central African Jewish Board of Deputies, tel (263) 4-723647. *Hindu Society*, tel (263) 4-740853; *Islamic Culture Institute*, tel (263) 4-791605.

CLIMATE The rains come in summer (November to February) and it can be very hot in the Lowveld and in the cities in the early afternoon. The winter months from May to August are dry and sunny but can be very cold at night. Autumn and spring are delightful. Zimbabwe can lay claim to an almost perfect climate, blighted by periodic droughts.

CONFERENCES Good facilities are found in the main centres as well as in the popular resorts, including some game parks. Contact *Zimbabwe Sun Hotels*, tel (263) 4-736644, fax (263) 4-734739, and *Cresta Best Western Hotels*, tel (263) 4-703131, fax (263) 4-794655. The *Harare International Conference Centre*, tel (263) 4-733741, fax (263) 4-735779. Private Bag 7752, Causeway, is the largest venue in the country followed possibly by the *Elephant Hills Hotel*, Victoria Falls. Tel (263) 13-4793, fax (263) 13-4655. P O Box 300, Victoria Falls. Smaller facilities are available at Leopard Rock Hotel, Bvumba, and Ruckomechi in Mana Pools.

DIPLOMATIC REPRESENTATION For a full list see Vol. 2 of the National Telephone Directory (Harare), Some 70 diplomatic missions exist in Zimbabwe. The country is a much sought-after posting for the diplomatic and donor community, as Zimbabwe offers the best of Western facilities with the best of African safari resorts.

Diplomats and Technical Co-operation Experts, interpreted by local wags as Terribly Clever Experts, have white number plates and usually white 4 x 4 landcruisers. Many Embassies are sited off Second Street Extension 2km (1.25 miles) from downtown Harare. Zimbabwe maintains diplomatic missions in the United Kingdom, USA, Australia, South Africa, Germany, France, Ethiopia, Japan, India, Kenya, Italy and some 25 other countries.

ELECTRICITY The power system is 220 volts AC; US appliances require an adaptor. Plugs are usually 13-amp square pins.

ENTERTAINMENT AND ART Music is the soul of Zimbabwe and the Shona and Ndebele equivalent of Top of the Pops shows on TV are really excellent. In addition, there are cinemas and rep theatres, museums, and the National Ballet and its offspring the internationally acclaimed contemporary dance group, Tumbuka. There are sculpture and art galleries, orchestras, and many traditional dance troupes in the main centres. Those from Chipinge are exceptional. Exhibitions and performances are held throughout the year and are well advertized. Zimbabwe is a major centre of stone sculpture with regular exhibitions abroad. There are fairly regular visits by international super-songsters.

EMERGENCIES Dial 999 and stipulate either Police, Fire or Ambulance. The **Samaritan Service** (suicide or just the need to talk) in Harare is on tel (263) 4-722000, and Bulawayo Tel (263) 9-65000. **Medical Air Rescue Service** (MARS), tel Harare (263) 4-734513/4/5, fax (263) 4-734517, or Bulawayo (263) 9-64082, fax (263) 9-78950. Insurance Cover can easily be arranged with MARS. But if this is not done and your travel insurance does not cover all emergencies one can encounter in Africa, then MARS will probably ask for payment upfront, before e.g. effecting an emergency evacuation.

FILM-MAKERS The movie industry in Zimbabwe has made great strides in recent years. For assistance or information contact *Rory Kilalea Films*, tel (263) 4-302369, fax (263) 4-302355, at 7 Everett Close, Avondale, Harare.

FITNESS The major centres and some hotels are well-equipped for the fitness-conscious guest. Swimming pools, tennis courts and aerobics classes can be found in most towns. Many sports clubs offer temporary membership to visitors, including squash, tennis, bowls, golf, swimming, cycling, jogging and running. There are also numerous health clubs with satellite TV to occupy you while you cycle, plus aerobics, callisthenics and aquaerobics in the summer. Jogging is safe but not allowed in the game reserves as it presents unbearable temptation to the local lions.

FOOD AND WINE There are Chinese, Indian, Italian, Greek and African safari restaurants in Harare and Bulawayo, and even one or two brave attempts at British-style pubs, and there are dozens of hamburger and chicken 'n chips joints. Zimbabwe's national dish *sadza* (stiff maize porridge) and relish is very tasty when freshly cooked. Steaks are invariably good.

Zimbabwe cuisine is generous rather than delicious. The wide range of local fruits is excellent, as are the vegetables. The best breads are usually made in Italian, French- or Swiss-owned bakeries. Zimbabwe actually has a 'national loaf' made from a mixture of wheat and maize meal, and is good when fresh. Wholesome home-cooking is the norm in safari camps, while in the cities the larger hotels have restaurants with French names.

Local wines, especially the Meadows Range, improve annually. Chose white rather than red, although Private Cellar's Cabernet Sauvignon has crossed the rubicon. Local lager, such as Castle or Zambezi, is average but goes down well after a long day in the bush. Drink Hunters Lager from Chiredzi if you can find it, while the best imported beer is a toss-up between Autralian Tooeys and Namibia's Windhoek Special. Mazoe Orange Juice is a national drink, followed closely by Coca-Cola.

GAMBLING Horse racing and betting is a popular pastime and there are casinos in the Victoria Falls, Juliasdale (Nyanga), Bvumba and Kariba. The cities have regular charity casinos. A state lottery offers a monthly prize in the region of US$10 000.

PUBLIC HOLIDAYS Zimbabwe has 13 annual public holidays: New Year's Day (January 1), Good Friday to Easter Monday (4 days), Independence Day (April 18), Workers' Day (May 1/2), Africa Day (May 25), Heroes' Defence Forces Day (August 11/12); Christmas Day (25 December) and Boxing Day (26 December). The school terms are divided into three per year with month-long holidays, normally over the Easter period, August/September and Christmas.

ICE This welcome relief is available at many service stations, either in large blocks or cubes. It is widely advertised, especially in hot places like Kariba.

LANGUAGES The three official languages are Shona, Ndebele and English. Practically everyone, everywhere, speaks English but seldom any other European languages.

MEASUREMENT Zimbabwe uses the metric system. Kariba Tiger fishermen, however, have a more expansive version of their own.

MEDIA

TV There are two local TV channels, ZTV1 and ZTV2, usually broadcasting from 15h00-23h00 daily and all day at weekends. The main news bulletin each day is at 20h00 in English. TV is government-controlled and thus tends to concentrate on the activities of the President and the ruling party, but intercuts these with CNN clips. There are occasional good programmes and imported films but very little is produced locally. The accent is on Australian and American soap-operas and rather old education programmes, but the standard of technical TV expertize is high. Satellite dishes afforded by many in the leafy suburbs, and provided by hotels and sports clubs, give access to international TV.

Press There is a very efficient press in Zimbabwe with both daily, regional and Sunday papers, plus a wide variety of magazines. Although largely Government-owned and thus reluctant to provide hard-hitting criticism on matters political, the level of journalism of the national dailies is high, and there are sufficient weeklies to provide comment on bureaucratic foibles and inadequacies. *Horizon* and *Moto* magazines and the weekly *Financial Gazette* are worth purchasing.

Radio Government-controlled and very popular with the majority of people, the radio stations feature popular modern music, Zimbabwe chat and magazine programmes. A little classical music is broadcast from time to time.

MEDICAL SERVICES Pharmacies sell all the necessary medicines. A list of medical doctors can be found at the front of each town's phone entries in the telephone directories. Public hospitals are well equipped and there are many rural clinics; however, visitors should take out their own medical insurance. In an emergency call *Medical Air Rescue Service (MARS)* or go direct to the Casualty Department of a General Hospital. Hospitals are listed under *Health* under the Government section after each city's phone numbers in the directory. To contact the private Medical Air Rescue Service, tel Harare (263) 4-727540, or Bulawayo (263) 9-64082.

PHOTOGRAPHY Most international film brands and sizes are readily available and same-day or one-hour processing can by done in the major centres. Note that certain Government, military and police buildings may not be photographed.

You will have difficulty in obtaining high speed film outside Harare, so bring all your own requirements and remember airport x-ray machines can damage films of 1000 ASA and above. Always keep your film cool, preferably in an ice-box, refrigerator or at least wrapped up away from the constant sun. Vehicles can get exceptionally hot.

Small instamatics are fine for snapshots to send home but not really adequate for wildlife photography. A 300mm lens is probably the best for game shots, and for birds, 400mm. A macro will be needed for close-up work and a wide angle to capture the lovely skies and open vistas of Zimbabwe. The sun is very bright in this country and 50 or 100 ISO/ASA rating is good workmanlike film. But a few rolls of 400 ISO/ASA will enable you to capture late evening and early morning 'magic time' shots. Bring a polarizing filter for the Zambezi River and rather use a bean bag than a tripod, which always takes a long time to assemble.

A word of caution: do not let your instinct to capture a view on film dominate your holiday. The memory of Africa's stillness and your own, will possibly be a more lasting gift of the wild.

Filming The law forbids anyone to take films for commercial purposes without the necessary work permits and permissions. These are readily granted.

Video Cameras Ensure you have an adaptor to run and charge video batteries from 12v DC vehicle batteries as well as a 220v AC power source and a long lead to enable you to move around your vehicle. Bring some video tapes as they are not always available in the more remote areas.

Camera Repairs Try *K. Kemp*, tel (263) 4-573703, 97 Harare Drive, Hatfield, Harare.

POSTAL SERVICES Most postal offices are open from 08h30-16h00 on weekdays and from 08h30-11h00 on Saturdays. Zimbabwe has an inexpensive postal service. There are a variety of courier services including *DHL*, tel Harare (263) 4-792881, fax (263) 4-790197, corner Fourth Street/Central Avenue; or Bulawayo (263) 9-74710, fax (263) 4-78885, 91A George Silundika Street.

PHILATELIC BUREAU Tel (263) 4-794491, P O Box 4220, Harare.

SECURITY In Zimbabwe, drugs other than *mbanje* (cannabis) are novelties, although in the past few years hard drugs have begun to appear and are deliberately sold cheaply to hook customers.

The country has to some extent been exploited as an entry port to access the huge South African market. Guns are rare (except on hunting safaris), but there is the occasional armed robbery. Cars, however, are a favourite target and BMWs fetch a high price in Zambia and Zaire. Petty theft and pickpocketing does occur, so backpackers should be wary of their valuables at camp sites, while putting forex under your mattress in a hotel is asking for trouble. Expensive clothes and running shoes are a potential magnet for thieves. Ignore black market forex touts – they may be plain clothes policemen plus you can get a better deal in a bank. Remember, a visible money-belt identifies you as a visitor.

SHOPPING Practically anything can be purchased, for a price, in Zimbabwe's modern city supermarkets, but the range is nowhere as vast as in Western countries. Most of the goods are Zimbabwe-made with South African products the next most popular. Deparment stores are usually open from 08h30-17h00, and on Saturdays from 08h30-13h00. Supermarkets and fleamarkets quite often stay open on Sunday mornings. There are new multi-boutique suburban shopping complexes, as well as (all-hours) small corner shop trading.

Sales tax At the time of writing all commodities (excluding unprocessed food) carry a 14% general sales tax surcharge. The quoted price is inclusive of this tax.

Many roadside crafts and good buys are to be had in Zimbabwe, including crochetwork, stone and ivory carvings, copperware, jewellery, tie & dye fabrics, elephant, crocodile and ostrich skin items, and pottery. Mavros' ivory and silver creations, Toby's emerald jewellery and Ros Byrne's potato-dye prints are top of the range.

Try to avoid anything made from wood except very small items, as irreplacable hardwood trees are often poached to make hippos and giraffes. Export permits are not required, but some countries have restrictions on import of items made from non-cattle leathers and ivory.

SPORT Soccer is the country's favourite sport attracting crowds of up to 45 000, followed by rugby (the fastest growing sport among schoolboys), cricket and tennis, but with a good climate, practically every other sport is played. The country's sportswomen particularly have had success internationally winning gold medals in hockey, bowls and swimming. Long-distance runners and triathlon athletes are now coming to the fore in international athletics, and the country's watersports success has included sailing and rowing.

Motorcross, gliding, motorcycle racing, netball, volleyball, squash, shooting, baseball, softball, cycling and archery all have an enthusiastic following. Horse racing attracts thousands of punters, the annual tote turnover approaching Z$50 million. May to July is the main racing season; Ascot in Bulawayo and Borrowdale Park in Harare the two main venues. Golf, however, is the arena which has won the country the highest sporting laurels. Nick Price has been voted the world's top golfer for several seasons with Mark McNulty not many holes behind. Zimbabwe has over 70 golf courses including those in Nyanga, Bvumba and Victoria Falls.

Golf courses:

Harare
Chapman, tel (263) 4-736940. 6514m 18 holes
Royal Harare, tel (263) 4-702920. 6467m 18 holes
Warren Hills, tel (263) 4-741874. 6384m 18 holes
Bulawayo
Bulawayo Golf Club, tel (263) 9-67067. 6431m 18 holes
Bulawayo Country Club, tel (263) 9-46473. 6186m 18 holes
Victoria Falls
Elephant Hills, tel (263) 13-4793/4503. 6204m 18 holes
Eastern Highlands (Bvumba)
Leopard Rock, tel (263) 20-60742. 6204m 18 holes

TELEPHONE STD dialling is possible to anywhere in the world on a usually fully automated system. Zimbabwe's international code is (263), followed by the town code and the number. To dial out, dial 110 to obtain the international satellite, then 44 (UK), 1 (USA & Canada), 27 (South Africa) or 61 (Australia), followed by the number.

In Zimbabwe every exchange has its own dialling code. Where dashes occur in this code, it is an indication that you should wait for a further (and usually immediate) dialling tone before dialling the main number. To obtain operator assistance for local calls, dial 967. There are public call boxes in most of the main centres. Two phone directories are printed, one for Harare and the other for the rest of the country.

Fax facilities are widely available; many organizations in resort areas still have Telex as an option, and a few, mainly in Harare, are using E-mail.

THE WOMENS' RESOURCE CENTRE AND NETWORK 'To enhance the Position of Women in Zimbabwe' in the gender development field. Sited at 288 Herbert Chitepo, P O Avenue/7th Street, Harare. Tel (263) 4-737435, fax (263) 4-720331, P O Box 2192, Harare.

TIME Zimbabwe is two hours ahead of Greenwich Mean (or Universal Standard) time, one hour ahead of Europe in winter time and seven hours ahead of the USA's Eastern Standard Winter time. Sydney is eight hours ahead of Zimbabwe.

VENOMOUS CREATURES & HEALTH HAZARDS
Aids HIV is a major disease in Zimbabwe. All visitors will be aware that abstention is the only 100% guarantee of avoiding this disease.

Bees, Wasps and Hornets African bees are known to be aggressive and swarming colonies can occasionally be dangerous. If you are stung, do not squeeze the poison sac of the sting. Remove it with a quick scrape of a knife. Anti-histamine cream, a bandage soaked in bicarbonate of soda or other alkaline solution or a cold compress will all give relief. A mild acid such as lemon or vinegar will usually counter the discomfort of wasp or hornet stings. (African honey from the Save Valley and Eastern Highlands is delicious.)

Bilharzia (Schistosomiasis) Do not swim in rivers and dams in Zimbabwe if you can avoid it. This does not apply to Kariba lake but does to the shoreline. The tiny bilharzia parasite buries itself into human skin, causing in the early stages (usually after six weeks) lassitude, ill health and eventually the passing of blood in urine and stool. Bilharzia can appear to lie dormant for a long time in a human being while quietly causing great damage to bladder, liver and intestine. If you have been in contact with water, especially still backwaters, take a bilharzia test. The cure is easy and effective.

Creepy Crawlies Zimbabwe has a bonanza of insects, but very few visitors get bitten or stung by the nasty ones. Pepper ticks in the grasslands of the Eastern Highlands can itch for a week; shorts are most congenial when walking in the bush and brush off after hiking. Blister beetles can cause a nasty rash; apply Stingose or a similar product.

Malaria Prophylactic treatment should commence a week before visiting any areas other than the main plateau towns or Nyanga in the Eastern Highlands. Note that some strains of malaria are becoming immune to chloroquine so check first with your pharmacist when buying prophylactics. You should also try and avoid being bitten by applying insect repellant on exposed skin areas and making use of mosquito nets.

Scorpions, Spiders and Snakes The simple precaution of shaking out shoes and clothes and checking firewood before handling it should keep the beasties at bay. Scorpion stings are inevitably very painful, the ill effect lasting for weeks. Aspirin and cold compresses both help, as they do with spider bites. But both rarely happen if the recommended precautions are taken.

Snakes usually try to avoid humans while scorpion and spider bites are hardly ever fatal. The most poisonous spider venom is that of the flat spider that lives on the interior walls of houses, but it is harmless as it cannot bite! Above all, a snake bite victim should be encouraged to remain calm to avoid circulating the poison. Sucking out venom is ineffectual and tourniquets are not advisable. Apply a pad and bandage firmly. While wrongly administered serum may kill the victim, current medical opinion advises its use only as a last resort. Get the victim to a doctor or hospital urgently, together, if possible, with the snake that bit him. In any event, the snake must be positively identified to facilitate treatment.

Sun Sunburn can lead to skin cancer; use a minimum factor 15 (preferably paba-free) cream and always wear a hat. Remember, a T-shirt is seldom sufficient protection against the sun's searing rays.

Tick-bite fever Not many ticks bite and few lead to tick bite fever. Ticks the size of a match head often affix themselves to your clothes when walking through the bush so brush your clothes off well. Tick bite fever is often like malaria with violent headaches, fever and aching bones. The infected bite, looking like a small boil, identifies the disease which can be quickly cured with tetracycline.

Water For those who like to play safe and take their drinking water in blue plastic bottles, there are several commercial brands available in hotels and shops throughout the country. Real mineral water is rare but the spring or mountain water tastes better than ordinary tap water. High in the mountains provided there is no human habitation above you, the stream water is delicious.

VOCABULARY Local slang expressions are sometimes a mix of Shona, Ndebele, English, Afrikaans and Portuguese.

Aiwa/aikona – No
Badza – Hoe
Biltong – Dried, salted meat; experts claim game is better than beef
Braai – A barbecue
Comrade – Expression used by government officials and broadcasters as an honorific, and with tongue in cheek by everyone else
Fynbos – Heath-type vegetation
Hwange Goat – Impala antelope
Kalahari Ferrari – Sun or rain spider
Kanjan – Howzitt?
Kopje/Koppie/Gomo – Small rocky hill
Kraal – Small village or settlement
Mabuggered – Broken down
Maningi – A lot of ...
Mushi – Lovely
N'anga – Herbalist and spirit diviner
Nose – Someone who is 'stuck-up' or superior
Pavement – Sidewalk
Penga – Daft
Povo – The people
Robot – Traffic lights
Sadza – National dish of stiff maize meal porridge
Safari – Literally (in Swahili) to walk, to adventure
Shamwari – Friend
Shateen – Loo in the bush
Shoopa – Nuisance
Shumba – Lion beer
Sterek – Strong, great (an expression used to give all-purpose emphasis)
Verandah – Patio, stoep.

BUSH AND CAMPING TIPS

* Animals are always dangerous. Never underestimate them or assume they will be friendly merely because they are temporarily ignoring you. They know very well you are there and can quickly turn on you.
* If you are sleeping in the wild, sleep in a tent under a mosquito net. The roof of a vehicle is always a safer spot. Lions and hyaenas will quite willingly sample you if you do not take adequate precautions.
* A zipped up tent keeps out such undesirables as snakes, scorpions and insects.
* Check that your vehicle is in good shape. Regularly.
* Leave radios, musical instruments and telephones at home. Let the sounds of silence, of the rivers and of the wild be your guide.
* Please do not throw any litter anywhere. Take it back with you in a plastic bag for disposal.
* Keep campfires small. Never chop down living trees for firewood.
* Please do not spoil rivers by using soaps, shampoos and detergents in the water. Wash outside the water using a container.
* It is common courtesy to ask permission before making use of village water supplies. Do not waste water by washing your vehicle at village pumps.
* Swimming in rivers and lakes (other than in the Eastern Highlands) is dangerous because of crocodiles and bilharzia.
* Pack away all food in tight containers and do not leave any food around that may attract scavengers. Taking meat or utensils and coolboxes smelling of meat into your tent can be highly dangerous. Never feed oranges to elephants or any food to any wild animal.
* Jogging in wildlife areas should never be attempted and never wander off alone into the bush. Always take someone with you if you decide to walkabout and inform the rest of the party.
* Do not get out of your car except at permitted view sites and camping/picnic spots.
* Always carry a flashlight at night. It is easy to bump into elephant, buffalo or a snake right outside your tent or safari lodge.
* Children must be specially protected in the wild as predators can seldom resist the young of another species, especially if they are attracted by running, playing or shouting.
* Buffalo, hippo, elephant. Be very wary of these three, especially buffalo.

INDEX

Page numbers in **bold** refer to main entries; page numbers in *italics* indicate photographs.